TRUE HEARTS AND PURPLE HEADS

TRUE HEARTS AND PURPLE HEADS
an unauthorized biography of a
football team BY JIM KLOBUCHAR

Ross & Haines, Inc., Minneapolis, Minn.
1970

In Memory of
Terry Dillon

Foreword

Pro football is the Roman Coliseum of the American society, the difference being that sometimes the Christians win on Sunday afternoon and the lions scream about the officiating.

It has now become the ultimate distraction of the casual thrill-seeker, replacing—according to the household and time of day—conversation, wild parties, the arts, and sometimes sex.

From 1960 to 1970 it graduated from the role of a popular curiosity to that of an institutionalized passion.

In Minnesota, a Sunday at the Met in 1969 became part of the quality of life. Thousands partied in the parking lots, a mass smorgasbord on a scale unimagined by the old Swede settlers. It was family day, jubilee day, crazy days, and atonement day in a package.

And on Jan. 4, of 1970 it bridged the final frontier when more than 400 snowsuited pilgrims attended a non-denominational church service two hours before the Viking-Browns title game kickoff, in the Met Center hockey arena 300 yards away. The service was conducted with a bright and eager solemnity, the text coming from one of the all-time athletic vets, St. Paul.

A church youth group provided the instrumentals and established a milepost in religion. It was the first time the choir sang in a penalty box.

What follows in these pages is an affectionate although frank and very personal look at a football team, the Minnesota Vikings. In character and performance graph it seemed to telescope pro football itself during those years of its rise to national mania.

If it appears weighted just a little on the side of the Vikings' Van Brocklin era, it is no accident. I lived daily with them for five years, as the correspondent of The Minneapolis Tribune. In those years, I admit, I acquired some of the traits of the large people I covered. These would include wary movements, nimble feet, and that rather prized property of being able to be defensive and aggressive in the same stance.

Most of these had something to do with years of skirmishing with Norman Van Brocklin, the team's combustible coach during its first six years (less one day, if you count his first retirement).

We had some near brawls and constant wrangles, but he was a joy to cover because he raged so beautifully and suspected so much. That he also was a first-order football coach simply added to the stimulation.

So you will find here the tempests of Van Brocklin, his dressing room tirades, his skilled manipulation of an undermanned team, his conflicts with Francis Tarkenton and some of his bizarre menagerie of athletes — one of whom threw lasagna at his wife more accurately than he threw blocks.

Later you will be introduced to the stationary front from Canada, Mr. Bud Grant, who in three years lifted the Vikings from last to first. And with him is Joe Kapp, the Mexican vagabond who is beyond all question the most absorbing football player I have ever met.

The book is written as a general chronology. But it is a history only in terms that this may provide a framework for the locker-room harpooning, the private dialogues, and the musky memoirs of a lot of free-falling characters. The names of some of them will endure, if not in the record book then at least in the sentimental treasure box of their sympathizers and baffled buddies.

Jim Klobuchar
July 1970

The Alumni

Adams, Tom (e) Minn-Dul, 1962
Alderman, Grady (t) Det, 1961-69
Arrobio, Chuck (t) USC, 1966
Barnes, Billy (rb) Wake Forest, 1965-66
Battle, Jim (g) So Ill, 1963
Beasley, John (te) Cal, 1967-69
Bedsole, Hal (te) UCS, 1964-66
Berry, Bob (gb) Ore, 1965-67
Bishop, Bill (dt) No Tex St, 1961
Bolin, Bookie (g) Miss, 1968-69
Bowie, Larry (g) Pur, 1962-68
Boylan, Jim (e) Wash St, 1963-64
Breitenstein, Bob (t) Tulsa, 1967
Britt, Charlie (db) Georgia, 1964
Brown, Bill (rb) Ill, 1962-69
Bryant, Bob (db) So Car, 1968-69
Bundra, Mike (dt) USC, 1964
Butler, Billy (rb) Chatt, 1962-64
Byers, Ken (g) Cin, 1964-66
Caleb, Jamie (rb) Gramb, 1961
Calland, Lee (db) Louisvl, 1963-65
Campbell, John (lb) Minn, 1963-64
Carpenter, Preston (e) Ark, 1966
Christopherson, Jim (k) Concordia, 1962
Clarke, Leon (e) USC, 1963
Coleman, Al (db) Tenn St, 1967
Cox, Fred (k) Pitt, 1963-69
Cuozzo, Gary (qb) Va, 1968-69
Culpepper, Ed (dt) Ala, 1961
Davis, Doug (t) Ken, 1966-69
Dean, Ted (rb) Wich, 1964
Denny, Earl (rb) Mo, 1967-68
Denton, Bob (de) Pac, 1961-64
Derby, Dean (db) Wash, 1961-62
Dickson, Paul (dt) Bay, 1961-69
Dillon, Terry (db) Mont, 1963
Donahue, Oscar (e) San Jose, 1962
Eller, Carl (de) Minn, 1964-69
Faust, Paul (lb) Minn, 1967

Ferguson, Bob (rb) OSU, 1963
Ferguson, Charley (e) Tenn St, 1962
Fitzgerald, Mike (db) Ia St, 1966
Flatley, Paul (e) NW, 1963-67
Franckhauser, Tom (db) Pur, 1962-63
Gault, Billy (db) TCU, 1961
Goodridge, Bob (e) Van, 1968
Grecni, Dick (lb) Ohio, 1961
Grim, Bob (e) Ore St, 1967-69
Guilford, Larry (db) Pac, 1962
Hackbart, Dale (db) Wis, 1966-69
Haley, Dick (db) Pitt, 1961
Hall, Tom (e) Minn, 1964-66, 68-69
Hansen, Don (lb) Ill, 1966-67
Hargrove, Jim (lb) How Pay, 1967, 69
Harris, Bill (rb) Colo, 1969
Hawkins, Rip (lb) No Car, 1961-65
Hayes, Ray (rb) Cent Okla, 1961
Henderson, John (e) Mich, 1968-69
Hilgenberg, Wally (lb) Ia, 1968-69
Hill, Gary (db) USC, 1965
Hill, King (p-qb) Rice, 1968
Hultz, Don (de) So Miss, 1963
Huth, Gary (g) Wake For, 1961-63
Jobko, Bill (lb) OSU, 1963-65
Johnson, Gene (db) Cin, 1961
Jones, Clinton (rb) MSU, 1967-69
Jordan, Jeff (db) Tulsa, 1965-67
Joyce, Don (de) Tulane, 1961
Kapp, Joe (qb) Cal, 1967-69
Kassulke, Karl (db) Drake, 1963-69
Keys, Brady (db) Colo St, 1967
King, Phil (rb) Van 1965-66
Kirby, John (lb) Neb, 1964-68
Kosens, Terry (db) Hofstra, 1963
Kramer, Kent (te) Minn, 1969
Krause, Paul (db) Iowa, 1968-69
Lacey, Bob (e) No Car, 1964
Lamson, Chuck (db) Wyo, 1962-63
Lapham, Bill (c) Iowa, 1961
Larsen, Gary (dt) Conc, 1965-69
Lee, Bob (qb-p) Pacific, 1969
Leo, Jim (de) Cin, 1961-62

Lester, Darrell (rb) McNeese, 1964
Linden, Errol (t) Hou, 1962-65
Lindsey, Jim (rb) Ark, 1966-69
Livingston, Cliff (lb) UCLA, 1962
Mackbee, Earsell (db) Ut St, 1965-69
Marshall, Jim (de) OSU, 1961-69
Martin, Billy (te) Ga Tech, 1968
Mason, Tommy (rb) Tulane, 1961-66
Mayberry, Doug (rb) Ut St, 1961-62
McCormick, John (qb) Mass, 1962
McElhenny, Hugh (rb) Wash, 1961-62
McGill, Mike (lb) ND, 1968-69
McKeever, Marlin (te) USC, 1967
McWatters, Bill (rb) No Tex, 1964
Mercer, Mike (k) Ariz St, 1961
Michel, Tom (rb) East Car, 1964
Middleton, Dave (e) Aub, 1961
Morris, Jack (db) Ore, 1961
Mostardi, Rich (db) Kent St, 1961
Murphy, Fred (e) Ga Tech, 1961
O'Brien, Dave (g) Bos Col, 1963-64
Osborn, Dave (rb) N Dak, 1965-69
Osborne, Clancy (lb) Ariz St, 1961-62
Page, Alan (dt) ND, 1967-69
Pesonen, Dick (db) Minn-Dul, 1961
Peterson, Ken (c) Utah, 1961
Phillips, Jim (e) Aub, 1965-67
Poage, Ray (e) Tex, 1963
Powers, John (te) ND, 1966
Prestel, Jim (dt) Idaho, 1961-65
Pyle, Palmer (g) MSU, 1964
Rabold, Mike (g) Ind, 1961-62
Reed, Bob (rb) Pac, 1962-63
Reed, Oscar (rb) Colo St, 1968-69
Reichow, Jerry (e) Iowa, 1961-64
Reilly, Mike (lb) Iowa, 1969
Rentzel, Lance (e) Okla, 1965-66
Rose, George (db) Aub, 1964-66
Rowland, Justin (db) TCU, 1961
Rubke, Karl (lb) USC, 1961
Russ, Pat ((dt) Pur, 1963

Schmitz, Bob (lb) Mont, 1966
Schnelker, Bob (e) Bow Gr, 1961
Sharockman, Ed (db) Pitt, 1962-69
Shaw, George (qb) Ore, 1961
Shaw, Glenn (rb) Ken, 1961
Shay, Jerry (dt) Put, 1966-67
Sherman, Will (e) St. Marys, 1961
Shields, Lebron (de) Tenn, 1961
Simpson, Howard (t) Aub, 1964
Smith, Gordon (e) Mo, 1961-65
Smith, Steve (de) Mich, 1968-69
Stonebreaker, Steve (lb) Det, 1962-63
Sumner, Charley (db) Wm Mary 1961-62
Sunde, Milt (g) Minn, 1964-69
Sutton, Archie (t) Ill, 1965-67
Swain, Bill (lb) Ore, 1964
Tarkenton, Francis (qb) Ga, 1961-66
Tatman, Pete (rb) Neb, 1967
Tilleman, Mike (dt) Mont, 1966
Tingelhoff, Mick (c) Neb, 1962-69
Tobey, Dave (lb) Ore, 1966
Triplett, Mel (rb) Tol, 1961-62
VanderKelen, Ron (qb) Wis, 1963-67
Vargo, Larry (db) Det, 1964-65
Vellone, Jim (g) USC, 1966-69
Walden, Bobby (k) Ga, 1964-67
Warwick, Lonnie (lb) Tenn Tech, 1965-69
Washington, Gene (e) MSU, 1967-69
West, Charlie (db) Tex-El Paso, 1968-69
White, Ed (g) Calif, 1969
Williams, A. D. (e) Pac, 1961
Williams, Jeff (rb) Okla St, 1966
Wilson, Tom (rb) no coll, 1963
Winston, Roy (lb) LSU, 1962-69
Yary, Ron (t) USC, 1968-69
Young, Jim (rb) Queens Ont, 1965-66
Youso, Frank (t) Minn, 1961-62

Chapter I

"On Sept. 28, 1969, Joe Kapp threw seven touchdown passes in one game—all to his own men."

Standing in the open basket of his securely-tethered balloon, 11-year-old Rickie Snyder paused to reflect on the simple airborne joys of life at 150 feet among the snowflakes.

From his bouncy outpost above midfield at halftime of the Minnesota Viking-San Francisco 49er game, the young aeronaut could just make out the sportive avalanches blowing down off the third deck roof and imbedding hundreds of happy customers in the grandstand drifts.

Glancing at the small sideline glaciers to obtain a new position fix, the balloonist could have sworn for a moment there that he was looking DOWN on the third deck.

By the time he was able to verify this eyeball reading, Rickie Snyder had cleared the Metropolitan Stadium scoreboard, quickly erasing all of Harmon Killebrew's marks and a few of Joe Kapp's.

And so it soared into history, the unscheduled flight of the hot air bag from St. Paul. The lack of radio equipment robbed posterity of the boy's precise rhetoric at the moment, but reconstructed later it sounded very close to: "Migawd, mother, I'm outa the ballpark."

Hours later, after the boy had been fished safely out of the Minnesota River, somebody awarded him an honorary game ball. He said he was grateful but would have traded it all for five pounds more of ballast.

Scholars who track the cyclical course of history claimed they were not surprised by the remarkable odysseys of Rickie Snyder and the Vikings. The stars had both programed for the year 1969.

Once every few generations, they maintain, the measured tread of civilization rebels against all rules of natural law and brings the world to one of those convulsive years for which not even the prophets are ready.

Those are the 1492s and the 1776s, the ones written in the galaxies and on the blackboards. They are the hash marks of history, the years that get chiseled on trees and shirtcuffs before finals.

The advance book on 1969 showed scant evidence that we were about to be overtaken by the cosmic events. It began with a new man in the White House maintaining we already had moved 10 years ahead of ourselves.

And yet within the next 12 months the world was numbed by a procession of deeds that will one day surely engrave the year 1969 in the ages.

Historians may argue that man walking on the moon was not enough to confer immortality on 1969. Still, it was a major celestial event. So was the close-up scrutiny of the planet Mars and the first flights of the jumbo jets.

But even beyond this in the realm of the implausible stood the saga of the New York Mets.

And beyond that, was there anything to surmount the voyage to the moon, the flight of the Explorer, and the triumph of the Mets as an adventure of the human spirit?

Of course there was.

On Sept. 28th, Joe Kapp of the Minnesota Vikings threw seven touchdown passes against the Baltimore Colts.

In one game.

With an official, standard-size football.

And all to his own men.

It is impossible to catalog the full chain-reaction of events that spun off from this magical afternoon. Its effects, culturally and politically, are still being measured and analyzed.

It was performed in full view of 47,000 people in Bloomington, Minn., including one vice president, Mr. Spiro Agnew, a Colt fan who at that time had not yet discovered the republic was in danger of being overrun by supercilious eunuchs and other college types.

Mr. Agnew spent the afternoon as guest of the Viking management. He agonized inwardly, inscrutably. At the conclusion of the game, Mr. Agnew vanished from the enclosed stadium-top penthouse in the company of ashen-faced secret servicemen. He was not heard from again in the news dispatches until weeks later when he appeared in full battle dress, the reconstituted Agnew, flinging thunderbolts at television, the press, demonstrators, liberals, professors and other perils too numerous to classify.

Until Sept. 28th, in other words, Mr. Agnew seemed content to rest his case for future enshrinement on such off-hand originals as "youth lacks, to some extent, experience." As quotables, these had a promising ring. But even then they were being outpointed in the public prints by the more punchy epigrams of Joe Namath, the most memorable of which was: "I'll never play football again if they make me give up the bar."

History may not record a definite connection between the spectacle of Joe Kapp throwing seven touchdown passes and the unleashing of Spiro Agnew.

But there it was. There is no doubt that Mr. Agnew's juices were irrevocably riled thereafter. By some strange chemistry in the atmosphere that day, flying footballs got mixed up with Mr. Agnew's flying metaphors.

Viewed in this perspective, Kapp's unheralded performance

now begins to take on larger-than-life dimensions. Dramatic and wholly unpredictable events sprang from it, some of them many months from the deed. In this way it was not unlike another un-prophesied eruption, the blowing-up of the volcano Krakatoa. The difference here was that Joe's performance was re-played on the spot on television while the volcano had to wait for 90 years.

What gave Joe's great day a special character was that it caught everybody totally unprepared.

Not the least in this category was the Baltimore defense. Without doubt Joe had been a good and sometimes great quarter-back in Canada. Plunged into the unfamiliar world of 11-man football and four downs, Joe made his debut with the Vikings in September of 1967 by getting thrown for a 10-yard loss.

In defiance of the law of averages and simple justice, his season then began to get worse. And yet by 1968 Joe's bandito gall and his reckless disregard of the weekly National Football League passing statistics—in which he was outranked not only by 15 quarterbacks but some of the extra-point holders—had lifted the Vikings into first place in the Central Division.

He was now duly established as one of the NFL quarter-backing regulars. By way of demonstrating that such fame carries with it high responsibilities, Coach Bud Grant kept Kapp on the bench to lead the Viking rooting section for the entire opening game loss to the Giants in 1969.

Taken in toto, this was not quite enough evidence to prepare the nation for the news that on the very next week Joe Kapp would become the fourth quarterback in NFL history to throw seven touchdown passes in one game.

Only the December before the Colts' last blitz of the day had interred Kapp on the 40-yard line in the mud at Baltimore and left him for the corpsmen.

But now, freshly exhumed, Kapp promptly played himself into eternity with seven touchdown balls, 28 completions and 449 yards.

The Colts immediately renounced all claims to another cham-pionship.

If Kapp's achievement alone did not impart an Olympian quality to the year, events that followed in its wake certainly did.

They can be chronicled as follows:

1. Despite the Detroit Lions' threat to give them nothing but ice water in their shower in reprisal for a plumbing breakdown in Bloomington, the Vikings won the division championship in a Thanksgiving snowstorm in Detroit. This vindicated the club's solemn pledge to clinch the division title before the lake freezeup in Minnesota.

2. In a game widely billed as a dress rehearsal for the midwinter playoffs, for athletes and fans alike, the Vikings defeated San Francisco 10-7 in three feet of snow at Metropolitan Stadium. The game substantiated league claims that conditioned football players are capable of performing under any adversity. The fans, however, choked up. More than 200 cars went smash on the freeways en route to the ball game.

3. The Vikings won the Western Conference championship by rallying to defeat the Rams 23-20 at Metropolitan Stadium Dec. 27. Five thousand fans swarmed the field after the game, producing the Twin Cities' greatest mob scene since the Lutheran World Convention. Few prisoners were taken in each.

4. Just 10 years removed from their creation in the maize fields and pine cones of their first summer camp at Bemidji, Minn., the Vikings won the National Football League championship by defeating the Cleveland Browns 27-7.

Granted, this spilled into 1970, which simply proved the Vikings of 1969 were too much an epic to be squeezed into one year. Their Super Bowl defeat by Kansas City on Jan. 11, unfortunately, cut short their dynasty after one week.

But were the pyramids built overnight?

Did the glaciers come special delivery?

Chapter II

"The Giants are penalized 15 yards for having an illegitimate man downfield." *—Bob Casey, public address announcer.*

Quite clearly the Vikings did not rush into greatness. Instead, they decided to lay siege to it.

Yet nobody who was present on that July day in 1961, when Norman Van Brocklin marshaled his first unsteady formation among the Bemidji conifers, seriously doubts that some supernatural forces had to be at work to put the Vikings into the league championship 10 years later.

Van Brocklin viewed his first assemblage with a mixture of tolerance and grief. Something of an historian himself, he mentally noted this was a day that probably would live in obscurity.

This was true, in a fashion. The world gave only passing notice to the occasion. It was doubtful whether most of the people in the National Football League noticed.

This was an undeserved slight because the Vikings were something of a novelty in the NFL, the only franchise that owed its existence to an act of piracy.

In the general upheaval in professional sports in the late 1950s and early 1960s, occasioned chiefly by the phenomenon of mass market television, it was clear the Minneapolis - St. Paul territory was important ground for new exploration.

Historically it was good if not passionate football country. As a potential baseball market it had a sociological profile not unlike Milwaukee's. Where it fell short of Milwaukee in per capita beer consumption, it compensated with a more stable, sedate temperament among the fans. Sellout crowds in later years, in fact, acquired fame as the forerunners of Nixon's Silent Majority.

It had the population, the stadium and a scorn of pari-mutuel betting to guarantee the success of bigtime baseball and football in the 1960s and in the indefinite thereafter.

Its one experience with major league professional sports was the Minneapolis Lakers of several affiliations. The enterprise flourished handsomely for a time. But it had the misfortune of falling into a basketball era that came somewhere between the sawdust circuit of the 1940s and the Park Ave. of the television millions in the '60s. The Lakers won and drew until George Mikan got old, after which they were spared from pauperdom only by the unsinkable energies and borrowed cash of the Twin Cities industrialist, Robert Short.

Their years of profit, however, were not lost on one Max Winter, a kind of promotional man-for-all-seasons. He had begun as a small-change boxing operator and graduated by degrees into restaurants, theaters, auto shows, real estate and later bigtime sports, including part-ownership of the Lakers.

In 1959 Winter tied in E. W. Boyer and H. P. Skoglund of Minneapolis in active pursuit of a pro football franchise. Boyer was a silver-haired Ford dealer whose persuasive, smooth-talking arts were honed in a business where they are not only helpful but a condition of life. By some vocalistic quirk he had acquired a permanent Southern burr despite a lifetime in the snowdrifts. Nobody had ever figured it out, because Boyer had spent less time in the cotton fields than in the Chevy salesrooms.

Skoglund was the charger of the threesome, a vast, billowing man of round-the-clock energies. He ran his insurance company from a variety of locations, including his office, airplanes, telephone booths and Swedish groaning boards. He was a favorite of Scandinavian royalty and once talked seriously of scheduling an NFL exhibition game in Stockholm—which according to all available statistics is one of the few cities on earth where an NFL exhibition game has not been played.

By the time of their alliance, the Twin Cities already had been test-marketed as an NFL site, but the early enthusiasm belonged unilaterally to the Twin Cities. The NFL played a few games at the Met all right. Yet it had no serious thoughts about handing out new franchises until the incubating American Football League actually went out and got a football.

Business interests campaigning for a pro football franchise in Minnesota put down $240,000 to bring into Metropolitan Stadium two home games of the St. Louis Cardinals in 1959. They strongarmed the tickets aggressively, in some cases ingeniously. They invoked the old appeals of civic pride, the prospect of a battle of the behemoths (a role the Cardinals until then had managed to conceal from their followers) and added the stirring disclosure that the football world was watching the Twin Cities.

In one fashion or other, most of the seats were filled for games matching the Cardinals against the Eagles and the Cardinals against the Giants. Lacking any emotional attachment to either team, the natives looked on with a benign neutrality. Observers thought they detected the same kind of seasoned restraint with which Minnesotans watch the ice form on lakes.

The games themselves (the Cardinals blew both) almost certainly would have been obscured in the archives except for ee rather historic fringe events.

The first of these was the inaugural appearance at the Met of Van Brocklin, quarterbacking the Eagles with his bury-the-bastards style that always gave him the appearance of George Patton facing third and eight. He threw three touchdowns and put a quick squelch on the Pug Lund-oriented natives who were asking "Dutch Who?"

Ranking right up there with Van Brocklin's bombs was the oratorical tour de force of the stadium public address announcer, Bob Casey. His fourth period announcement to the crowd in the Giant-Cardinal game has easily repulsed all challengers as the most inspired malaprop of the post-war era.

Charlie Conerly was cheerfully throwing passes to all fields when the officials called one back under a fusillade of flags. A Giant offensive tackle was spied roaming illegally in the Cardinal secondary.

"That completed pass has been nullified, ladies and gentlemen," Casey revealed in the doomsday baritone of the dedicated

P.A. man. "The Giants are being penalized 15 yards for having an illegitimate man downfield."

Visiting New York reporters in the press box stared at each other aghast. Did Casey know something they had missed in the dressing room?

Before the next play Conerly lectured the transgressing tackle, explaining there were such things as setting examples.

Whereupon he called the same play and threw another touchdown pass.

Of more enduring significance, however, was a telegram from the Bears' George Halas to Charles Johnson, then the sports editor of the Minneapolis Star and Tribune, released to reporters as Conerly was throwing his last touchdown pass.

Halas was the chairman of the NFL's expansion committee. This functioned as a sort of dummy corporation until it began to look as though the AFL organizers were serious about the madness of forming another pro football league.

Johnson was the Dag Hammarskjold of the Minneapolis major league sports campaigners, the behind   negotiator, adviser and intermediary. The community's new stadiu...   on the hook at the time. Its private bondholders had invested milln ns in the arena on the expectation of bringing in major league tenants, and none had signed in at the moment.

The chief recruiters were Johnson; Sid Hartman of The Minneapolis Tribune, a kind of one-man conglomerate of the Twin Cities jockstrap trade; Gerald Moore of the stadium commission; and the Winter-Skoglund-Boyer group.

The sticky wicket of the whole campaign at this point was the organizational meeting of the AFL, in Minneapolis, on the very day Halas' telegram arrived.

Halas' telegram said in effect the NFL was on the verge of offering a franchise to Minneapolis-St. Paul.

This sowed some consternation and a little pique into the ranks of the innocent young millionaires assembled for the AFL meeting, because Winter, Skoglund and Boyer were on the brink of putting Minneapolis into the AFL as a charter member.

As a matter of unvarnished truth, they did.

The new league was midwifed at the Pick-Nicollet Hotel in

Minneapolis by a cast that included the determined young millionaire from Dallas, Lamar Hunt; a considerably more effervescent millionaire, Bud Adams of Houston; the undeflatable ex-sports announcer, Harry Wismer of New York; ex-Notre Dame coach Frank Leahy, wearing his minstrel show bow ties and the colors of Baron Hilton's Los Angeles Chargers; plus others who kept getting crowded out of the captions.

The Minneapolis operation was never taken seriously as a permanent AFL franchise by the National Football League sympathizers among the local promoters. With a rival league now formally in the market if not on the field, Halas' committee clearly was going to counsel some form of expansion, to protect uncommitted TV markets if nothing else.

Dallas and Minnesota would be the first. Still, to nudge Halas' committee a little, Boyer and Skoglund gave off noises that made it sound as though the boys actually planned to play ball with the AFL.

The first was to announce the signing of a couple of free agents, whose names easily slipped from public consciousness between the morning and afternoon editions.

They also made a genuine offer to one of their high draft choices who, by a gentle spasm of irony, turned out to be one Dale Hackbart of Wisconsin. Hackbart eventually materialized five years later as a defensive back shopping for a job with the Vikings after unspectacular careers with the Green Bay Packers and Washington Redskins.

Released by the Vikings in 1965, he reappeared the following year and ultimately ended his long search for identity by becoming the concensus all-league hatchetman in 1967 and 1968. His new coach, Grant, admired his belligerence but was offended by the huge acres of territory it was costing the team in penalties.

Grant therefore altered Hackbart's psyche once more and turned him into the image of decorum in 1969. From this stance of the mellowed headhunter, Hackbart recalled the airy few days when he was one of the only college athletes in the country solicited by four leagues. In alphabetical order these were the American Football League, the Canadian Football League, the

National Football League and the Class C Northern League of organized baseball.

"Some guy from Minneapolis called me in Madison when I was out and left a number. I called back and found out he represented the Twin Cities team in the AFL," Hackbart recalled. "He told me they had drafted me very high. I asked him what he was offering. He said $7,000. I asked him what they were paying the lower draft choices, wheat shucks?"

"So then I asked him for a ballpark figure on the bonus they planned to offer me. He said as a matter of principle the club was not offering bonuses. I told him I was the last guy who would want to corrupt their principles, so I hung up."

As far as can be determined, this was the Minneapolis AFL's franchise only assault on the power structure of organized football or baseball. The forts held up remarkably well. As a threat to the economic integrity of the NFL and the Class C Northern League, the Minneapolis offensive could be described as brief but inglorious. Hackbart was so confused by all of the attention he tried baseball first before signing with the Packers, who could never quite decide what prompted him to change his mind.

It wasn't until he had gone through the wringer of trials and releases with the Packers, Redskins, Vikings, and Winnipeg that Hackbart finally landed upright with the Vikings in 1966.

At about this time Boyer and Skoglund received fresh evidence of the Halas committee's growing ardor for the Twin Cities as an NFL property. They had maintained all along that Minneapolis had never officially enlisted in the AFL and was simply being carried on the temporary duty rolls.

Still, they wanted to tag along on the chance that Halas was unable to deliver an NFL franchise. Wismer snorted at this as a cynical piece of streetwalking, but the AFL could hardly kick out a potential franchise on a point of pride—especially since Lamar Hunt himself was still cultivating an NFL offer.

In the early winter of 1960 Winter, Skoglund and Boyer met with Johnson and two prospective new members of a Minnesota-wide corporation, Bernie Ridder of St. Paul and Ole Haugsrud of Duluth, to actively court an NFL franchise.

Chapter III

"Getting a franchise for $600,000 compared with getting Lake Superior for the price of Mud Creek."

The battleground was Miami, the site of the NFL's winter meetings. Politically at the time, the league was a loose confederacy of a handful of feudal baronies. The oldtime commissioner, Bert Bell, was dead and a successor had to be chosen.

The hazy prospect of television millions hung somewhere in the distance, but nobody in 1960 grasped the enormity of the ultimate bonanza. It was a simple matter to ridicule the awkward new league publicly but not hard to imagine privately what damage it might do in a bidding fight. The question of voting new franchises therefore became a crucial issue.

The NFL, as then constructed, had impressive reserves of Neanderthal thinking for a stubborn defense against the inroads of progress. As an illustration of these rare wall-butting qualities, the owners needed three days of round-the-clock balloting to elect a commissioner. Their eventual choice was a man whose name was dragged in almost exclusively as a concession to sleep. He was approved because the owners in their somnabulent daze could not think of another soul to run through the electoral logjam. And thus did the NFL stumble, accidentally and almost blindly, into the man who steered them to the Shangri La ahead— Pete Rozelle.

The expansion question came down to Dallas and Minneapolis-St. Paul. Dallas' application was put in by the Murchisons, representing enough oil money to transfer the whole league to Mars.

The owners therefore decided Dallas deserved a franchise, to begin operating in 1960.

Now they turned to the fur-parkaed emissaries from the northern prairie.

These delegates offered no oil millions but did present a unified front of Minnesota's various geographic interests, which was more than could be said for the State's delegations to the political conventions.

They also offered a fair amount of ready cash, of which the league tapped $600,000 as the entry fee. In retrospect, coming just two or three years before pro football burst into everybody's living room as the ranking leisure time passion of the decade, it was comparable to getting Lake Superior for the price of Mud Creek.

Ridder published the St. Paul Dispatch and Pioneer Press as a member of a 19th Century-style newspaper dynasty with publishing roots in Europe. He was a massive, Boston-accented patrician with an amiable manner, an obsession for golf, and a calmly civilized approach to the problems of the conference table and the problems of people.

He would be the stabilizing figure of the Viking board in the years ahead, and very often its conscience.

With him came Ole Haugsrud, representing Duluth and its muskeg swamp satellites of the north and the legacy of another geological age in pro football.

Ole was a gentle gnome, a bald little man who grew up on the Duluth-Superior waterfront. His stock was energy and a rhapsodic fondness for the make-believe world of the athletic gladiator. Although never shovy nor strident, he had some craft as a promoter. He thus found a way to merchandise his dreams. He started hawking early, and as a newspaper boy acquired a lively education in the techniques of the sales business by observation along his route—which included daily deliveries to one of the Superior whore houses.

In later times he maintained the Superior whores were among the best read in his experience as a carrier salesman. Unfortunately, their work hours kept them away from the football games he promoted in ensuing years.

Ole was an authentic museum piece, one of the fife-and-drum promoters of pro football from the days when they played the games on graded potato fields. For a time he operated an NFL franchise called the Duluth Eskimos, featuring one of the genuine super-heroes of the 1920s, Ernie Nevers of Stanford.

Long before the era of Jimmy Brown and long after it, Ole Haugsrud would talk about Ernie Nevers as the apotheosis of the great football rusher. Friends would rate the staying power of a new acquaintance on the basis of how many beers it took him to get through Ole's monologues on Ernie Nevers.

He was a loveable little guy and, beyond that, he was absolutely indispensable to the Twin Cities promoters in one rather unique way. They needed him to get the franchise.

As the resident NFL dowager in Minnesota, Ole had what amounted to first option to buy in if and when the time came for a Minnesota franchise to be reactivated. It was there in some musty bylaws, and if there was any disposition on the part of the league or the Twin Cities applicants to overlook it—which there wasn't—Ole carefully had it notarized.

As it was finally set up, the organization allocated 60 percent of its stock to the Winter-Skoglund-Boyer group of Minneapolis, 30 percent to Ridder, and 10 percent to Haugsrud.

That basic formula held through the first decade of the Vikings' operation, although each of the charter owners sold some of their stock in splinters to a collection of pals, business associates, and miscellaneous hangers-on as it ballooned in value. The original five, however, retained exclusive voting rights.

(The actual worth of the Vikings ten years after their formation has been a subject of lively parlor debate within the club ownership and in investment circles. Its original market value, presumably was the $600,000 it cost to get into the league, plus the $400,000 assessed later. The club could not be bought today for less than 15 million and possibly not for 20 million. The original stock was priced at $100 a share. Its value obviously has multiplied 10-fold and more since then, but in a literal way it is impossible to set an actual value on it at any given time. The Vikings stock, in other words, is worth whatever a potential buyer is willing to pay for it today—assuming the figure coincides with what the owner is willing to accept.)

Having approved Dallas for field membership in 1960, the league owners in Miami yielded to Halas' urgings and bestowed a second expansion franchise on Minnesota, to begin play in 1961. Almost all hands expressed delight except the AFL, which now described itself as jilted, hornswoggled and short-sheeted by Minnesota.

As one condition, the NFL stipulated that Metropolitan Stadium in Bloomington be equipped with 40,000 seats by the 1961 opener. Further, the Minnesota organization was required to have 25,000 season tickets in the bank for its maiden season.

In the year 1961, a season ticket sale of 25,000 was well up in the troposphere, at least 10,000 beyond what any previous new-boy franchise had ever delivered in the NFL.

It left the candidate tycoons from Minnesota panting, but the tough provision was sound. Minnesota plainly was going to lose a lot of football games in its first three or four years. It was not likely to be subjected to immediate adoration from the public, especially in a town paternally devoted to university football and with a major league baseball team probably headed there to thicken the competition.

There remained, for the new commissioner to handle largely by decree, two sensitive matters of organizational business.

Of the five partners, Skoglund, Boyer and Ridder came in as bushy-tailed rookies. Haugsrud had run the Eskimos, but that had been in the years when Pola Negri was still a household word.

Winter, however, had managed a sports organization for a time, the Lakers. He was also immersed in other athletic and commercial promotion from time to time and was regarded as canny and competitive.

He was largely a stranger to pro football. Still, it was natural for Max to see himself, by experience, time and inclination, as a logical man to handle most of the duties if not the title of general manager in the new organization.

In this at least one of the Viking owners, Ridder, did not concur. The two later acquired a mutual regard. The problem at the beginning was that they entered the big business penthouse through different doors.

Winter came from the Minneapolis North Side, where money was almost always in short supply and usually wound up in the hands of the early-risers, the jungle fighters, the shrewd and the non-stop runners. Robert E. Short, who eventually owned the Lakers, the Washington Senators and a fair part of the Democratic Party, came from there. So did Sid Gillman, the Los Angeles Rams and San Diego Chargers coach. So did Biggie Munn of Michigan State.

Ridder's milieu, on the other hand, was the country club, the yacht club and the chandeliered board rooms of high finance. He was no stuffed shirt but he came by his money and his wealthy friends as a matter of heritage. He wore his status easily, without display or raised voice.

Their styles were not necessarily antagonistic. But they approached their business encounters with a mutual wariness that never completely disappeared. Ridder accorded Max the respect the financier gives to the nimble broker. Winter trusted Ridder but at times wondered if the publisher had convinced himself somewhere along the line that his money had a special kind of pedigree Max's didn't.

Whether Winter had any thought of pushing his candidacy, Ridder preferred to have a professional general manager installed in the Viking administration office. Rozelle, the new commissioner, considered this absolutely essential. To make sure there was no misunderstanding, he made that arrangement part of the league's operating guidelines for the new franchise.

Max' rising temperature at this point was not soothed by a second league stipulation, that the Vikings set up a permanent voting trust consisting of Ridder, Boyer and Skoglund with the ultimate authority to settle any major dispute involving the entire five-member board.

The provision was still in there heading into the club's second decade of operation, but it has never been used. Despite substantial disputes within the board on such matters as the firing of Bert Rose as general manager and the appointment of a successor, the Vikings' five-headed ownership has functioned well, to the mild astonishment of the league. Winter himself served as president during the important years of transition leading up to the Vikings' drive to the league championship in 1969.

With the franchise awarded, the AFL was now effectively shoved into the river in Minneapolis. This caused no great wave of sympathy in Minneapolis, or St. Paul, but did bother the hell out of the AFL. For the record the new AFL commissioner, Joe Foss, and the head organizer, Lamar Hunt, blistered the Minnesota ownership for its defection, double dealing and four flushing. Some of this happened to be true.

Boyer insisted, however, that he and Skoglund never intended to tie in with the AFL forever, and had not put up the $100,000 in earnest money that would have bound Minneapolis to the AFL, possibly for better but undoubtedly for worse.

There were threats of lawsuits against Boyer and Skoglund. Most of this was public bombast permitting the new league to yield with a certain amount of frayed dignity. It not only yielded but returned to Boyer and Skoglund the original $25,000 intended as Minneapolis' share of the early league operating expenses.

The hostilities were resumed for real sometime later in an antitrust action brought against the NFL at a time when the AFL was trying to shoot its way into a merger. The action went in favor of the NFL, Winter delivering some of the crucial testimony.

So where do you begin to catch up when the Bears and the Giants and Packers and Lions have a 40-year headstart?

"The first thing," Rozelle said, "is get yourself a good scout. You've got a chance to look at the college spring practices this year (1960), looking toward your first draft in the fall. Even before you need a general manager you need a scout."

Rozelle's recommendation was a 35-year-old football knockabout with a good head for appraising talent and the bachelor status that made this kind of vagabonding not only uncomplicated but positively inviting.

Rozelle had known Joe Thomas from the time when both were with the Rams, Thomas as an assistant coach and Rozelle in the front office. He was unemployed in the winter of 1960, having been washed out of a coaching staff job in Toronto with the ouster of the head coach, Hampton Poole.

The Vikings hired Thomas and commissioned him to begin bushwhacking for prospective all-time greats without delay. He brought to the job a sociable temperament, ability and a flair for periodic personality collisions with Van Brocklin. His first-year work with Rose in recommending the draft of Tommy Mason, Rip Hawkins, Francis Tarkenton, Ed Sharockman and Chuck Lamson represented a piece of high professionalism.

Rozelle also had some notions about a prospective general manager who knew the league, had experience with sound front office administration, and progressive ideas about organization of the draft and personnel.

To Rozelle, all of this was synonymous with the Los Angeles Rams, with whom he was one of the office stars for several years. The public relations man for the Rams at the time of the Vikings franchise grant was Bert Rose.

In the Twin Cities they remembered Rose from his publicity excursions into the territory in behalf of the University of Washington football team. He was bright, entertaining, a good companion over a martini, and ambitious. He had done well in Washington and also with the Rams, for whom he worked from 1955 to 1960.

Rose was with the Rams at the Redlands, Calif., training camp in the summer of 1960 when he got a call from Skoglund. The insurance man said he was in the Los Angeles area on company business and invited Rose to lunch with him in Santa Ana.

Chapter IV

"The Swedish Underground was sent into action when Bert Rose began ignoring hints to resign."

"Tell me," Skoglund said, "how you would go about it if you were us and had to start a National Football League club."

"Would you like the long-form exposition or the abridged version?" Rose asked.

Skoglund said he had no objection to small-print details. These Rose provided in a well-modulated monologue that stretched into two hours and left Skoglund outwardly interested, privately convinced, and physically worn out.

He asked Rose to fly to Minneapolis two days later for a conference with the board. He was supposed to be the first of ten prospective candidates interviewed by the directors, but the others never got in the door. Rose was hired, and the press was duly summoned to inform humanity.

Of all the Viking movers in the organization's formative years, Bert Rose has been granted the least recognition, charity and calm detachment. Although he was a first-rate public relations man, he had—in dealing with people new to pro football—a trace of arrogance and defensiveness that made him downright feisty now and then.

He went through the motions of genuflecting before some of the local sacred elephants—University of Minnesota athletics, the sports editors Johnson and Hartman, and others—but these ceremonials lost some of their thrill after a time. This may have been human and understandable, but it was not very good politics.

Van Brocklin later joined an impressive roll call of those

alienated or otherwise bothered by Bert. From there it was a mathematical cinch that the names of Boyer, Winter and Skoglund would be added to this increasingly distinguished list.

As one of the journalistic witnesses in those days, I admit not being overwhelmed with sympathy for Rose. Yet it is probably true that despite some personality flaws and his occupational evasions, Bert eventually was done in because he happened to be the Vikings' first general manager and not because of his administrative sins.

The circumstances of his removal have never been given a good public airing and it is a pity, because for unrehearsed slapstick espionage, they represent a small epic in NFL history.

The miracle was that Rose lasted as long as he did, into the spring of 1964. It was a suspenseful siege. The one at Leningrad lasted longer, but not by much.

At its height the befuddled general manager was under direct assault or lively enfilade fire by a majority of the board, two sports editors, the head coach, and miscellaneous magnates around town. In his spare time he faced some rather heroic sabotage between the lines by a talkative secretary, and a heavy-footed tail job by the organization's resident Sherlock Holmes.

The code name for this last was "The Swedish Underground," a one-man operation that constituted the Vikings' CIA. It was run out of the insurance company headquarters of one of the owners, Skoglund, a devotee of continental-type intrigue.

The Swedish Underground was, in reality, one Ray Johnson, a former FBI agent. He was a likeably surreptitious character who had the vague cover title of security officer for Skoglund's company.

Among his several duties in the Vikings' early history was to compile a sort of vice index of the Hennepin Av. area of Minneapolis, where the Viking warriors might be exposed to various social pitfalls. Part of the street was declared off-limits to NFL players during Rozelle's hard-line austerity program in the wake of the Hornung-Karras gambling suspension.

Acting on intelligence reports from The Swedish Underground, Rozelle blanketed every joint from 10th St. to 4th St. on Hennepin and condemned them for NFL patronage.

Some of the joints, of course, were stubbornly reputable, such as the White Castle Hamburger Stand and Fitwell Pants.

It was during a routine scrutiny of the embargoed six-block strip that The Swedish Underground discovered a horrifying truth: Among the establishments it had condemned was none other than the 620 Club, one of whose custodians was Max Winter, the Vikings' president-elect.

In the range and ferocity of its activities The Underground functioned as a lutefisk-and-meatballs version of Inspector Cluseau's office in the Paris constabulary.

The Underground was sent into action hurriedly at a time when Rose began ignoring reasonable hints to resign. Bert at this point had developed erratic driving habits, some of which wound up with citations and at least one in a trial.

The presumption now was that if Bert couldn't be induced to resign in the board room he might be drummed out of the job in traffic court.

Sports page offices and suburban police departments began receiving anonymous telephone calls detailing Bert's current whereabouts and his programmed route of travel, together with anticipated times of departure and arrival.

Cluseau could not have performed with higher dedication or a lousier track record. Rose stayed clean automotively, although he was sinking fast administratively.

Part of the problem was a not-uncommon clash between a strong personality in the head coach's office, Van Brocklin, and a general manager who had ability but declining popularity with the ownership. Rose retreated about as far as he could in yielding his authorities, at which point the directors invited him to complete the process by retiring.

Bert was no martyr. He might have hung around and outlasted Van Brocklin if he lowered his pride and stopped pretending to be the general manager when most of his power was gone. It also would have helped if he had lengthened his traditional Lenten interludes of abstinence. His fondness for the executive institution of the pit-stop was hardly original or even excessive. But it did make him very vulnerable in the gossip chambers on the fringes of the organization and at times it made him very pugnacious.

In the end it came to a vote for or against Van Brocklin, which made it practically an uncontested match. It was never an actual power struggle. What Dutch wanted around the organization, with the exception of more stock in 1963, Dutch usually got. Bert tried to be adaptable but wound up making people uncomfortable. When this growing number came to include Skoglund, Winter, Boyer, Haugsrud and finally Ridder, Bert hung up the paper clips.

His achievements, however, were considerable. Among other things he enlisted a clan of exuberant civic boosters and tipplers called the Minneapolis Minutemen, toward the goal of selling 25,000 season tickets.

The Minutemen are the ticket-peddling militia of the Twin Cities. When the money establishment of Minneapolis built the stadium in the mid-50s, it quickly became apparent there would be no stampede by small businessmen to pick up the bonds necessary to underwrite the project. The Minutemen hawked them around until the thing was solvent, after which the boys lapsed into repose, awaiting new Bunker Hills.

Rose furnished one in the fall of 1960—25,000 season tickets to sell by the summer of 1961. There were problems. By popular demand of the American Baseball League, Calvin Griffith disengaged from Washington, D. C., and moved to Minnesota.

To further murk up the ticket hustlers' prospects, the University of Minnesota Gophers picked the fall of 1960 to burst fully conscious from the football graveyard. They not only beat up on almost everybody in view but won the national championship and stretched the season into the Rose Bowl.

Yet the Viking tickets were sold by the time of the final audit, satisfying the hard-hearted accountants from Rozelle's office and putting the franchise into an unexpected glow of health, no matter what happened in the stadium.

At the urging of the board Rose hired, with no runaway enthusiasm, the former Minnesota football star and high school coach, Billy Bye. Bye was a figure of wide popularity within the sporting society and newspaper crowd in the Twin Cities, an engaging good fellow and a gifted salesman. But he was miscast as the ticket manager, and was looked on as something of a threat by the general manager. In later years Bye became an office handy-man and general-manager-in-waiting. He left to enter the banking business when he was passed over in the choice of a successor to Rose.

But in the fall of 1960 Bert Rose, freshly-crowned general manager, viewed the horizons and saw two challenges worthy of the undivided energies of a dynasty-builder. He could foresee himself picking a head coach in a fashion so audacious as to rock the jaded trustees of pro football's high councils. And he would preside over the Vikings' first year draft with the same verve and unexpected savvy.

So, all right, everybody was in the middle of a football season, and all the coaches were busy with Xs and Os on the blackboards. The times, reasoned Bert Rose, called for boldness.

He put in a call, therefore, for Ara Parseghian at Northwestern.

Chapter V

"Rose knew all about Van Brocklin's flair for rages and his capacity to generate enemies."

From his days in the service, Bert Rose had learned the wisdom and the intramural politics of the protocol system. He was, in short, an establishment man, right down to the long, legal-size tablets on which he made notes and occasionally wrote memos to himself.

As a newly commissioned general manager about to recruit a coach, Bert understood there was such a thing as etiquette and prescribed form in launching the search. There would be time later to lift the league's eyebrows with a brash trade here and a daring appointment there.

First, though, respects had to be paid. Bert would make courtesy calls on Cleveland's Paul Brown and Green Bay's Vince Lombardi, the latter relatively new in the league as an all-around muse but even then in the early stages of veneration.

Bert asked each how he would proceed. The conversations were conducted in strict privacy. So it will never be confirmed whether either one or both told Rose the best arrangement in the NFL was have one all-purpose virtuoso calling all shots as both head coach and general manager.

At the time there were two such prodigies in the league, Paul Brown of Cleveland and Vince Lombardi of Green Bay.

Since Rose's only experience as a coach was in the Sunday Afternoon Vesper Service League in Seattle, he fell short of qualifying. Whatever their recommendations, Bert made a very nice, respectful impression—which didn't hurt him a bit a year later when he called Brown about a trade.

Since Max Winter and Sid Gillman were old North Minneapolis confederates, Bert viewed it as additional good protocol to talk to Sid about the Viking coaching job. Gillman had been the Los Angeles Rams' coach in the middle and late 1950s, a career notable for a division title in 1955 and a noisy disharmony involving the coach and his quarterback, Van Brocklin.

In the end, Van Brocklin temporarily retired to escape Gillman and got himself traded to Philadelphia—which at the time was like the German emperor getting traded to Liechtenstein.

Gillman was fired a couple of years later, completing the circle.

Students of the cyclical theory of recurring catastrophes recalled this sequence of events nearly ten years later. Then, another quarterback named Francis Tarkenton temporarily retired to escape a coach named Van Brocklin and got himself traded to New York—which was several leagues beyond Liechtenstein financially but not exactly overrunning the continent competitively.

Like Gillman, Van Brocklin departed as coach, thus concluding the Grecian melodrama in which all parties to the brawl exited from opposite ends of the stage and jumped off the cliff simultaneously.

In 1960, Gillman was coaching the Los Angeles Chargers of the AFL. His name appeared first on what Rose described as his ready list of coaching possibilities, and later on the more exclusive "general manager's short list."

Among the others were Otto Graham; Nick Skorich, an assistant on the Eagles staff at that time; Mike Nixon, another of the accredited members of the league's revolving fund of coaches; Ara Parseghian, Norman Van Brocklin and Bud Grant, then the coach at Winnipeg and quite clearly the winterbook favorite of several of the directors.

Rose and Gillman had been associates in the Rams' organization. They talked about the Viking job, and Gillman appeared interested, but the general manager plainly was shooting for an administrative coup. The franchise was new. It was going to lose a lot of football games, but it needed a fresh coaching personality to stir the fans with instant name identification. The word was Excitement.

There are few coaching personalities on earth who generate more excitement than Parseghian. Bert Rose, sitting in a hastily-requisitioned swivel chair in the Vikings' temporary offices at Skoglund's insurance company, examined his options. Van Brocklin, he determined, probably would be his No. 1 choice if available. But at that time the Dutchman was in the midst of quarterbacking the Eagles to the league championship and was under the impression that his next job would be coaching the Eagles. The Minnesota owners wanted Bud Grant, but what did Bert Rose, NFL man, and a Los Angeles Rams one at that, know about Canadian Leagues and rouges?

So Bert viewed Parseghian as a fascinating and serious possibility to be the first coach of the Vikings. True, he had no head coaching experience in the NFL but he had been in the league, and his offense at Northwestern had a distinctly pro coloration.

He was a headliner, an able coach and electrifying sort of character. He could epitomize an impulsive, eager young football organization hurling itself at the hoary ranks of The Structure.

The more Bert Rose thought about it, the shorter his short list shrunk.

The fact is that Ara Parseghian might very well have been the first Viking coach, save for the never-sleeping intelligence network of columnist Sid Hartman of The Minneapolis Tribune, the constant presence of the Twin Cities newspaper trade. Sports-page readers in Minneapolis have come to expect a Breathtaking Scoop from Sid as a matter of routine over the years, and the Extraordinary Expose as a regular weekly bonus.

As a combined columnist and radio interviewer—a dual role that frequently created the illusion that Sid was in two places at once—his feats of transmogrification are without parallel in media history. Readers going through one of his dispatches from the Vikings' training camp, for example, would be startled to hear Sid interviewing the Twins' manager on the radio in New York at that very moment. He must have been in New York because he kept using phrases such as "I see that Perry is warming up," information that would have been tough to come by in Mankato, Minn.

What it was, naturally, was the miracle of electronics plus a certain amount of dramatic license. Sid could see that Perry was warming because the manager had just revealed it in their little pre-tape jam session by telephone from New York to Mankato.

The tape recorder is Sid's Excalibur, the armament and shield of a man born to chronicle the deeds of the mighty.

One of his machines already has been spoken for by the Smithsonian, the one used by Sid in his celebrated underwater interview with Joe Namath.

Hartman had covered the widely-publicized first competitive meeting of Namath and Tarkenton in the Giants-Jets exhibition in the Yale Bowl the summer of 1969. Tarkenton had been one of Sid's professional favorites, having earned Hartman's affection by declining to join the other 99 percent of the Minnesota jocks who needle the hell out of Sid in the lockerroom.

Namath and the Jets demolished Tark and the Giants. Realizing Francis would understand, Sid hurdled three puzzled professors strolling the Bowl caverns so that he might be the first to interrogate Namath.

As an interview subject, Broadway Joe retains the artist's prerogatives. He is choosy about such things as setting, time and room temperature. On this night he chose to ignore all questions by the assembled authors, claiming he needed an extended, 45-minute shower because of his well-known partiality to impeccable hygiene.

With their deadlines fast encroaching, the journalists sadly gazed at the departing merman and settled for Weeb Ewbank.

Not, however, Hartman.

With undeterred purpose and high dignity, Sid grabbed his tape recorder and walked right into the shower with Namath.

A veteran New England sportswriter who had covered the raising of the sunken submarine Squalus told me later that fathom for fathom, Hartman's performance surpassed anything he had witnessed in 20 years on the marine beat.

"I refer both to his seamanship," the journalist confided, "and his agility in avoiding a case of the bends. He was the only guy in the lockerroom who talked to Namath, and he did it right in the middle of the shower, fully clothed, with the faucets going 50 barrels a minute.

"What he did was to stand beside Namath and stick his microphone into the cascading water for Namath to answer his questions while Sid would try to stand as far away from the torrent as he could. This wasn't very far because the microphone cord was only a couple of feet long. One time there, Sid stuck what he thought was the microphone under the shower, but he must have put out the wrong hand because Namath wound up talking into a cake of Sweetheart Soap.

"The rest of us stood around by the drain trough, protected from the spray, but Namath wouldn't give us the time of day. We thought of sending a guy in there with an umbrella, but he woulda looked like a pansy alongside Hartman, who was up to his socks in standing water.

"Namath was barely visible in the clouds of steam and the pouring water. Once in a while you could catch a glimpse of him, lathering leisurely. When he got to the more intimate part of his ablutions, it demanded some advanced acrobatics by the reporter to maneuver the microphone in such a way as to stay with the conversational flow and still hold on to his professional dignity.

"I know that Namath agreed to this acquatic interview as a put-down to newspapermen, but between you and me I'm positive that the sight of this Hartman sloshing through the groundswell in his leather shoes completely unnerved Broadway Joe. I swear I heard him say, 'good Christ, they finally found one who actually believes he can walk on water.'

"So he told him all about the game plan and the turning point and how Tarkenton could have done just as well as Joe if he had the Jets' offensive line to play behind. And then in one of those great second-effort bids for the poignant quote, Sid asked Joe if he ever dreamed he would some day be playing before 70,000 screaming fans in the Yale Bowl. And Joe rose splendidly to the occasion by turning down the nozzle of the cataract so that the mike could pick up every word, and he said, 'I never dreamed that I would some day be playing before 70,000 screaming fans in the Yale Bowl.'

"Well, never let anybody tell you that Namath isn't responsive to a question."

The interview ended, Namath toweled, dressed silently and left the rest of the press box crew grubbing in the soap trays for Hartman's discarded tapes.

Sid's remarkable feat of sonar journalism is chronicled here as the backdrop and alibi for the demise of Bert Rose's first undercover operation as Viking general manager.

Bert knew he would have to chart the shrewdest kind of diplomacy to meet and confer privately with the lively Armenian in the middle of October with the football season in full uproar.

Parseghian agreed to take a day off from practice at Northwestern to fly to the Twin Cities for a preliminary talk with Rose. Lunch would be fine, Bert proposed, at some out-of-the-way table at the Edina Country Club.

Rose was aware that the Edina Country Club is not listed among ranking retreats for the meditative and the solitude-seekers. It is, in fact, the Happy Hollow of the more sociable and sporty residents of America's fourth-most-prosperous-suburb-per-capita.

With the operations planner's sure grasp of the big picture, Rose conceded that lunch in a crowded room just might compromise the mission. But a lunch at the anonymous hour of 2:30 would—in the wry language he used occasionally with his intimates—remove all of the hazards to privacy in one swell foop.

Parseghian arrived by plane around noon and dined with Bert at the appointed hour. Only four or five stragglers remained of the daily martini sweepstakes. Clearly, there was no problem with security.

Bert and Ara talked for a couple of hours about the Vikings' plans, the organization, prospects for the draft, the pro football potential of the Twin Cities and how the Vikings' first coach would face a magnificent if unsurmountable tomorrow.

Parseghian obviously was interested. A football coach could not fly from Chicago to Minneapolis in the middle of the football season and still pretend to be bored. They did not talk specific terms, nor could any firm offer be made in the absence of a consultation between Rose and the board.

One thing Parseghian did stipulate to the general manager. If news leaked about their conversation, he would have to disclaim any remote notions about leaving Northwestern and probably renounce the whole thing as preposterous.

What, Bert agreed, could be fairer?

They finished and Ara headed for the airport to rededicate his thoughts to the latest crises at Northwestern. Rose returned to his office. The country club stragglers, however, all sprinted to the telephones independently to inform the newspaper that the Vikings' general manager was seen talking that very afternoon to Ara Parseghian, and they weren't discussing the latest tariff on rugs.

Authenticating the story was a simple, three-telephone romp for the peerless columnist, and Sid made an item out of it.

The wire services moved it around the country briefly, and Parseghian arrived at the Chicago airport to be met by a hive of sports reporters inquiring about his adventures in Minnesota.

So ended the Vikings' first excursion into the coaching markets. Rose's short list shortened by one and was reduced eventually to Bud Grant and Van Brocklin.

Rose and Grant discussed the possibilities at an afternoon meeting in the insurance building late in 1960. Some of the owners already had indicated they preferred Grant for the job. It was his if he wanted it. But in midstream of a highly successful career in Winnipeg, Grant could not have been overpowered by the thrill of coaching a first-year franchise in the National Football League. Unquestionably he wanted to get back sooner or later. And he was as logical a man to consider then as he was seven years later when he did accept the job.

But, after Rose had scheduled another meeting the morning of the next day, Grant advised the owners to withdraw his name from consideration, explaining that he preferred to remain at Winnipeg.

At this point in the action Rose was still moving laterally but had a lot of field left. The preliminary negotiations with Van Brocklin would involve a delicacy rare in the rhinoceros-style diplomacy usually practiced in the NFL. Bert Rose therefore packed his swallow tails and headed for Philadelphia, ostensibly on other business.

Van Brocklin was then quarterbacking the Eagles in the direction of the championship. It was generally understood that Buck Shaw, the coach, would retire at the end of the season and that Van Brocklin might be the one to succeed him. The Dutchman was close to Jim Clark, the Eagles' board chairman, and was doing a fair amount of Shaw's coaching as a player.

Rose and Van Brocklin knew each other well from their years together in the Rams' organization. Rose knew all about Van Brocklin's impulsive temperament, his flair for rages and his capacity to generate enemies.

He also recognized Van Brocklin's extraordinary power to lead, a football mentality matched by few playing the game and few coaching it, and a disposition that could be abrasive but also could be captivating and persuasive.

So he telephoned the Dutchman and invited him to drop over to his hotel room, from where they would go to dinner. Van Brocklin agreed to stop in about 6:45.

Being an industrious man and not enraptured by the dinner hour cartoons on television, Rose then invited Nick Skorich of the Eagles staff to come up for a chat at 5:30. Nick was down near the water line on Bert's short list. But he was a very estimable man and would, by the way, get the Eagles head coaching job just two months later.

Rose presided cordially over the meeting with Skorich, reciting the now familiar timetable with which the Viking organization planned to assault the challenge of tomorrow. The session lasted a trifle longer than planned and Rose was pressed to get Nick out of the door tactfully.

Nick boarded the left car on the double-elevator shaft, waved a fraternal goodbye, and descended. At this precise moment the door of the other shaft opened, disgorging Norman Van Brocklin.

Rose stifled a quick impulse to swoon at the thinness of the escape, and shifted fraternal waves in midstride to greet his old colleague Van Brocklin.

They had a leisurely dinner, merely skirting the question of the Viking coaching job. Van Brocklin's coaching ambitions did not go beyond Philadelphia at that point. And Rose, always protocol conscious, was in no position to shop the Viking coaching job to a man under contract to another organization. The manual was clear on this: You had to have the other organization's clearance to talk. The manual said nothing, however, about between-the-salads burps and other code forms with which the general manager may communicate his intentions.

In any event, they parted without seriously discussing the Viking position. Van Brocklin went back to his projector and Rose plunged into the Vikings first draft, in late November of 1960.

In mixing the essential elements of a pro football team, you have a formula that is simplicity itself. No matter what you stir in afterward, you start out the mix with a quarterback. Rose reasoned that a franchise could survive a rookie general manager and could even survive a rookie coach, but it might not survive a rookie quarterback. He would therefore deal for a veteran quarterback and then choose a rookie high in the draft to learn the mysteries of pro football at a leisurely pace under the tutelage of the old head in front of him.

Rose's nomination for the old head was George Shaw, then in the midst of a routinely troubled season as backup man to Charlie Conerly with the Giants. George was a calm, thoughtful, junior-broker type of professional athlete. For a time in the mid-50s he seemed to verge on star quality, as the young quarterback for the Baltimore Colts. But the Bears busted up his leg, bestowing on George one small footnote of NFL celebrity: He was the man who lost his job to a hungry kid from the coal fields, Johnny Unitas.

Of all the No. 2 quarterbacks in the league—presumably the only ones available—Rose viewed Shaw as the most desirable to anchor a new team. He had demonstrated ability, he had good character and intellect, and he was young enough to play for at least five or six more years.

Late in November Rose telephoned Wellington Mara, the keeper of the Giants. "George will cost you your first-round draft choice," Mara disclosed.

Bert treaded water easily, pausing to ask Wellington whether he also wanted the Minneapolis Grain Exchange and University of Minnesota cyclatrone.

"Okay, your first draft choice for next year," Mara amended.

Rose concurred. On the basis of this understanding, he was now prepared to dazzle the old guard at the draft table.

According to Joe Thomas' computations and finger-in-the-wind reckoning, the 1960 college football player most likely to make important waves in the NFL for years to come was Tommy Mason of Tulane, a young man with a slashing running style, a fondness for guitar picking and an easy, coachable disposition.

Chapter VI

"I started out as a future, and damned near wound up as a past."—Ed Sharockman, Viking defensive back.

The Vikings picked first in the draft and chose Mason.

Nobody in the organization would ever regret the choice. Wounds of various description would deny him the professional fulfillment his gifts and competitive will deserved. But for a couple of years at least he was the best halfback in the league and he would be remembered by the men he played with for his reckless, unflinching effort and the sunny decency of his character.

"We wanted a running back high in our first draft," Rose adjudged, "and we wanted a young middle linebacker as the glue of whatever defense our first coach would put together. The quarterback we rated No. 1 in college football, and the one the others rated the same way, was Norm Snead of Wake Forest, who went to the Redskins after we drafted Mason. The guy we had rated as the No. 2 quarterback was Francis Tarkenton of Georgia, but because we had Shaw already pledged we went after a middle backer on the second round, and Rip Hawkins of North Carolina—a very good one—was available. So the question became, how much chance did we have of getting through the rest of the second round without losing Tarkenton before we drafted again at the top of the third round?"

It got down to the thin hairs near the bottom of the list, with only two teams remaining to select on the second round. In those years the teams conducted their draft in a hotel ballroom, usually in Chicago. The high command of each organization would congregate around a felt-topped round table, a few feet from the nearest rival. Telephones were hooked up for instant communication with the young gladiators around the country, their coaches and even their girl friends. Beside each deliberating team was its file of scouting reports. The dimensions of these depended on the zeal with which the organization conducted its scouting. If it was Pittsburgh, a small memo pad could have handled all of the organization's confidential data. If it was the Los Angeles Rams, they needed half of the 5th Army's foot-lockers.

Rose and Thomas, both of whom had some experience with the Rams, dragged the equivalent of half the 47th Division's footlockers.

Nowadays the teams conduct the draft from their home offices, indicating their choices electronically to the league headquarters. When they were all under one roof, however, it was customary for the drafting organization to write the name of its next choice on a slip of paper and to convey it to one Harry Standish of the league office, standing at a lectern on the stage. He would then announce to all assembled in apocalyptic tones:

"Dallas selects . . . on the second round . . . R-E-N-F-R-O, Renfro, Mel, halfback."

As they neared the conclusion of the second round, with Tarkenton still unselected and Rose, Thomas and Viking owners grimly holding the left one of everything in pairs, Wellington Mara passed his slip forward.

Standish began reading, "New York selects . . . on the second round . . . T-A-R . . ."

Rose and Thomas exchanged the looks of sinking pilgrims.

". . . -B-O-X, Tarbox, guard, Syracuse."

Thus was Francis spared from the clutches of Broadway and Wall Street, six years before he finally got maneuvered there.

The only question about Tarkenton's qualifications for pro football was his ability to throw long. Thomas concluded he could throw long enough, and the Vikings speedily drafted him on the third round.

Rose now opted for some giddy aerobatics at the draft table, intended in part to startle the beetled old heads into low whistles of amazement. Somewhere along the line in each draft, most clubs will select a "future"—a player with college eligibility remaining but currently draftable because his class will graduate the following June.

Most of these are selected in later rounds, after all of the immediately available good players are taken. Once in a while teams with a large reservoir of talent will pick a future early in the draft, a luxury the weaker teams rarely consider.

Without warning, and with the impressario's casual art that conceals true art, Bert Rose drafted Chuck Lamson, defensive back, Wyoming, on the fourth round—AS A FUTURE, for 1962.

All hands were predictably flabbergasted, including Norman Van Brocklin when he heard about it two months later. History probably will record that of all of Bert's first-draft conjuries, the choice of a future on the fourth round was the least blessed with logic.

To prove it was no fluke, however, Bert did it again on the very next round, at least on the surface. Ed Sharockman was a tough, untamed kid from the coal towns who played quarterback for the University of Pittsburgh. He had a good mentality and basically good impulses, as his subsequent maturing was to demonstrate. But at the time he was an athletic gypsy at Pitt, a free-ranging maverick. His class was graduating and he still had another year of eligibility left, making him a potential "future" in the NFL draft.

But Thomas had learned something few of the other gumshoes were aware of. Eddie was not being invited back to Pitt and wasn't going to get his last year of competition. Which meant he could play in the National Football League the following fall, instead of waiting for 1962.

Bert Rose had Harry Standish announce, "The Minnesota Vikings . . . on the fifth round . . . select Ed Sharockman, University of Pittsburgh, quarterback and defensive back."

This time there was no Dutch Uncle amusement from the league elders but the spluttering rage of the Pittsburgh Steelers' Buddy Parker, who had already banked Ed Sharockman for the Steelers as a probable future in the next few rounds.

"You can't do that," Parker shrieked. "Not another goddamned future. What in the hell season are you getting ready for, 1984?"

Thomas tenderly broke the news to the storming Steeler coach, about Sharockman's immediate eligibility. Recovering, Parker now tried to make a flat-out deal for the young renegade. Rose declined, explaining Sharockman undoubtedly would be the Vikings' No. 1 rookie defensive back in the 1961 season.

He wasn't. The forces of the cosmos were on Parker's side, even if his scouting system lined up wrong. After three days in Viking camp, Sharockman headed for the Chicago All-Star camp, from which he returned with a broken leg to miss the entire 1961 season.

"I started out as a future," he told a pal, "and damned near wound up as a past."

Chapter VII

"You're a goddamned phony hunkie newspaperman."
—Van Brocklin in easy stride in an interview.

"The Eagles were nothing before I got here," confided Norman Van Brocklin in one of the frugal farewell addresses of the 1960s, "and they'll be nothing when I'm gone."

As a valedictory, there was a nice blend here of disdain, malice and truth. From the mid-50s to 1958 the Eagles pursued the role of cheerless mediocrity with a stubborn resolve. Van Brocklin overtook them in 1958 as part of his penance for his private rebellion against Gillman and the warring Ram owners.

By 1959 the Eagles were back from exile and in 1960 Van Brocklin took them all the way to what the NFL in those days called the championship of the world. It may not have been a misnomer at that. Any time you beat Vince Lombardi in the 1960s you were entitled to global considerations. Lombardi's glowering overnight rehabilitation of pro football in Green Bay was as impressive as Van Brocklin's wisecracking reclamation of the Eagles.

Their championship game was a match of a reformed and defiant old guard making one last bid for big money and vindication—the Van Brocklins and Bedthe Hornungs, Starrs, Dowlers and Taylors who would command the league for the rest of the decade.

The Eagles won with a fourth period touchdown, 17-13. Norman Van Brocklin regarded this as a culminating act in his forthcoming installation as the Eagle head coach. It was the ceremonial knighting of Lancelot with the championship ring.

It would be followed a couple of days later by the bestowal of the clipboard, whistle and paranoid tablets that are the coach's badges of office.

It might have worked out that way. Van Brocklin was absolutely convinced he had the Eagles' moral commitment to succeed Buck Shaw as the head coach. Whatever promises were made by whom, it became clear that the enthusiasm for Van Brocklin as coach was not unanimous.

It was not hard for Vince McNally, the general manager, and Frank MacNamee, the president, to see more logic in a Van Brocklin as quarterback and assistant coach. The lockerrooms were full of potentially good coaches but had no such largesse of all-pro quarterbacks. Van Brocklin would be a mere 34 in 1960. There were quarterbacks in the league five years older who were still on their feet and very often hitting the receiver.

Van Brocklin was offered this role of quarterback and auxiliary mastermind for a figure that might go close to $45,000. With animation and short words he made it clear where the Eagles could dispose of this offer.

To friends and sometimes simply to nosy hangers-on he said things about the Eagle patriarchs that had to be classified as unfriendly at the very least. Some of it got back to McNamee, et al. Conversations shortly blew up and the Eagles wired Bert Rose in Minneapolis, "Philadelphia hereby gives Minnesota permission to talk to Van Brocklin about position or positions interested in."

Rose was waiting in Los Angeles when Van Brocklin arrived to begin practices for the Pro Bowl, his last as a player. Shortly afterward they flew to Palm Springs, Calif., to meet Skoglund. Like Boyer, Skoglund was one of those hard-headed business captains who melt boyishly in the company of a linimented hero. He was captivated instantly by Van Brocklin, whose naturalness, sociability and spasmodic giggles away from the lockerroom make an enormous impression on somebody offering friendship.

The Dutchman was asked to fly to Minneapolis the day after the Pro Bowl for a meeting with the rest of the Viking board. Rose by now had made up his mind to recommend him for the coaching job. Skoglund, at that time the most forceful voice on the Viking board, obviously would endorse him.

Rose later was fond of portraying his decision to go after Van Brocklin as a gamble. He suggested that the hiring of an un-inhibited star player with no coaching experience could jeopard-ize the formative years of the Viking franchise, and he gave the impression it was an act of bravery to sign him on.

The real gamble, as it turned out, involved Rose personally, the future of his job in an organization Van Brocklin came to dominate.

Fired general managers do not usually write memoirs until they have exhausted all other available general managerships. Bert, however, is a man not without a certain historical presence.

"For a brand new manager to recommend a guy as coach who had never coached before, well, I would not exactly say this was playing it safe," he says. "The thing that appealed to me about Dutch was that I was confident he had certain leadership qualities. I had seen some of those get him into trouble. But he had a certain kind of flamboyant leadership and I was willing to take a chance on the coaching. I knew from my days with the Rams' organiza-tion that there were only a few essential elements in coaching.

"One was technical knowledge of the game. I think you almost have to assume—if he's a guy who has been coaching or quarterbacking—well, they all can do the Xs and Os pretty well. Some maybe have a sharper football mind than the next guy.

"And then the other thing, the unknown, is the motivation quality which to me is maybe 70 percent. Who does the best to motivate 40 different individuals to a common goal, so that they're playing to the utmost or close to the utmost of whatever is their capability, Sunday after Sunday. To me, that's the big part of coaching.

"And I thought Van Brocklin would have that to a large degree, almost by a follow-me attitude if nothing else. We were going to have a bunch of rookies and a bunch of veterans who were not particularly wanted where they came from. They might respond pretty well to this guy who they knew by reputation or from the Sunday battles.

"From a public relations standpoint, he would be a plus—a

big name, a guy who would generate interest with the ticket-buying public. He was just the biggest name in pro football at the time.

"With Grant out of the picture, one alternative was to hire an acceptable, experienced assistant coach from within the NFL. This would have been safer, I suppose, but Van Brocklin had a lot more potential and, let's face it, he was a lot more exciting. The risk was his personality, which is a risk I suppose is still there even after his eight years of coaching in the NFL.

"So that was an unknown. But all things considered, I thought from a club standpoint . . . I guess I'm trying to say this, that my recommendation of Dutch was based on what I thought would be best for the organization, and not necessarily what would be best for the man making the recommendation."

The Van Brocklin personality had already been the object of years of energetic Freudian analysis around the NFL. This took place recurrently in such widely diverse forums as the sports pages of the Los Angeles and Philadelphia newspapers, the club-houses of the league, the coaching sanctums, and the saloons where the ballplayers beered.

He was a creature of will, impulse, intellect and ego. His greatest single virtue as a competitor and a human being was his unbreakable belief in himself. It lifted him to rare levels of performance under duress and, when rubbed off on his team-mates or players, could do the same for his team. When it spilled into impatience and frustration, it pushed him into spasms of cruelty, vindictiveness, and just plain bad-mouth.

He had a positive genius for spontaneous fury and a bewilder-ing private roster of encircling villains, some of them clearly imagined. But when the demons were quelled, he was a merry, needling leprechaun in the clubhouse or at the bar. His fondness for the old days of the NFL was profound and almost tender. But it also acted as a dividing line in his mind between the "real ones," the achievers, as opposed to some of those who followed or hung around. These Van Brocklin would classify as phony pencil-pushers (front office men), phony newspapermen (the ones with whom he quarreled), phony Notre Damers (not to be confused with phony Big Tenners), phony owners (the ones he began to suspect), and various sub-orders of phonies.

It was a convenient word, generally applied to people who didn't agree with Van Brocklin or saw some edge of hypocrisy in his one-sided renditions of the truth. He spoke emotionally about the value of the bedrock qualities of loyalty, pride, family devotion and personal discipline, but he had a hard time crediting the men who played under him or against him with the same.

His off-the-field warmth, generosity and spontaneous good humor made hundreds of friends, but he alienated many of those who felt that no man-to-man relationship is very good very long if one party to it has to accommodate to the wraths and whims of the other. His ballplayers smouldered and bitched under it and those who could afford to deal with him independently often wound up telling him to go to hell—without really losing their respect for him as a football man.

I covered the Vikings daily for five years when Van Brocklin coached them. There were times of mutual mischief and easygoing confidences at training camp when I saw him as a buddy, notwithstanding the generally understood professional barriers we kept between us. Van Brocklin was at his rollicking, chummy best in the rough-housing of the evening chugalugs or yarn-telling sessions with football people, up to and including newspaper people. In these nobody's thin skin was spared and there was no problem on earth that could not be solved by (a) another Sammy Baugh story or (b) a quick run to the Mileage restaurant for a breakfast of abominable greasy eggs to finish off the camaraderie at four in the morning.

And yet it was probably true that no newspaperman covering Van Brocklin is earning his salary unless he has at least five fights per season with the Dutchman, and it does not really matter who does the provoking.

In normal years, I over-subscribed my quota by a few.

The question of who was the guilty party troubled me, although I admit not much. Finally I discovered an airtight formula for ascribing blame, especially on road trips with the Vikings.

When Van Brocklin and I got into a name-calling session somewhere en route, it was prima facie evidence of Van Brocklin's guilt if I got a phone call at 5 the following morning. The voice usually bespoke a faint residue of Budweiser beer and a twinge of conscience. "You had breakfast yet, you son of a bitch?" Van Brocklin would ask cordially.

"I thought you only ate general managers," I would respond.

"I got a six-pack left over by some freeloader," Van Brocklin would announce. "It's better than eggs in this lousy hotel."

These reconciliations would usually last the better part of two weeks, after which we would lapse into another furious round of silence. The Dutchman took the institutional view that newspapermen covering the team really were a part of the team, and ought to bear that in mind when they wrote. This viewpoint, if adopted by the journalist, would soon convert him into a ghost writer for the ball club's coach or its general manager.

As far as I can remember, our random skirmishes threatened to come to blows only once. Whenever the Vikings played the Detroit Lions in his early years, Van Brocklin would recall his psyching-up days as a ballplayer and pitch himself to a level of dark pugnacity the night before.

He did this because the Lions had the kind of defense that only a Kamikaze pilot could truly admire, or view with any detachment. It mauled and bullied and ground and crunched. The object of most of this intimacy was the enemy quarterback. Some quarterbacks, like Bart Starr of Green Bay, took a fatalistic attitude about facing Alex Karras, Roger Brown, Sam Williams and Darris McCord. They were going to get bombed a half dozen times and they may as well face it. Francis Tarkenton of the Vikings took the position that nothing short of all-out flight could save him against the Lions.

Van Brocklin's trouble was that he knew Tarkenton was right, and it galled him. He hated the thought of his shrewdly-laid offensive schemes reduced to tatters by (a) Karras and the rest of the Lions' brutes and (b) Tarkenton's unscripted romps miles behind the line of scrimmage.

As a result, whenever the Vikings played in Detroit Van Brocklin would get off the airplane ready to take on General Motors and any other handy ogres.

Occasionally, I happened to be the nearest one available.

We were to meet in one of the small bars of the Sheraton Cadillac about midnight the night before the game for a light nightcap. Van Brocklin arrived in the lobby with his coaching assistants after a late dinner and spotted me through the beaded curtains of the barroom chatting with Bert Rose, with whom he was then feuding.

Van Brocklin suspected some act of betrayal. Thrusting himself through the beads, the Dutchman demanded a meeting. We got together in the lobby. I really don't recall the exact nature of the charge and Van Brocklin's accompanying suggestion, but it was very novel. He concluded it by offering to take our disagreements up to his room for a man-to-man settlement.

Normally, before plunging into a gallant defense of honor, I take a calm reading of my chances for victory, stalemate and survival. At the time Van Brocklin was approximately 6 feet 2 inches tall (and still may be for all I know) and weighed approximately 220 pounds.

In those years I had the general contours of a dissipated jockey. I would not only have to give away height and weight but faced the further discouragement of having to write a fight story with my head packed in an ice bag.

"Save it for Karras, Rocky," I counseled.

"You goddamned phony hunkie," Van Brocklin blurted.

"You forgot phony newspaperman," I corrected.

"You're a goddamned phony hunkie newspaperman," Van Brocklin shouted. By now he had removed his jacket and obviously would next kick some sand in my face from the lobby cigarette cylinder, the ultimate in disdainful gestures.

Resigned, I took off my jacket and asked him if he had last words. The only thing I could promise myself as we headed for the elevator was that it was going to be a short fight and might even threaten a few records.

Whereupon Van Brocklin jammed his jacket back on, made some endearing comment about all the nosy lobbyists, and disappeared.

My room telephone rang the following morning at 5.

"What caused you," I asked, "to chicken out?"

"I'm giving you a chance to apologize for your crude grandstand play in the lobby," Van Brocklin croaked. "I'd flip for breakfast but since it would break precedent for you to pick up the tab, we can split what's left of the beer."

I can recall Van Brocklin actually swinging only twice. The first was in the summer of 1963 at Bemidji when he threw a right into the gut of a noisy customer at Jack's roadhouse while Ron Vander Kelen was leading the All-Stars to a surprise victory over Green Bay on television. The Dutchman's blow was distinguished chiefly by its needle-point accuracy. It was a looping overhand right that barely missed Viking director Bernie Ridder at the height of its parabola and had to get through a tiny opening between assistant coach Stan West's paunch and the bar on the follow-through.

The other was a bizarre encounter with Dallas sportswriter Gary Cartwright outside a Birmingham, Ala., supper club the night before the Viking-Cowboy exhibition game in 1965. Cartwright, well-greased, challenged the Dutchman with a fierce stare and a clumsy left. Van Brocklin's return was a helpful forearm which he later explained was intended to prevent Cartwright from falling and injuring himself.

The Dutchman, apparently rehearsing for even more dramatic press conferences ahead that year, took the unusual step of having public relations man John Thompson summon all available journalists for a bedside announcement at 8:30 a.m.

I was surprised they didn't call it for 5 a.m.

Eyewitnesses, the Dutchman explained, had absolved him of all blame and clearly established him as the victim of a wanton, unprovoked attack by the sportswriter.

It was the only time I have ever heard Van Brocklin likened to Little Red Riding Hood.

These small bursts of boyish effervescence had long ago persuaded Bert Rose that Van Brocklin needed a broader canvas for his creative urges, and that only coaching the Minnesota Vikings could provide the full horizons the Dutchman needed to stretch out artistically.

So Van Brocklin made plane reservations to Minneapolis and went ahead with the final game of a truly remarkable 12-year career. He had fully expected to lounge around as a bystander for the East team, grandly palming off the quarterback honors to Pittsburgh's Bobby Layne. The ball game, however, did not quite dovetail with Layne's plans and the Dutchman, as league's most valuable player, was hurriedly enlisted as an active combatant.

Van Brocklin responded with three touchdown passes in a losing mission. The L. A. press surrounded him for auld lang syne after the game and asked him, not surprisingly, what were his immediate plans.

"To get the hell out of this town," Van Brocklin replied economically.

By way of fulfilling this threat, the Dutchman flew out the next day and checked into the Biltmore Motel not far from the Edina Country Club.

Rose's plan was for Van Brocklin to be auditioned for the coaching job by the full Viking directorship gathered that evening at Boyer's home. Despite Skoglund's early approval of the Dutchman's style, Rose was jittery as the confrontation approached, anxious that his nominee make the very strongest and most alert impression.

For one thing, Rose was aware Max Winter was still waging a mild rear guard action in behalf of Sid Gillman and also would have preferred Grant. The Winnipeg coach had withdrawn, however, leaving the field to Rose's recommendation if this night's meeting went reasonably well.

The Dutchman arrived shortly after 3 p.m. and joined Rose for a labored dinner. He was travel-bushed and aching a little from the Pro Bowl. He had been courted off and on by the Vikings for the better part of a week. He assumed he was going to be offered the job, but the way he felt it wouldn't break his heart if he weren't.

While Rose chattered happily about the prospects of overthrowing the Packers within a couple of years, Van Brocklin tried to avoid dozing despite the thrilling vistas.

They headed for Boyer's to meet with the assembled chieftains—Boyer, Skoglund, Ridder, Winter and Haugsrud. To the best recollection of all concerned it was one of the few times in pro football history when a candidate coach fell asleep in the middle of his application for the job.

Rose was silently horrified. He had formally unveiled this exciting nominee to lead the owners into a new world of pro football glamor, and the candidate looked ready for the oxygen tent.

"When they got to the part of his coaching philosophy," Rose recalled, "I was going to suggest that maybe all of us should trot around the block, partly for physical rejuvenation but mostly to get the Dutchman awake."

The owners later admitted a pang of disappointment over Van Brocklin's responses. When you are about to offer a man a three-year contract you expect some fugitive spark of interest.

"The Dutchman wasn't rude intentionally," Rose said later, "I don't think. He just seemed to be getting closer to a coma as the night wore on."

Van Brocklin was finally excused and told he would be contacted the next day after the owners had the opportunity to digest his testimony in private.

They conferred the following morning for two or three hours. One ventured the helpful comment that the Dutchman appeared to be in mourning and obviously would improve in his mental approach. Another agreed, arguing he saw nothing inconsistent with an attitude of mourning and what Van Brocklin was getting into.

Max Winter, always the cool professional in the business, conceded he had not been overpowered either by Dutch's performance or the urgency to hire him. He had nothing especially against Van Brocklin but thought there might be other choices. If it were the wish of the rest of the board, however, he had no objection to making the selection unanimous.

They voted unanimously to give Van Brocklin a three-year contract starting at $25,000 with escalations to follow.

Rose joyously telephoned Van Brocklin at the Biltmore and the Dutchman was revealed to the local press at 4 p.m. at the Leamington Hotel. By now he was fully awake and eager and responsive, and had only one question on the subject of the Viking draft:

"Francis who?"

Chapter VIII

*"The first time I got a questionnaire from the Vikings
I thought they were a six-man team."* —Tommy Mason,
Viking halfback.

Hugh McElhenny awoke on a winter day in San Francisco to
discover that as a reward for nine years of stardom in pro football he had been consigned to Minnesota.

The King was not familiar with the recent map changes
within the National Football League. Because of this and financial problems in the operation of his supermarket, McElhenny's
first reaction to the newspaper headline was fatalistic: He thought
he was being deported.

His actual status, as one of 36 NFL veterans dispatched to
Minnesota for $600,000, might have been even shakier. In the
small, muted huddles where it was discussed among the exiled,
The List was regarded in biblical terms of excommunication in
which the lost souls surrendered all further hope of redemption.

"It's a helluva fate," McElhenny decided, "just for fumbling
twice against the Rams and getting Red Hickey mad."

The presence of Hugh McElhenny's name on the list of NFL
expendables available to the Vikings in 1961 momentarily
soothed Van Brocklin's growing fears that the whole NFL was
conspiring to turn the Vikings into the ash bowl of the league.

The list contained some of the all-time deadheads of postwar
football. In his preliminary offensive plans that spring, Van
Brocklin seriously considered punting on first down. He was
bequeathed the wilted flowers of football, the abused, the misused
and the confused.

The rival teams generously agreed to make eight players available each (from which the Vikings would choose three) and then packed the list with every cripple, dud, pensionaire and mutineer in hand at the moment.

The Baltimore blue ribbon group, for instance, included Alan (The Horse) Ameche, who had played with high distinction for years but who also had a wrecked Achilles tendon that would disqualify him from any more football.

The Vikings nearly went broke checking the medical histories, police records and Wasserman results of all the prospective new employes before finally arriving at a list of 36. The group was undoubtedly clean medically, politically, and legally. But it was in unpromising shape physically and psychologically.

"Stiffs," Van Brocklin brooded, "they gave me 36 stiffs for a football team."

The usual attritions of training camp shrunk the 36 elect— via squad cuts, resignations, wounds, and in one case enlistment in a monastery—to less than half still serviceable for the start of the 1961 season.

But it would be rank dereliction not to assemble them all for one final memorial. The 36 originals were not the mightiest football force congregated. But at least they never fell prey to overconfidence.

The mention of a name here and there might stir the zephyr of a memory.

From the Baltimore Colts the Vikings received Don Joyce, defensive end; Lebron Shields, defensive end; and Zeke Smith, a linebacker who vanished immediately.

From the Bears they got Glen Shaw, fullback; Charley Sumner, defensive back; and Bill Bishop, defensive tackle. The Browns gave them Fred Murphy, tight end; Gene Selawski, offensive tackle; and Rich Mostardi, defensive back.

Dallas, freshly organized, was exempt from the lottery, but Detroit bestowed Dave Middleton, a flanker; Dave Whitsell, who refused out of hand to join the Vikings and later got traded; and Grady Alderman. Grady's presence on the Vikings 10 years later as the last member of The Survivors was no tribute to Detroit's generosity. It simply proved that the Lions in those

years had so much talent even their orphans made it to the
Pro Bowl.

To finish the litany: Green Bay—Ken Beck, defensive end;
Dick Pesonen, defensive back; and Tom Winslow, running back.
Los Angeles—Don Ellersick, flanker; Jerry Stalcup, linebacker;
and Charlie Janerette, offensive lineman. New York—Frank
Youso, offensive tackle; Bill Kimber, receiver, and Don Boll,
tackle. Philadelphia—Gerry Huth, offensive lineman; Bill Lapham, center; Gene Johnson, defensive back. Pittsburgh—Tom
Barnett, halfback; Byron Beams, offensive tackle; Jack Morris,
defensive back. St. Louis—Ed Culpepper, defensive tackle; Mike
Rabold, offensive lineman; Perry Richards, spread end. San
Francisco— Hugh McElhenny, running back; Clancy Osborne,
linebacker; Karl Rubke, linebacker. Washington — Dick Haley,
defensive back; Bill Roenhelt, linebacker; Red Stephens, offensive lineman.

Of these, a half dozen either retired on the spot when the
announcements were first made, sought refuge in assistant coaches
jobs or otherwise managed to escape into obscurity.

A few, such as Joyce, Bishop, Sumner and Middleton, had
been first-rank National Football League players for years and
were driven to a final season or two with the Vikings either by
an overpowering ardor for the game or the demands of creditors.

Younger ones, such as Youso, Rabold, Huth, Osborne and
Rubke, had days of distinction in the Vikings' first couple of
years. They would be remembered best on the club's honor roll
for special valor in the Battles of Bemidji, which occupy a unique
niche in the annals of scorched earth campaigns.

It was the habit of the time to describe the player pool as an
array. It was only rarely accorded the prestige of being called
a group, except in the Vikings' press books. McElhenny and
Alderman alone rose above the burlesque in the final accounting.
And it is a testimonial to his pride as well as his admiration for
cash currency that McElhenny's two years with the Vikings did
nothing to demean a career that is now permanently preserved
in the Hall of Fame.

Among those least smitten by the McElhenny style and Hall
of Fame prospects in those years was Red Hickey, the coach of

the 49ers. This lack of esteem reached the point in 1960 where McElhenny was not playing at all. One of the reasons was Red's switch to the shotgun offense, which put a huge premium on versatile quarterbacks but made nimble halfbacks practically extinct.

The market value for nimble halfbacks—even aging, discontented ones—remained strong. McElhenny could have commanded a good return at the trade counters. Red, however, plopped him on the expendable list.

Van Brocklin and Rose clomped on him like drowning men.

McElhenny's first disposition was to call it a career. His second, after viewing his financial posture, was to demand a raise on his $20,000 salary.

Rose's policy was to offer each of the 36 a flat $500 raise from their 1960 salaries. This was deemed round enough to prove the Vikings wanted to be hospitable to the incoming mercenaries, but low enough to allow for the fact that they really weren't wanted where they were coming from.

McElhenny was granted a special dispensation from this policy and signed a three-year contract guaranteeing him $21,500 the first year, $23,500 the second, and $25,000 the third—which he played with the New York Giants.

While the Vikings were thus marshaling their legion of the disinherited, recruiters were scoring a sweep of the several galahads chosen in their draft. Rose signed Mason, the No. 1 draft choice, with a low-key pitch that was assisted by a $10,000 bonus inducement. But the salary increments—$12,500, $15,000 and $15,000 for his first three years—were almost comically low in relation to Mason's contributions over that span.

And what kind of resistance did the happy guitar-strummer offer to the carpetbagging smoothie?

"I suppose an agent would have pointed out," Mason recalled later, although with no anger, "that I ought to give myself a little more flexibility to allow for good seasons. At the time I signed, I didn't know who was going to coach the Vikings. I really didn't care. As a matter of fact, the first time I got a questionnaire from the Vikings I thought it was a six-man team. I didn't know much about pro football. So I didn't give them any trouble. To tell the truth, I probably would have played for free.

"I never stopped to think there were others (in the league) who got more than I did in bonuses and other things. I just wanted to play in the National Football League. It is really hard to blow your horn when you haven't done too much. At Tulane I was getting $15 a month. If I had gotten more, I don't know if my folks would have let me take it. My mother and father both worked, and the bonus the Vikings gave me was more than both of them made in one year.

"So how was a guy like me going to negotiate very hard, even though I had a good offer from the other league? I didn't know whether I was good enough in the first place. And the kind of money I was used to in those days — it was a chore to scrape up enough for a banana cream pie and a glass of milk."

They signed Hawkins without difficulty but almost lost Tarkenton to Boston of the AFL because of Francis' wounded feelings over the NFL's tardiness in drafting him—on the third round.

And so with a teeming roster of nonentities, tired vets, nondescript free agents, sulking second-year pros and visionary kids, the Dutchman pointed his wooden shoes for Bemidji.

He told his loved ones not to worry, expressing the hope that somehow most of them would make it back.

Chapter IX

"He's not the grocer, he's one of our free-agent tackles." *—Bert Rose to Norm Van Brocklin at training camp.*

The town of Bemidji, argued at least one Minneapolis sports editor, was too deep in the tamarack groves of northern Minnesota to afford the Vikings the kind of publicity a pro football team warranted.

Van Brocklin dismissed this objection effortlessly. What the Minnesota Vikings of 1961 needed was concealment, not publicity.

It is a matter of record that the first man to board the Viking bus bound for the sylvan hermitage that July was a 320-pound bartender from Ishpeming, Mich.

He was not going along as a caterer. He intended to try out for offensive tackle.

"I tried to discourage him," Rose said somewhat helplessly. "Look, I refused to answer his first 12 letters. I declined to take his long-distance phone calls. We were a brand new football team in sore need of manpower but we DID, I told him, have standards. Besides this, I knew Van Brocklin would raise hell if I went around giving contracts to every guy who claimed to be the most valuable man in the credit union tug of war championships.

"But he showed up the day we took the rookie draftees and free agents up to Bemidji and I didn't have the heart to run him off. He told me he never played football in college but learned the technique of line play by watching 'Knute Rockne of Notre Dame' 14 times on television."

He wore squat baggy trousers with a copy of Street and Smith's football annual in his back pocket, and a tight yellow sweater that crept above his rolling midriff when he reached into his chest pockets for fresh supplies of mint cremes. His face was puffed and florid but his eyes bore the zealot's fierce resolve to make them forget about Pudge Heffelfinger.

Van Brocklin first spotted him when the candidate hove in view in the chow line of the Bemidji State College cafeteria.

"Bert," the Dutchman screamed, "the town grocer just crashed into our chow line."

"He's not the grocer," Rose said wretchedly. "He's one of our new free-agent tackles."

Van Brocklin subsided, groaning. Tarkenton, seated at the next table, later expressed serious fear that the coach had suffered a cardiac arrest.

Van Brocklin summoned the team physician, the internationally-renowned physician and specialist on athletic injuries, Dr. Donald Lannin of St. Paul.

"Doc," he said, "I'm never going to tell you about how to diagnose another case. But when you get to this one, I don't care what the goddamned thermometers and enemas show, you tell this guy he's got Artie's Incurable Lockjaw or some other dread condition. I don't, and I repeat, I don't want him even putting on a jockstrap. He's just one heartbeat from collapse right now, picking up his tray with three T-bone steaks on it. You ever put a uniform on him, we'll all be accessories to involuntary manslaughter."

Lannin found this presentation extremely persuasive and escorted the intended Hall of Famer out of the training room, as gently as possible.

There is a recurring legend in the clubhouses of the league that the bartender showed up again one year later at the training camp of Harry Wismer's New York Titans. Despite having lost some of the conditioned tone of his one day in Viking camp, the story goes, he not only got through the medical exam but played most of the season as a regular before being suspended for smuggling a six-pack into a dummy scrimmage.

As a training site, Bemidji was a happy choice from a standpoint of (a) preventing mass defections of Van Brocklin's first-year recruits and (b) protecting the innocent season-ticket buyers to the south from the sobering truth.

Few of the early arrivals had cars and the only alternate means of escape was North Central Airlines frequently operable and often heroic fleet of DC-3s. Confronted with these options, the potential escapee almost invariably stuck with Van Brocklin's training camp, although at least one or two of them did attempt the overland route by way of Turtle River and Puposky before foundering in the swamps near Nebish.

The route had first been pioneered, according to mythology, by the giant lumberjack Paul Bunyan, in whose image much of the town's tourist industry and most of its beer schooners were designed.

The training facilities were adequate. But Van Brocklin's long-term observations in the field of boy-girl phenomena told the Dutchman there was something unmistakably perilous about dumping 80 football players into a nest of 500 coeds. He announced:

"There will be no fraternizing. Period. By fraternizing I mean dating, dancing, saying a hello or smiling. I'm not doing this for your protection or the girls' protection. I'm doing it for the simple and selfish protection of the Minnesota Vikings.

"Rest leave will be available for those who show signs of getting buggy. I repeat. THERE WILL BE NO FRATERNIZING WITH THE COEDS. We are not going to fine you. We are not going to suspend you. We are just going to kick your ass off the ball club."

Van Brocklin's edict was rigidly observed on the campus. But by common consensus of the ballplayers and the coeds, it was deftly outflanked at a hilltop 3.2 beer joint called, in a coy twist of irony, The Dutchess.

Except for a bowling alley near the college where the players consumed vats of beer after hot practices, The Dutchess was the only watershed in town where the athletes could congregate without drawing $100 from Van Brocklin or cold stares from the mothers.

The coaches, writers, owners and the addendum of the Viking

party drank their beer and drew their consolation from the wailing saxophones of the juke boxes at Jack's roadhouse, the Turtle River Restaurant up the other highway, the MuniSIPal Liquor Store or the Elks Club.

The ballplayers were stuck with The Dutchess. It looked like a converted stockade that had survived the Chippewa Wars. On a windless day, it was touched by gently colliding aromas reminiscent of the town zoo. The interior decor came under the general heading of Early Period Shambles and, as a convenience, the men's biff had been moved to the parklot bushes.

It was the players' dance hall, wailing wall, drinking trough, confessional and lovers' roost. Its ownership was never clearly established, but there had to be an awful lot of charity in the hearts of the local gendarmes and sheriff's deputies to keep it open.

At times, when complaints about wild parties were heard from as far away as Walker 40 miles to the south, the local enforcers would stage a combined operation officially classified as a raid but actually an extension of the social hour.

The operators the first year were quickly befriended by two seasoned NFLers with long-standing reputations for sympathizing with the workaday problems of saloon owners. To these, Don Joyce and Bill Bishop, the owners gratefully turned over duplicate keys so that The Dutchess should not stand idle in the hours of the ballplayers' most urgent needs. These turned out to be the hours of 3 a.m. to 6 a.m. on nights when the Vikings returned from exhibition road games.

Joyce was one of the registered headhunters of professional football in the 1950s, a defensive end on the Baltimore Colt championship teams of the early Johnny Unitas vintage. By the time he got to the Vikings he had lost most of his lateral movement, and practically all ability to move hurriedly in ANY direction. But he had lost none of his profound admiration for bottled beer, and nobody messed with ole Don, on the ballfield or in the tavern. He admitted falling under the roster classification of "fat but ornery."

His running mate, Bishop, also was on the shank side of a brawling career. He was a brooder, a man of innumerable angers and suspicions, most of them centering on his old keeper, George Halas of the Bears. He still hit like a truck at defensive tackle. But at the moment he was carefully pondering the best routes to retirement.

His dilemma subsequently was solved on the final day of the season when Bishop in all seriousness threatened to throw Van Brocklin off the airplane on a champagne flight celebrating the Vikings' survival of their first year in the NFL.

Joyce's ability to withstand vast infusions of beer was a matter of common knowledge when he first appeared at The Dutchess. He was accorded all courtesies due one of the trade's recognized masters in this activity.

The standing NFL record for beer consumption in one 24-hour period had been in dispute for some time. Joyce had never filed a formal claim but was generally conceded a rating with the all-time top five in anybody's listings—and these included the wire services, the NEA, Collier's, and the late Walter Camp.

In August of 1961, however, he broke all barriers and set a mark that would have achieved the combined accreditation of the NFL and the Beverage Dealers Association except for a technicality. The technicality was that all of Joyce's buddies had passed out by the time he had buried the last soldier. Nobody was able to notarize the feat.

According to village lore, however, from the end of a night exhibition game in Fargo-Moorhead to the 11 p.m. curfew the next night in Bemidji, Joyce emptied 75 bottles of beer.

It will have to go in as an asterisked record for the simple reason that some of those bottles were middleweights, what the boys call splits. Witnesses were inclined to dismiss this as a quibble, claiming Joyce was fully geared to go the distance whatever the label listing.

When the cases had been stacked from floor to ceiling, Joyce voluntarily called off the uneven struggle. With an agreeable burp he roused his sagging buddies. He then called in to Hernando's Hideaway for an order of pizza to take back to Pine Hall and strode into the night, fulfilled.

It was a virtuoso display, but the lingering fragrance was too much for his confederates. For the next two scrimmages Joyce's teammates on the defensive squad refused to huddle for signals and, instead, audibled their way out of it.

In ensuing years, Van Brocklin's training camps became the scenarios for some of the most gripping horror stories in the football player's underground. By reputation they fell somewhere between Valley Forge and Buchenwald. The calmer test of time, however, would locate them closer artistically to the Little Big Horn, since the attrition rate was approximately as high.

Yet it was the Dutchman's honest intention to run a loose ship in the first months of creation. He did this as a gesture of charity toward some of the aging swaybacks who occupied critical positions on his team—meaning there was nobody else to play there.

But temperamentally he was still as much a ballplayer as a coach. His contempt for some of the nickel-and-dime training camp rules was still too fresh to permit him to start acting like Zeus immediately. There would be time enough for that.

Too, there was the business of the psychological makeup of his team. All of the veterans were rejects in some fashion. A number of them were habitual soreheads, deadbeats and bitchers. A few of those might be rescued by an act of comradeship.

Truthfully, Van Brocklin's first camp was not a continuous hothouse. Agreed, it was not standard practice to order pads and scrimmage on picture day.

Van Brocklin is an impetuous man. The sight of a half a hundred bodies romping about the football field—HIS bodies—momentarily overpowered his cooler judgment. Van Brocklin swore he saw at least a half dozen all-pros out there during the rookies' first calisthenics.

By 1 p.m. he had ordered all of the photographers off the field and by 2 p.m. Tarkenton had called his first pass play. It wound up in a scramble that put Tarkenton within five yards of running into Lake Bemidji before Van Brocklin blew his whistle and asked Tarkenton whether he planned to pass or snorkel.

Aware of his inflammatory reputation as a player, his novice ballplayers—all except Tarkenton and Rip Hawkins—looked on the Dutchman with mingled wonderment, fear and disbelief.

Except for rare interludes, he left the football alone. He might have joined the passing drills. But he would not allow himself this harmless piece of showmanship that would have been forgiveable in a man who retired six months before at the pinnacle of his calling.

He did not try to dominate the field that way. But his personality—profanely autocratic, unpredictable, fierce sometimes and puckish others—engulfed his team. From the very start his moods dictated the atmosphere of the camp, the clubhouse and the field.

One of his early-period rookies, still active in the game, saw him from this stance (and presented a theory of how the Dutchman could be handled by a new man with presence of mind):

"You would come in and sit on Van Brocklin's first playbook session and get the feeling that this man knows so much football and you could never possibly know that much ball. It wasn't just what he did with the X's and the O's but the way . . . well, what the hell, whoever heard of a guy practically declaring war when he showed how to execute a simple dive play.

"When he did give you a game plan later, he presented it like a hard-boiled salesman would. Every good salesman has to exhibit a degree of confidence, and you believe him. And Norm presented the game plan in a way that really convinced you, so that when you went out on Sunday, nearly everything on that list was ready to work, and they did just about exactly what he anticipated them doing. And when this happens time and time again, you know it's not a grab-bag situation. You know the man has talent and brains even if he is so damned abusive to guys, and you know if you do what you are supposed to do and execute properly, it is going to be successful.

"He treated me okay, but he said things to other players, publicly, in front of the squad, that were pretty awful. I disliked him for it because some of those people were my friends and didn't deserve it.

"The thing about this guy and his strong personality is that he likes to run the show. Some of the rookies would come in really naive, or at least impressionable, and were just over-awed by the guy. Some of them, though, and I think I was one,

would just let it run off their backs—just take him as a bull-
shitter with all that Captain Bligh attitude and rough language.
I don't mean he was putting on a performance. I just mean that
he never realized that some people would really take all that
stuff as though it was the end of the world."

But some of them did, especially a few of the black players
who were never sure they were being chewed out as muddling
rookies or muddling nigger rookies.

In this connection Van Brocklin had the racial attitudes of
most of his contemporaries. He was no better nor worse than
most. But he might have been better if some of his pals had
not persuaded him of the easier coachability of the Southern
Negro as opposed to the California nigger—the one allegedly
being docile and humble, and the other being independent and
intrusive.

On the field, however, he was impartial enough. He would
often question the heroism of a black halfback like Bobby Reed,
but he would do that same of a white quarterback like George
Shaw or a kicker like Mike Mercer.

Roiled by this, some of their pals in the dorm rooms and
lockerrooms wondered where Van Brocklin developed all the
bravery to give him the right to demean a man like that.

In those years, the veterans reported at least a week or ten
days after the rookies. This permitted the Dutchman and his
charter staff—Walt Yowarsky, Harry Gilmer, Stan West and
Darrel Brewster—to separate the rookies who were merely god-
awfulgreen from the ones who might not be able to defend themselves when the crafty old pros arrived.

Van Brocklin's first blush of enthusiasm in his role as field
commandant began to ebb noticeably when they packed Sharockman, Mason and Hawkins off to the All-Star game. This left
him with the authentically interesting Tarkenton and a few other
marginal rooks. He also had a swarm of free agent stumblers, a
handful of early-arriving but unsensational vets, and very dark
notions about the immediate future.

At this somber moment the Dutchman chanced to look up on
the slope rimming the Bemidji practice site and recognized the
slimly tapered form and battle-stitched cheekbones of Hugh

McElhenny. His hair was a little long and his tan spoke of a hundred lazy hours in the sun, but brothers, there was nothing on that field within three galaxies of Hugh McElhenny.

"King," Van Brocklin shouted with the joy of the delivered, "you got here just in time. Jimmy Eason will get you some boards and the rest of the stuff. This place is beginning to take on the look of a National Football League camp."

The aging thoroughbred viewed Van Brocklin with immediate alarm.

"Dutch," he said, "I just remembered I got two days left before reporting and I think it would be a damn shame if I took some of the attention away from these deserving kids of yours out on the field. By the way, which one is Mason?"

The Dutchman caught this casually-launched glimmer of professional wariness, and thought he would bounce it just as casually off the King's exposed flank.

"He's gone to the All-Star camp," the Dutchman said. "He's green, but he's fast and he doesn't mind hitting. I think he's going to be a great one."

The King greeted this intelligence with fresh interest. "Where," he asked, "can I find this equipment man, Eason. I may drop in tomorrow for a little light work, huh?"

McElhenny's sudden zeal for practice so impressed Van Brocklin that he decided a few days later the King would be his offensive captain. Bishop would be the defensive leader, but it was Mac who was going to be the spiritual lion.

"King," Van Brocklin said in a private devotional, "they will need a leader, somebody to look up to, somebody who can tell them what training camp is all about, that it's bush to break curfew and not only bush but expensive. And if they start doing it here, they're going to get run off the team."

The venerable but still-prime halfback gave Dutch a solemn nod and a fraternal grip, and headed back to the dorm.

The next morning Van Brocklin's sleuths reported the first curfew violation in camp.

"Who in the hell is the ungrateful violator?" the Dutchman roared.

"He gave his name," the sleuth said, "as McElhenny."

The Dutchman had scheduled McElhenny to start in an intra-squad scrimmage that morning. It was clear to all of the compassionate journalists present that McElhenny was in distress. The evidence for this was the olive cast to his face and the fervor with which he clung to the ground in the pre-scrimmage calisthenics.

"McElhenny," the Dutchman announced, "starts."

I need hardly add that while McElhenny may have started, he did not finish. Before finally collapsing within grasp of the sideline oxygen inhalator, McElhenny set the Vikings' first-year mark for consecutive end sweeps with a hangover.

"From such adversity," Bert Rose mused, "are great organizations welded."

On that, everybody headed for the Mun-i-Sip-al to drink a commisserating toast in honor of the stricken King.

Chapter X

*"I'm thinking, reverend, how bad it would be for me
if the linemen ever caught up."* —*Francis Tarkenton,
Viking quarterback.*

It must have been one of the regrets of Van Brocklin's life that
he was not born in Nashville, Tenn.

Van Brocklin liked the droll, twangy back-40 style and philosophy of the southern football player; and he respected the
disciplines many of them brought from the football collieries
of Bear Bryant, Bobby Dodd, and the other coaching oligarchs.

Most of his closest friends as a pro football player were men
from that geography and mold. Against what they considered the
phony tinsel of pro football—the front office posturing, the
publicity accents on glamor names from Notre Dame and big
northern schools—they formed a private, inner club of "the
real pros," the doers and the spade-callers.

This state of mind explained a lot of Van Brocklin's personnel
decisions and moves at the draft table in his early years, not all
of which were sunny successes or even very logical. But he
related extremely well with the southern football player, and
endorsed the Vikings draft of Tommy Mason (No. 1) from
Tulane, Rip Hawkins (No. 2) from North Carolina, and Francis
Tarkenton (No. 3) from Georgia.

Mason was a happy, earnest young troubadour and Hawkins
was a commanding, courtly, ante-bellum figure out of planta-
tion literature.

But Tarkenton was the one that drew the Dutchman immediately.

He was the rookie quarterback, which was explanation enough. But there was a sauce and a spunk to him, an easiness in the crowd and clearly a facile mind.

He had a schoolboy's freshness and a preacher kid's respect for the dignity of his teammates and his elders. It was almost impossible not to like him, and Van Brocklin found himself fascinated.

The coach was going to try, as he put it, "to make a hero out of George Shaw, because we need a veteran quarterback like him." But he had seen George in the last couple of years in the Eastern Division. George projected the appearance of a pretty competent quarterback mechanically. But his bad injuries of a few years ago had made him a cautious football player. An intelligent young man, he spoke softly and, in the huddle, gave the impression of being the chaplain rather than the general. In manner and professional approach, he was the polar opposite of Van Brocklin.

The Dutchman was aware of that, and certainly had to think of it when Tarkenton arrived with his verve and eagerness. He grasped the basic concepts of the pro football offense quickly. Van Brocklin had been through it, and realized that here was not just another kid from the campus trying to make a showing.

Francis and I walked to the college cafeteria seven or eight days after the opening of practice and talked randomly of the future of a rookie quarterback in pro football.

He talked without bravado. But he seemed to understand exactly where he stood and where he was headed.

"I like George and respect his head and experience," Francis said. "But I don't think he will quarterback this team for too many years, or even all of this year. He is a fine fellow. You can see he's thinking about what happened to his legs. I don't get the impression he'll be a leader over the long haul.

"I think I have an opportunity here. The best thing that happened to me was not getting picked to play in the All-Star game in Chicago with Tommy and Rip and Sharockman. I'm getting in the ground floor. With George the only veteran quarterback around, they're going to need a rookie not only to learn but to play. I think I'll play this year."

From the first Van Brocklin never rated Tarkenton's mechanical ability as much better than fair by professional football's standards. But then, Van Brocklin's appraisal of almost any quarterback resembled Erwin Rommel's critique of the Italian General Staff.

He used to call Earl Morrall a ragarm and could not quite figure out how Billy Wade ever won a football game. He was convinced the Vikings were keeping John Brodie in the league and he never thought much of Bart Starr when the Packers got behind. Mercifully for Green Bay—if the Dutchman's judgment was correct—it didn't happen very often.

He made pardonable exceptions of Johnny Unitas, Bobby Layne and Y. A. Tittle. But even in the case of the Baltimore quarterback, he nearly convulsed a Viking squad meeting one day by offering his tribute to Unitas: "Johnny isn't a great passer, but he's willing to pay the price."

"Imagine," declared a marveling Viking defensive back who had made a career being stripped nude by Unitas' passes, "imagine the guy saying Unitas isn't a great passer. Only Van Brocklin could say it. I mean, say it and mean it."

But in a way that aroused Van Brocklin's private admiration, Tarkenton's inquisitive mind dug into the complexities of the pro offense. Where the average rookie quarterback would go through the familiar cycles of bewilderment and despondency, Tarkenton had time for neither.

There were seven quarterbacks in camp when the training season opened, but it was clear after two days that all but Shaw and Tarkenton were heading for early retirement. Before he played a game, Tarkenton was a recognized leader among the rookies, partly because of his progress with the team but also because of his buoyant good temper and rosy view of the world around him.

He brought to pro football a peculiar amalgam of the choir boy's naivete and the self-confident athlete's grasp of the opportunities ahead. He was a minister's boy who didn't swear, smoke or drink—although the erosion of time has seen to it that Francis does not have to carry the burden of all of that purity into his second decade of pro football.

Yet he made no display of his temperance and no pretense of any special nobility. He went around with the boys at night, into the saloons at times, but simply passed when it came to the booze order.

Gingerly, he let the rough-housers of the clubhouse use the purple words he would have used if his daddy hadn't told him no. In the hair-down banter of the locker room, somebody was forever calling somebody else a bastard or a son of a bitch or combinations thereof, and Francis would bound to his feet gleefully and shout, "that's right, you're exactly what Bill Brown called you."

In the early years, especially, he practiced his Methodism. He might counsel a man who would come to his room with one of the end-of-humanity problems that so often afflicted rookies in training camp.

Nobody ever really pinpointed the day Tarkenton first decided that the scrambling style of quarterbacking would offer the soundest route to preservation in the NFL and, ultimately, to Broadway and Wall Street.

I would put it, though, reasonably close to the first time he handled the ball for the Vikings.

In the team's prime years of splendid futility, the Vikings' offensive line was frequently described by football economists as the Appalachia of the NFL.

The orthodox procedure for a drop-back quarterback in pro football is to withdraw seven yards behind the line of scrimmage and throw. Either that or to step forward in the protective pocket when the pressure of enemy bodies dictates some form of evasion.

This assumes the existence of a pocket.

In his first couple of years with the Vikings Tarkenton could count on an extremely heterogeneous pocket, consisting of one or two falling Minnesota blockers and three or four very hostile enemy linemen. The latter almost always got there first.

As a result, Tarkenton adopted as a standard policy the

principle of Headlong Flight. In this he would describe spectacular, marathon figure-eights far behind the line of scrimmage.

Van Brocklin at first viewed this aberration through the clenched teeth of a gruff, forgiving parent. "I suppose it's no more than right," he would tell himself. ":The kid has got no protection. He's trying to get something out of the play by running around back there. But it does look like hell."

By upbringing, Van Brocklin was a stay-put, quarterback fundamentalist—meaning he had no inclination, talent or zeal for running with the ball. In time he concluded that Tarkenton was really over-reacting to the pressure of the rush, and scrambled when most other quarterbacks would wait another split second to deliver the ball downfield.

Besides, it was messing up his game plan.

Rival linemen first encountering Tarkenton's behind-the-line adventures were dumbstruck and infuriated. A few thought it was illegal. The Colts' Gino Marchetti offered the blunt prediction that Tarkenton was going to get killed.

"The game," Marchetti declared after his first meeting with the scrambler, "was not invented by God to be played that way." As he spoke, Marchetti was inhaling large amounts of pure oxygen. He appeared to be in a semi-coma, and there was an internal rattling as his great chest heaved.

"It's the kid I'm thinking about," he said. "He seems like a pretty good kid. Personally, I'm not a man to bear grudges. But there are defensive ends in this league who don't think they should be playing fox-and-hounds when the temperature is 85 degrees. The reason is that a lot of them are fat and out of shape, and something terrible could happen to Francis if they get mad some day. Like I say, it's the kid I'm thinking about."

Van Brocklin himself was baffled at times by the apparent madness of Tarkenton's death-defying loops and pirouettes, in which he would very often fake one rusher into the very jaws of another to escape almost certain catastrophe.

"What are you thinking," a solicitous minister once asked, "when you have a man like Roger Brown chasing you from one direction and Alex Karras from another?"

"I'm thinking, reverend," Tarkenton replied, "how bad it would be for me if they ever caught up."

Yet Francis eventually developed an ad lib artistry that convinced opposing players Van Brocklin actually had drawn up some plays to exploit it. In other words, "The Scrambling Series—Right or Left, on Two."

This attitude overtook Grady Alderman on his first appearance in the Pro Bowl when the Packers' Forrest Gregg asked him flat-out:

"What blocking does Van Brocklin give you when Tarkenton lights out on one of those scrambles?"

Teammates had to help Alderman to his feet five minutes later. He was still limp and powerless from the effects of uncontrollable laughter.

"Listen," Alderman explained, "the only way you can keep your sanity when Tarkenton starts to scramble, let alone your job, is to approach the whole thing like a World War I fighter pilot. You have to look for targets of opportunity.

"You never know which way to block a guy because you never know where Tarkenton is running by now. Blocking for Tarkenton is like trying to stand still in the school hall when somebody rings the recess bell. There's a big rush of humanity in many directions. When we played the Colts, I spent more time blocking Mick Tingelhoff, our center, than Ordell Braase, the Colts' end.

"In other words, it was every man for himself, and that included the rushers. I've seen guys collapse in front of me when they did nothing but trip over a blade of grass, they were so bushed.

"If you were still on your feet—and you always had time to get up several times on Tarkenton's best days—you just looked for any guy in an opposing uniform who looked a little more tired than you were, and you tried to cream him.

"I did that once to a tackle from the Rams, and he fell on top of me and said, 'why did you put the knock on me? I was just standing there wondering whether Tarkenton had the guts to come back this way the fourth time on the same play.'

"And you know, sometimes he did exactly that. I remember one play with the Bears when I had already hit somebody, maybe it was Doug Adkins, two or three times, and we were lying on the ground figuring the play was over or was way downfield by now, and Tingelhoff yells, 'look out, here he comes again,' and we all stomped to our feet and started hitting again, except Adkins. As I recall, he just walked off the field in disgust."

Tarkenton's defense of his free-lancing heresy was pretty tautly-reasoned: "I just couldn't see standing in there in the pocket and 'eating the ball' the way you were supposed to, by the book. What for? If there was a chance I could salvage something out of the play by scrambling, what was so wrong about that? I think the guys I played with will agree that I never rapped our offensive line the way some others did. I never rapped it at all. They knew they weren't all-pros. I can't remember them objecting very much when we tried to wing it. And really, I didn't scramble all that much. I got a big reputation for it, and I suppose two or three times a game I'd give it that round-the-world business way back there. Believe me, I didn't have the faintest idea how it was going to come out, whether I'd keep running or find a way to get rid of the ball."

"I'd be the first to admit," he said some time after leaving the Vikings, "that there were times when I shouldn't have gone off on those wild scrambles. Van Brocklin's beef was that I could have gotten rid of the ball quicker, and a lot of the times he was right. As the years went on, I worked on that. But he was wrong when he said I was doing it for selfish reasons. He gave people the idea I was trying to put on a show to make myself bigger box office, and that I was sacrificing the good of the team. That was a lot of bull. Football players are a blunt bunch, sometimes brutally. They would have been the first ones to let me know. I know there were a few guys on the Vikings who didn't exactly love the way I quarterbacked the team, but I can't remember any of the players accusing me of being selfish."

Tarkenton started those gyrations as a condition of life in his first year of quarterbacking. Gradually he refined what enemy linemen swore was a form of football ESP. He learned the best escape routes, what decoy moves worked on one kind of rusher but didn't on another. Above all, he made an art out of locating friendly ends and backs far downfield, while dashing in several directions at once.

"The Vikings," observed one of their winded pursuers, "had the only unrehearsed, unlisted offense in football."

This was a fact, not only out of necessity but because of the renegade temperament the team acquired after a couple of years under Van Brocklin. The Vikings answered the snickers of the pedigreed teams with an unbuttoned defiance that was the essence of Van Brocklin.

It didn't win many games for them in those first few years. But from the time they played their first exhibition game, nobody laughed at them. The Mets, Astros, Senators, Cowboys, Expos, San Diego—all of the first-termers in the expansion years went through the pimply embarrassments of being everybody's rubes.

But not Van Brocklin's team. Whatever his future in the trade, he may have been the perfect expansion coach. He had a nails-hard scholarship as a football man and an indomitability that transmitted itself to the struggling kids and sulking outcasts who made up his first team.

They developed an offbeat spirit of the corps, the pooled fervor of the banished and the impetuous novices.

Tarkenton was the natural fulcrum for these diverse passions. He played a zany potato-patch kind of football, and it infected the others. There were days Van Brocklin would swear Tarkenton called his plays not in the conventional cryptology of the blackboard, e.g., "open 2 right, 29—GO," but: "Reichow, you run as far as you can; Mason, you head for Row 25 and then cut for the air blowers; Brown, hang around me because they're a gonna be comin' like bulls."

Actually, there was precedent for it. No football training camp has ever been spared the one about how Sammy Baugh used to call his pass plays in the wartime days when they never had the same team on consecutive weekends. "Right end," Baugh would drawl, "you go down 15 yards and angle for the middle; right half, you follow him out and look for fumbles; left end, just fug around awhile to keep the rest of them confused."

Before many games the Vikings with Tarkenton quarter-backing had acquired a reckless elan that sometimes made them look like The Beaver Boys playing their season opener. Everybody watched for laterals, especially after the Viking-San Francisco game in 1962 when the play went Tarkenton to Reichow to Brown to Mason to Reichow to Alderman to Tingelhoff and collapse.

"I damned near called a double dribble," one of the harrassed officials admitted afterward.

And the legends about the scramble inevitably became reality. Tarkenton actually DID call a scrambled play in the huddle several times, the most notable of all being the climactic pass play in the Vikings' first victory over Green Bay, in 1964.

Tarkenton's Huckleberry Finn style of offense bothered Vince Lombardi, almost personally. Vince was the meticulous shaper of grand designs, a field marshall among strategists. He would devise defensive plans of exquisite beauty and resourceful scope.

And Tarkenton would scramble them into misshapen ruins, like a mischievous kid tumbling sand castles at the beach. But until this day in Green Bay in 1964, he had merely offended Vince's esthetic values and sensitivities.

This time he beat him.

With less than a minute left Francis and the Vikings stood fourth and 22 at their own 36, trailing by two points. They had a maximum of three plays left. In the mild suspicion that the Vikings might pass, Green Bay spread seven men downfield—as far as 40 yards away. Van Brocklin's offense was the most sophisticated in the league, but there was nothing on the ready list to beat a seven-man secondary with a 22-yard pass.

In almost so many words, Tarkenton told the huddle: "Everybody eligible get on your horse."

He had no intention of dropping back classically. The Packer defensive front four would be coming full-voltage. The only hope, he knew, was to kill time scrambling until somebody got open downfield.

This was the one redemption of the scrambler's craft. If you let the receiver run long enough, sooner or later he had to come open. The defensive back knows all about the receiver's pass routes and patterns, but once they start going pell-mell, all of the science is out and the defender is going to get lost eventually.

Tarkenton swung to the right sidelines with Willie Davis

churning and grunting in pursuit. Davis swiped at Tarkenton's heel and just missed. Tarkenton did one of those arabesques followed by a good old-fashioned buck and wing, and by now the the confusion downfield was becoming general. To old timers in the stands who remembered the silent movies, it resembled the last reel of The Great Train Robbery.

So now Francis spotted Tom Hall alone 30 yards out. He threw. The ball was on the money near the Packer 20. Hall was uncovered. He was going to catch it. And suddenly there was another horned helmet intervening. It belonged to Gordie Smith, the silent end from Missouri. Tarkenton was thunderstruck. The ball was practically in Hall's hands and Smith was jumping in there and he was going to screw up the whole thing. Tarkenton actually yelled "NO, GORDIE, NO."

But yes, Smith went up for it, and he caught it, and he dropped out of bounds. And after they sorted out all of the exhausted bodies Freddie Cox jogged in and beat the Packers with a field goal.

By then, Tarkenton had generated a sort of sub-culture in the society of pro football quarterbacking. Other quarterbacks, especially the ones operating behind collapsible offensive lines, felt suitably liberated by Francis' example to try their own version of the scrambling offense.

Nobody handled it with quite the gall and hair-raising sense of melodrama as Tarkenton. He gave the impression of constantly running a half step in front of a speeding train. But a lot of the time he made it work because he had receivers like Paul Flatley who learned to tune in on the same madcap frequency, when the whole field seemed a carnival tilt-a-whirl gone berserk.

"My thought about going out for a pass when Francis quarterbacked," Flatley would say, "was that if you kept running, you always had a chance. Actually, he was good for me. I was never the fastest guy. I have to depend on quick breaks to beat a defensive back. With Francis running around, the number of these quick breaks tended to multiply.

"Now when Francis would start running, the first, fundamental thing to do was try to locate him.

"If he wasn't where he should be, well then you'd find him and parallel his route. In other words, if I'm on the left sidelines and I see Francis is scrambling to the right, he sure as hell is never going to see me so I would make tracks to get to the right side of the field. Now he knew I was thinking that way, so if he could stay away from these monsters long enough I was always going to be on his side of the field eventually.

"People used to ask me if I had one, unforgettable play with Tarkenton, and I'd say, 'yeah, about a half million,' and that's about the truth. But if you really want to know one to take the marbles, it was this day late in the season when we were playing in Chicago, and neither one of us is going any place.

"It's late in the third period and Francis is running around like he's got pepper on his rump. It was even tougher than usual for me because I had a terrible hangover. But the guy covering me, Dave Whitsell, kind of compensated for that because he had one, too. Anyhow, it's second and long and Tarkenton covers half of the Chicago North Side on a scramble and I, being a receiver, have to cover half the South Side. I'm really bushed going into the huddle. Out of the corner of my eye I can see that Whitsell isn't feeling too hot, either.

"So somebody calls the play back and Francis does it all over again. Whitsell is all over me, going four directions simultaneously. The play was supposed to be one of those little hitch-outs, but I ended up in the end zone 60 yards downfield. He never did throw the ball. Francis was the only passer I ever saw who could turn a five-yard sideline pass into the Drake Relays.

"Now it's third and even longer, and I start downfield on one of those straight-down-the-field routes that Van Brocklin called an 'up'. Others call it the 'fly' because you're supposed to fly down the field, but I wasn't doing anything better than a slow drag. Whitsell is after me, huffing and swearing. He finally catches up and grabs my belt. 'Tarkenton is scrambling again,' he yells in my ear. 'I'll be damned if I'm gonna chase you any more.'

"Well, I grabbed at his wrist, but I want to tell you I didn't grab too hard because I don't want to run any more, either. As a matter of fact, I couldn't run any more. You ought to see the film of the play. I'm struggling there making it look as though I want to kill Whitsell so I can get downfield, but all I want to do is fall over exhausted. No, I can't remember what Tarkenton did with the ball. I did have a couple of suggestions along those lines, though."

No scrambler, the football oracles tell you, is ever going to win a title.

Maybe not. But in the fall in the Twin Cities he pioneered a whole new life vogue. At the stadium, even the ushers scrambled.

Chapter XI

"It was like Luxembourg beating the Kaiser's Army."
—Baltimore writer after Vikings defeated Chicago
Bears in their first game.

His name, the Cleveland Browns' Paul Brown told Bert Rose by telephone, is Jim Marshall.

"He could become a great football player," Brown said sadly, "but he's just recovering from a form of sleeping sickness and we just cannot wait on him. We will give you our last six players to be cut from the roster, including Marshall, for your second round draft choice in 1962."

There was a twinge of gloom in Brown's voice because it always depressed him at this stage of the pre-season when pure mathematics—the number of vacancies on the roster—forced him to unload potential all-stars to undeserving rivals.

For this reason Paul Brown scanned the rolls of the various undeserving rivals, searching for potentially the most harmless recipient of his bounty.

He immediately seized upon the Vikings, and telephoned Rose.

"Come to think of it," he said, "I think for public relations purposes we'd better throw another draft choice in there, so our people won't think this is a giveaway. Nothing much, sort of middlish. You name it."

"Like," Rose cooed, "about No. 11?"

"Eleventh will be okay. As soon as we decide, we will put these boys on waivers, and since you have first claim they will be yours."

Subsequent Viking trades had louder heraldry. But this one

ranked with the best and was a tribute to Brown's magnanimity, an admirable quality he had managed to conceal until then.

From Brown the Vikings got linemen Paul Dickson and Jim Prestel, receiver Justin Rowland, defensive back Billy Gault, linebacker Dick Grecni, and Marshall—who was some day going to be both great and historic.

With these and other trades and pickups the Vikings chinked up the airy gaps that divided their roster between the unmentionable and the presentable.

These included such as Mel Triplett, Bob Schnelker, A. D. Williams, Bob Denton, Jim Leo, Will Sherman, and one of those homeless victims of football's age of specialization, Jerry Reichow.

Reichow may have been the toughest football player who ever wore the Vikings' uniform. The pros really had no position for him. He played quarterback at Iowa, but this was no special recommendation considering his predecessors. He was bony, rangy, faintly awkward in stride, a good pass-catcher, and a bad man to hassle with.

The Lions discovered he could hurl the football with the strength of a discus thrower, but they don't play ball with platters in the NFL. Besides this, Bobby Layne could hit the target whereas Jerry usually threw in the general area of the stadium.

They tried him at two or three end positions but they had men faster, more agile and more experienced. They traded him to Philadelphia, where he ran into the same parlay. They tried to trade him to Washington and he said, "so long, boys, I'm going home."

This touching farewell undoubtedly was inspired by Van Brocklin, who had long eyes for Reichow. The two had been teammates with the Eagles. In any case, Reichow wound up with the Vikings in time to play flanker in their final exhibition game with the Rams, the team's fifth straight pre-season loss.

The team's first play in actual hostilities was one of those prophetic strokes of destiny. They started their exhibitions against the Cowboys and Triplett fumbled the ball at the Viking 15 on the opening snap from scrimmage.

"It could have been worse," Van Brocklin temporized on the sideline, "Dallas could have intercepted the first pass and scored."

They did, for their second touchdown.

Yet the Vikings played with unexpected stubbornness in the exhibitions until the Bears flattened them at Cedar Falls, Idaho.

It was fairly evident by now that George Shaw was not going to challenge for all-pro honors in 1961. Still, with the season opener against the Bears five days away, Van Brocklin grappled with the quandary of which to start at quarterback — Shaw or Tarkenton.

During those interludes in the wrangling when Dutch and I spoke to each other, we had a custom of riding together from the Viking practice site at Midway Stadium in St. Paul to the Viking Fan Club meeting in either city.

It annoyed both of us to use Front Page-style language like "off the record" and "on the record", so it was never clearly understood when the conversation was social and when it was professional. It was a comfortable relationship. And it had the added virtue of igniting a few hysterical outbursts now and then when one of the parties felt injured.

I asked Dutch whom he planned to start at quarterback.

"It's the damndest thing," he said, "I think we're a better football team with the kid in there, even now, let alone a few months from now. George is a decent-enough guy, I know all about that. But he really isn't sticking it in there. I wish the hell he wouldn't play the game so tenderly. Maybe I'm wrong. He's been pretty fair in the exhibitions. But they caught a little fire there when Tarkenton played the second half against the Rams."

I hummed a little, not having been in a confessional lately. I sympathized with Dutch's dilemma. He respected George's years in the NFL and there were such qualities as the fitness of things and the sensibilities of the veteran.

Van Brocklin gave my head a cuff. "Okay, coach," he said wryly, "who would you start?"

"I think," I responded with the other side of the needle, "I'll withhold my decision until just before the kickoff. But I'm pretty sure about one thing."

"What's that?"

"I think you are going to start George Shaw."

Van Brocklin nodded. "That's right. I'm going to start George

Shaw. You are accepted into the society of coaching geniuses."

It was not hard to like Van Brocklin's offhand sentimentality at that moment. The scales would go the other way a year later, almost to the day, when he would upbraid Shaw to his hometown newspapermen in Portland, Ore., in a merciless post-game indictment that marked the end of Shaw's career in the NFL.

So Shaw began against the Bears at Met Stadium and was muddling halfway through the second period despite doors-open chances. The Bears were playing quite possibly their worst game in history. The first suggestion of this was the Bears' initial punt attempt, when the snap from center soared into the stands.

When Shaw failed to produce a touchdown from short range, Tarkenton entered, without the prescribed glazed eyes and fidgety fingers. In three minutes he had his first touchdown, a 14-yard pass to Schnelker. He got two more in the third period, to McElhenny and Reichow, and another to Middleton in the fourth. Despite the temptation to go rocketing clear to the moon amid all this eruption of touchdowns Francis stayed around long enough to run the fifth touchdown by himself.

37-13. A football team playing its first game in the NFL. Against the Chicago Bears and George Halas!

The innocent thousands at the stadium applauded respectfully. A visiting writer from Baltimore had more trouble believing the fans than the ball game.

"Look at them," he said. "They really don't know the enormity of this. It's like Luxembourg beating the Kaiser's Army. Oh, Lord, Lord. I would hate to be the Bears when Halas gets to them."

And yet, unaccountably, there was no screaming, blast-your-eyes speech from Halas in the Bears' dressing room. There was, in fact, an utter, smothering silence.

It continued through the dressing period and the embarkation from the stadium. It continued on the bus ride to the airport and through the final boarding process.

Finally, the weather-gnarled old coach made his way to the head of the aisle as the defeated gladiators sat in brooding contrition. It had been a full life for Halas, fraught with triumphs and pratfalls. Nobody in his employ, however, had ever fallen on his prat more ingloriously than today.

Halas turned to face his mercenaries. He had fought the good fight to restrain his boiling wrath, the humiliation, the bitterness of a man wronged by blackguards.

But now he had to give them the coach's terse, explicit summation of their performance. It began in his abdomen and worked its way slowly through the various tracts, gathering speed as it passed the larynx and finally bursting through Halas' gnashed teeth:

"You goddamned PUSSIES," he said.

Whereupon, he sat down.

It was the shortest and most eloquent post-game oration in football history.

I think he did it for the Gipper.

Tarkenton's tenure in Valhalla lasted one week. The Vikings lost to Dallas 21-7 in the Cotton Bowl broiler despite Van Brocklin's halftime advice to Tarkenton "to forget about reading last week's newspapers and get your mind on today." To give Tarkenton added time for reflection, Van Brocklin reinstated Shaw the following week in Baltimore—and after ten years the game still stands as the most theatric and downright mortifying of all.

His reappearance in the stadium where he experienced his most blissful moments as a pro seemed to lift the introspective George Shaw. He passed well, he stood up to the rush of Marchetti and Braase. What he couldn't get done Van Brocklin ordered Mike Mercer to do. Mercer was one of the classic football hoboes of the era, an aspiring quarterback who became an intercollegiate turnpiker carrying his kicking tee and his field goal shoe. He started at Minnesota and made stops from there, in varying lengths, with the U. S. Marines, at Florida State, Hardin-Simmons, and Arizona State at Flagstaff. He was the only pro footballer who needed a separate chain to handle all of his fraternity keys.

He had a great leg but a nail-biter's temperament. It produced some of Van Brocklin's more memorable sideline commentary and led Mercer into the most resourceful cross-country routes ever pioneered in football to get him safely from the field to the bench after he had blown a field goal.

No matter how round-about his exit, however, Van Brocklin's rasping maledictions would reach Mercer somewhere between the hash marks and the water bucket.

"Mercer," Van Brocklin screamed one time, "you couldn't kick a whore off the pot."

Judgments such as these frequently failed to inspire Mercer on his next effort. They would so unhinge poor Mike, in fact, that his only escape from Van Brocklin on his next cross-field odyssey was to vanish into Section 32 and come back disguised as an usher.

But in Baltimore, before discovering how screwed-up he was as a field goal kicker, Mike pumped four through the posts and, with Shaw and Mason, kept the Vikings alive until it got to be Minnesota 33, Baltimore 31, with four seconds left. The Colts stood on the Viking 45. If anybody was going to win the game for them with a field goal, the ball would have to travel 52 yards, and it would have to be kicked by Steve Myhra, a friendly North Dakotan who that very day had lost his job as the kickoff man because he couldn't get the ball downfield more than 40 yards.

Myhra was rushed into the game, an improbable prospect for lionization. It was going to be one of those forlorn, doomed gestures.

But it not only went 52 yards, it went through the goalposts.

On the way from the ballpark to the airport, the bus broke down. It was 91 degrees. Van Brocklin sat mired in his agonies and his sweat.

There is no justice, he was thinking, that would let me get beat by a 52-yard field goal on the last play of the game—by fat-assed Steve Myhra, of all people.

Chapter XII

"Wouldn't football be a beautiful game if everyone played it like Hugh McElhenny?" — *Inscription on plaque presented in Chicago.*

Football players who had been around the horn maintain that nobody died losing a football game like Van Brocklin died. Yet—and this was one of the contrary twists in his makeup—his conduct with outsiders after the battle was often exactly the reverse of what his reputation would suggest.

In his press conference after a tough defeat he would rarely rage or condemn-to-hellfire. He might take a pensive, fatalistic tack that would seem to put his Psyche in another room. The awful reality would set in later—like Tuesday at the squad meeting. There was an interview session after another Viking-Colt game in Bloomington when Van Brocklin's team was struggling passionately to crash into the sunshine of respectability, and had the Colts beaten with 80 seconds left.

But Unitas took the Colts 75 yards in 75 seconds. And with one play left, he threw to Jimmy Orr in the end zone for the winning touchdown.

Van Brocklin sat in the swivel chair behind a desk in his office ten minutes later and answered questions in a tired monotone. Yes, he said, the Vikings should have won but Unitas, well, he was a guy who knew what it was to eat potato soup seven days a week as a kid, and that is what beat the Vikings and . . .

One of the interrogators was the barber-journalist from Bemidji, Cliff Morlan, an extremely large, well-meaning fellow with various portfolios including haircutting, sportswriting, fish-guiding, basketball-refereeing and fry-cooking. Cliff felt the need at this touching moment to extend the arm of kindred understanding.

"Dutch," he said dolefully, "I think I know how you feel losing this game to Unitas and the Colts. Up in Bemidji Friday, we lost one just like it, 7 to 6 to Brainerd."

Now there was some kind of parallel there all right, but Van Brocklin at that precise moment could not quite tie the two together as identical personal tragedies. He dearly admired Bemidji but these were the Colts, and he had to get his team up there where it could breathe, and there must have been $4 million worth of players out there, and he could still see Orr juking his corner back and going for the corner and he wanted to scream, "Flag! Flag!"

"We lost it just about the same way," Cliff was saying.

Van Brocklin looked up with large, weary, spaniel eyes and said softly:

"Aw, Cliff, for chrisesake."

The kick by Myhra could not really undo an extraordinary effort by his football team in Baltimore, and Van Brocklin, realizing it, was privately proud although still seething over the nearness of it. Three games—a win over the Bears, a near win over the Colts. Others would have to say it but Van Brocklin also knew at that moment he was a football coach because just nine weeks before all the team had, as a literal truth, was a two-page paper roster and 40 boxes of empty shoes.

They beat the Colts two months later, 28-20, after seven straight losses. Nobody demolished them, and they scored points, but the territorial losses by their undergunned defense approached the Russian withdrawal of 1941. When Joyce and Bishop played on the front line, the defensive four was usually characterized as experienced but slow. When Prestel and Leo played, it was usually described as young and slow. Marshall could move, but wasn't healthy. The other defensive tackle, Culpepper, was a willing boy but acquired his chief prominence for his ability to swallow schoonersful of goober peanuts at the bar, without gulping.

Behind these various mainstays Van Brocklin and Gilmer manipulated relays of defensive backs with the gray foreboding that the situation, while bad, at least was going to get worse.

Gilmer changed secondaries so often his own defensive linemen had to check the program before introducing themselves in the huddle. The harrassed sentinels included Mostardi, Morris, Johnson, Pesonen, Sumner, Dean Derby — acquired in midseason from Pittsburgh, Sherman, and others whose names never were released to next of kin.

Mostardi was a kid who looked frail but was sturdy enough to put in time in the purgatory of pro ball, the corner. He was a Kent Stater and the team comic. And he established a still-revered league record by getting beat by 40 yards on a routine pattern to Boyd Dowler in Green Bay's first scrimmage play at the Met.

"It was one of those play-action passes," he explained to baffled questioners afterward, "where Starr sends a back into the line pretending to hand off. Unless the man is careful, this may make the defensive back covering Dowler forget all about Dowler and go for the fake.

"I am covering Dowler. Starr sends Taylor into line. I'm damned if I don't take the fake and come up on Taylor. Then he sends Hornung into the line, and I'm damned if I don't get faked by Hornung, too. So I'm trying to sort them out, but neither one has got the ball.

"By deductive reasoning I decided there is only one place where the ball can be at that exact moment. Right. It is floating high overhead. By the time it comes down to Dowler on the sidelines he has been standing there so long he is tapping his foot impatiently and telling Lombardi, 'no, no, I swear they lined up with 11 guys on the field.' "

Eventually they won three games of 14, a record that may have been more remarkable than the team's 12 straight in 1969.

Mostly it was Van Brocklin, and Tarkenton, throwing 18 touchdown passes, Reichow catching 11, and the rekindled bravura of Hugh McElhenny. His art was the fluid gymnastics of the professional open-field runner. Never simply for show. It always had meaning—a limp leg here, a dipped shoulder there. The football fan who understood the nuances of his craft prized Hugh McElhenny almost above all other great football players of the era because he appealed to the aficionado's admiration of grace and style. His kind of football theater took him a little beyond the spectators' emotional partisanship. He might have beaten you but he rarely wounded you. The fan whose team lost to the Packers' power or the Cowboys' speed might have found scapegoats and villains in his own ranks, but McElhenny rarely left him with any such hostilities.

He flung his skills and technique against the maulers, the speedsters and the pursuers. It was irresistible drama for the fan because it was the jaunty cavalier defying the onrushing macers. And when he won he did not evoke the instant thunder that followed a spectacular catch. The reaction was closer to the bravo applause of the opera hall. The greatest McElhenny plays were pure concert, and it was not until they were over that he would allow himself that pardonable flourish of showmanship to which the great ones are entitled—a high stride into the end zone with his head thrown back.

His last such performance was on a sunny October day at the Met when he reached back into his prime for a valedictory run that represented the signature of a grand career. He made other runs in his last two years and scored again, but against the 49ers themselves on this day—

The King swung to the left behind two running guards, dipped back slightly and started to turn the corner. He needed only 32 yards. But the guards disappeared somewhere around the line of scrimmage. McElhenny ducked away from the cornerback and, spinning, slipped the corner linebacker. He slanted toward the center of the field, in glides and bursts. Linemen hit him at the hips and shoulders but they never hit him hard. He was always a half step away from the crunching shoulder or the tripping hand. He dodged Matt Hazeltine once, ironically his insurance broker. He was now at the 20 and he straightarmed the strong safety. Even while he was in full career the spectators' gaze fell behind him to a remarkable graveyard of fallen and sprawled bodies. By actual count seven players had open tackle on him but caught only a swatch of nylon or a vanishing pad. He was in high stride now, swinging toward the goal line, and here was Hazeltine—again. McElhenny pulled his shoulder in, the rhythmic, conditioned reaction of the matador, and Hazeltine flew by.

The end zone underfoot, McElhenny raised his knees a little and majestically pranced in. He stopped, turned, handed the ball to the official and trotted to the Viking bench.

"I wanted," Tommy Mason said, "to ask him for his autograph."

Van Brocklin clasped his hand, and he might have been telling an audience new to professional football, "this is what the game is when it is at its best."

It was almost exactly what the Chicago football writers said, in fact, when they presented McElhenny with a plaque 10 minutes before the Bears-Viking final game of the season.

"Wouldn't football be a beautiful game," the inscription read, "if everybody played it like Hugh McElhenny?"

Fifteen minutes later Hugh McElhenny ran back an Eddie Brown punt 81 yards into the end zone.

He was not an especially heroic man, although he had nerve enough when he needed it. He didn't function well when injured, and he never pretended any differently. He didn't dog it in practice, but he was also abundantly aware that he didn't sell any tickets with practice performances. Van Brocklin treated him deferentially his first year, considerably less so the next when his injuries and the grind of time left him outdistanced by the strong, young and reckless Tommy.

In a way he was the last issue of a breed, the halfbacks who saw the field as tapestry and read the texture on the fly, the ones who lived on wits and instincts and a decoyed hip. Even before time overtook him, the game itself did. A McElhenny might turn a five-yard sweep into an 80-yard frolic in 1950, but within ten years there were new hostiles for the open field runner to worry about—the men on the opposite side of the field.

"The football people call it pursuit," he said. "Years ago if you turned the corner you only had a couple of guys to beat.

You could put some moves on the linebackers and defensive backs. By the time I finished playing ball it wasn't the linebackers in front of you who were breaking up the long run necessarily. It was the guys coming all the way from the other side of the field, the ones nobody blocked because they weren't supposed to be in the play. It was a tough combination for a runner as he got older: The linemen were getting bigger and faster and they were in great shape, which put them three-up on me for openers."

And so the new great runners became the ones who approached McElhenny's finesse and speed but had more natural power to handle the encroaching musclemen—the Jimmy Browns and Calvin Hills and Gale Sayers. And even Sayers does not appear to be strong enough to sustain a long career.

McElhenny's personal code was the philosophy of the escapist. He never construed football as a game where he had to establish his enduring manliness on every play. He expressed it offhand in the daily lockerroom repartee when George Shaw brought up some recollections of his days with the Baltimore Colts.

"A guy who was really dedicated to football," Shaw said, "was our center, Dick Syzmanski. He was a bachelor then. Dick would lie awake nights trying to figure out new ways to hit people."

McElhenny allowed himself a moment of pained reflection. "Me," he said, "I used to lie awake nights trying to figure out new ways to avoid getting hit."

From his very first week with the Vikings he sensed the competition and threat of young Mason, yet he gave him as much advice as any veteran could reasonably be asked to give a rookie who eventually was going to take his job. Whatever know-how he offered Tommy was never going to cost the old man his job, he knew. He would lose it to Mason's young legs and Tommy's own very considerable skills.

Mason was moved by the veteran's willingness to help him, and the casual decency with which he did it.

"I'd see McElhenny run a play," he said, "and I couldn't imagine a guy having that much rhythm and balance in a hairy game like football. It made me feel like a sandlot player. But then I'd come off the field in scrimmage or in a game, and if McElhenny had something good to say about it, it puffed me up. We'd talk about technique, in a way I do with younger players now. I feel like McElhenny did then. There is nothing I'm going to keep from them that will keep them off the team. I never have felt that I knew anything that would make or break the situation.

"In those days he would tell me things to look for, things to be aware of. If we were running a screen, just before he would get the pass from the quarterback, he'd check things out downfield. Then he would make a move with his back to the line of scrimmage. Let's say you're off to the side of the field on one of those screens. Just before you turn back to catch the ball you see the linebacker recognizing the play . . . Well, you know he's going to be coming in on you, but you can make him miss because he doesn't think you know where he is. It sounds like chess and that's what it is, except that the guy weighs 250 pounds and he hits a helluva lot harder than the bishop. I used it a few times, and it seemed to work. Mac would say, 'now listen, if you can, check just before you get the ball; it'll put you ahead of the game.'

"For a while, I tried to cut like he did. But I decided it wasn't as good for me. McElhenny's stride was a smooth, weaving thing. When he would decide to make a sharp cut left, he would come up with his right foot and do a crossover fading away and falling back from the man bearing down on him. Mac would just sort of roll. He's one of the few guys I've seen cut like that. I often thought it would be easier on my knees, but I wasn't built that way and I went back to my natural style—which was to go slashing in there when the traffic got heavy. I never did quite get the mileage Hugh got, but at least I got more injuries."

They finished the year in a riot of touchdowns at Chicago, where Van Brocklin arrived at halftime with a police escort and boiling insides after getting delayed by storms en route from the East. His mission had been to sign an end from Miami, Bill Miller, the top choice in the Vikings' new draft. Miller listened respectfully to Van Brocklin but signed gratefully with Dallas, which offered more money and potentially less trauma in training camp. Gilmer as Van Brocklin's alter ego had managed to hold the Bears to 21-21 at halftime but the Bears added a few grains of lye to Van Brocklin's fermenting disposition by winning 52-35.

A freight handler's strike at the airport delayed the return flight to Minnesota by five hours. This interlude the furloughing warriors used constructively by doing some preliminary elbow calisthenics at the terminal bar in preparation for the commencement party on the plane.

It was a ritual in which most of the coaches enthusiastically joined. By the time the champagne was open over central Wisconsin the Dutchman's fellowship at the terminal had yielded to the more conventional smouldering fury. He remembered the games they might have won and he disclosed his suspicions that some of the sly old castoffs had taken their money fraudulently by loafing through the season.

These suspicions he voiced in ferocious nose-to-nose dialogues with the alleged offenders in mid-aisle at 30,000 feet. The most spectacular matched the Dutchman against Bill Bishop, a 260-pounder whose dislike for coaches was almost religious.

They stood in the center of the plane, Van Brocklin holding a bottle of Grain Belt in his right hand and Bishop a half-empty magnum of champagne in his. They shouted various discourtesies, the burden of Van Brocklin's being that Bishop was full of himself and the burden of Bishop's being that Van Brocklin was full of manure.

Whereupon Van Brocklin fired Bishop in mid-air. He also fired others in small-lot loads. In the field of spontaneous eviction, the performance reminded old heads of the day Buddy Parker of the Pittsburgh Steelers put his whole 36-man squad on waivers after the wretches had blown a ball game in the fourth quarter.

Dutch stopped while he could still field a team but he did outstatistic Parker in one category. He fired Jimmy Eason, the equipment manager, who was mysteriously blamed for putting on the plane in Chicago one Bill Bloedel, a well-known Twin Cities football camp follower.

Eason was about to bite a large chicken leg when he was duly indicted. The news temporarily numbed the little equipment jockey, who dropped his tray on the floor. Rising, he asked

Dutch to please get his hands off Eason's jacket. "You can't fire me," Eason announced.

"Give me one reason," Van Brocklin demanded.

"Because I quit. I wouldn't want to work for a mean bastard like you."

The Dutchman called Eason the following morning, presumably at 5, and disclosed brightly it was about time for him to be getting down to the stadium to clean the gear. Eason was too groggy to resist reinstatement. Six years later Van Brocklin asked Jim to accompany him to Atlanta. Too deeply rooted in the Twin Cities, Eason stayed with the Vikings. The Dutchman was one of the first to call him when the doctors amputated his leg, mauled at the Battle of Salerno.

"I've always figured Dutch was okay," Eason will tell you now. "The fight we got into could have happened to anybody."

"Then you didn't mean it, what you called Van Brocklin?"

"Who the hell said I didn't mean it?"

The dismissals, naturally, were unofficial. But a lot of the bodies were gone the next summer at Bemidji.

Bill Bishop graduated to the trucking business.

Hugh McElhenny begins memorable run against 49ers as Leo Nomellini reaches for Tarkenton (1); McElhenny twists from Hazeltine (2), and Baker (3).

The King slips by Colchico (1), then breaks through Mertens' arm tackle (2) and bursts into end zone full-stride.

He was never very heroic and never great but he was a good and typical pro, Gordie Smith.

It was just another fumble, but Jim Marshall turned it into an epic in 1964 with his 66-yard run into the wrong end zone in San Francisco. Jim burst clear in midfield (1), charges majestically across the goal line (2), and then bows his head when he learns the dismal truth. He became a great player in ensuing years, and the fans forgot.

Paul Flatley does a headstand after making a catch against Green Bay.

Two at cross-purposes: The Vikings' Tom Hall goes for the ball but catches the head of Chicago's Bennie McRae and draws 15 yards.

Van Brocklin, with Harry Gilmer, smoulders on sidelines.

Tommy Mason, interred under bodies. scores for Vikings but Bowie is nearly decapitated.

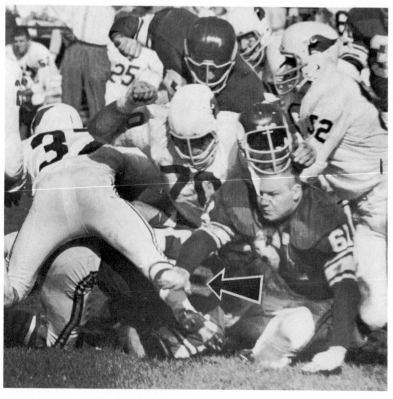

Francis afoot on the scramble. He spent most of his Viking career
a half stride ahead of disaster, in this case named Willie Davis.

Chapter XIII

"Take me to the church; I think I am going to die."
—Rookie tackle after 12 minutes in Van Brocklin's
camp.

Survivors of Van Brocklin's training camps have come to acquire the unbreakable bond of men who have shared the rack. It is a kind of togetherness that would be understood by the inhabitants of Devil's Island.

The Dutchman candidly confessed his first year camp had been too lenient, an admission that stunned the players. Most of them thought of it as a two-a-day Spanish Inquisition.

"I'll tell you," explained a much-medaled veteran who went through practically all of them, "it wasn't so much the physical part of it—although when you go through three straight days of full-pads contact work TWICE A DAY like that stretch in 1962, you know what it was like in The Crusades. I remember the first day in camp. The linebackers were running backwards across the field for openers, across and over, across and over, and it's real tough running backwards.

"Then we went to a whole series of drills and calisthenics so you worked up a helluva lather even before you started practice.

"But we were supposed to be okay for it because we had just one helluva medical exam, electrocardiograms, x-rays, hammers, needles, forceps, the whole armory.

"So this big rookie tackle starts coming through the ropes on opening day and he goes through four times. He's got up a real sweat, and on the fifth run-through he does a big half-gainer off to the side and flops to the ground, with his eyeballs rolling around. He's groaning and the sweat is pouring off him. The trainer, Fred Zamberletti, and Stubby Eason, the equipment man, come over and the tackle recognizes a friend in Stubby. He's lying there exhausted and he looks up to Eason and he says:

" 'Friend, take me to the church. I am going to die.'

"For a while I thought Eason was going to dig under the guy's jersey and shoulder pads to find his dog tag so he could get the right church. But Van Brocklin comes over about then and decides what the guy needs is not spiritual comfort but a one-way ticket out of Bemidji. The guy really thought he was going to meet his maker. When he saw Van Brocklin he must have been convinced of it. Anyhow, they put him on the bus and he was on the DC-3 heading home, five hours after he drew his equipment. I'm not sure what the elapsed time was from the start of practice to his voluntary retirement in the ropes, but I think it broke all previous standards."

It did. The officially logged time for the resignation of Jim Hayes, a very pleasant and willing young man who really WAS suffering, was 12 minutes.

Not surprisingly, the physical exertions and psychological stresses of Van Brocklin's camps occasionally stirred the inmates into some form of rebellion. The most promising and least harmful was a wee-hours escape to The Dutchess or similar refuge. Aware that his ranks include a formidable number of roisterers and kindred knaves, Van Brocklin tried in his first year to make himself a friend of the casual curfew-breaker. He decided not to impose maximum security measures.

Thus it was theoretically possible to duck out if the fugitive observed the standard precautions of stealth, camouflage, and noiseless re-entry.

Karl Rubke, the thirsty linebacker, developed a nearly flawless modus operandi by which he was able to enjoy the cool vapors of The Dutchess taps for an extra hour or so. Rubke would station himself in the pay telephone booth just off the main hall of the Pine Hall dorm at 10:58 p.m., a couple of minutes before curfew. Then, just as the officer of the guard was about to set out on his first dormitory tour, Rubke would thrust his head out of the booth and cheerfully identify himself, reminding the innocent coaching adjutant that he was present and accounted for.

The coach, West or Yowarsky usually, would return from the upper floor dorm inspection a few minutes later, notice the phone booth empty and assume Rubke was snoring in the sleep of the just.

Actually, he was already at The Dutchess happily chugging his first draught.

It all blew up a few weeks later, however, when Rubke and a dozen others were done in by an early morning dragnet laid out by West. Among the flushed-out was the onetime Van Brocklin teammate at Philadelphia, Lapham, a rustic fellow and the Vikings' first year center. He was one of those journeymen of pro football. This is a term eagerly seized by the club publicitors as a serviceable label to hang on the ones who play in constant fear of eviction.

A couple of hours before Van Brocklin's sleuths had apprehended the fugitives, Lapham appeared in the coaches' quarters with the earnest announcement that he wanted to see Van Brocklin. The time was 10:45 p.m., 15 minutes before curfew. Van Brocklin wasn't in, so Lapham withdrew courteously. It was a ruse, you understand. By presenting himself to the high command on the brink of curfew, Lapham had clearly established his whereabouts in the dorm in the event there might be suspicions later.

Lapham knew, although the coaches didn't, that there would be a mass bug-out around midnight and he was going to make damn sure he would not be counted among their number.

Lapham marveled at the cool, shrewd simplicity of this ploy as he drained another mug with the boys at The Dutchess an hour after curfew. It might have been hasty, his decision years ago to turn down the CIA people on campus at the University of Iowa.

The following morning Lapham and the 11 other miscreants were summoned to Van Brocklin's command post.

"All of you get nicked $100, you clowns," Van Brocklin snorted, "except Lapham. He gets $200."

Lapham was now willing to admit his culpability. But he

reeled under the dark injustice of a double fine. "What for?" he groaned. "All the rest get $100."

"You get $100 for missing curfew," Van Brocklin roared, "and $100 for being so goddamned stupid to think you could get away with that grade school stunt."

Although jarred by these heavy-handed judicial blows, the Viking rakes made another gallant bid to preserve their life styles the next weekend despite a new demoralizing experience of one of their buddies.

This one cannot be identified for several cogent reasons. What happened was that the ill-starred warrior was spotted by the campus cop in the act of trying to smuggle one of the town honies into the dorm.

Discouraged, he repaired to a nearby parking lot and the sanctuary of his automobile. As a love nest, it offered less comfort than his couch but did have more mobility.

The trouble with this alternative plan was that he forgot the time.

It got to be 1:30 and Van Brocklin, duly informed of the vacancy upstairs, exploded and set off on a personal patrol of the parking lots. It took him only a few minutes to detect suspicious coos emanating from the back seat. Peering inside, the Dutchman found his missing halfback locked in the very arms of amour.

Unsentimentally, Van Brocklin reached into the backseat and pried his astounded athlete from the caressing limbs of his adored.

Even the most calloused swains would have to agree it was a terrible predicament for the un-pried, to say nothing of the pry-ee, who found herself in a position that may be charitably portrayed as compromising.

I mean, they didn't even get a chance to kiss goodnight.

Van Brocklin ordered his man back to the dorm, and the tryst so ended. The Dutchman always contended he would leave no doors closed in the pursuit of duty. A man made sacrifices. It may have been the worst breach of chivalry since Errol Flynn sprinkled garlic salts into the atomizer bottle of a love rival.

It was left for the last Sunday of camp, however, for Van Brocklin to deliver the final retribution. The calling of the roll at midnight revealed the absence of two of the wiliest and most indomitable, Bishop and defensive back Charlie Sumner. A third absentee was Raymond Hayes, a rookie fullback.

The Dutchman had made a point of warning about any further offenses against the order and tranquility of camp that weekend. He interpreted the defiance of Sumner, Bishop and Hayes as a personal goosing. At 8 in the morning he rumbled into the dormitory room of the equipment man, Eason.

Van Brocklin grabbed the foot of Eason's cot, collapsed the legs and spilled the startled occupant onto the floor.

"Wassa matter," Eason said, "It's Sunday, We don't have to eat breakfast."

"We're going to have an extra workout this morning," Van Brocklin declared. "Get down to the dressing room."

Eason made no further objection. He had a running start on a hangover and, observing Van Brocklin's red-streaked eyes and owly manner, concluded privately that the Dutchman didn't look so irresistible himself.

Sumner, Bishop and Hayes appeared at 9 a.m. Eason issued them full battle gear—helmets, shoulder pads, blocking pads, the works. From the training room they walked the quarter of a mile to the practice field. There was a foreboding in their hearts and a funereal rhythm to their tread, as though they were walking in front of a caisson.

Van Brocklin was waiting for them in the middle of the field. The late August sun was rising in the cloudless sky, pouring near 90 degree heat onto the steamy greensward. Birds fluttered in the nearby oaks and the other innocent sounds of Sunday morning in the pines played lightly on the sylvan scene.

On another day it might have been a time for poets, but Keats never had to play the Bears six days later.

Van Brocklin stopped the approaching trio at the goal line.

"All right," he said, "I want you to roll end over end down the field to the other goal line."

They rolled to the goal line.

"All right," he said, "I want you to roll back to the other goal line."

They rolled to the other goal line.

They rolled back and forth, 100 yards at a time. And then they leap-frogged and they somersaulted. Even when performed by a healthy man, these are unnatural acrobatics that can cause upheavals in the several abdominal tracts. Sumner, Hayes and Bishop were already carrying the handicap of dark spots and queasy innards. After an hour they pleaded for a time out, but Van Brocklin seemed not to be able to make out their anguished mouthings. They were reeling, splay-footed and approaching a 4-G blackout condition.

The temperature mounted past 90. In scores of dormitory windows and from behind oak trees, awed teammates viewed the staggering tableau.

Two of them got into a rowboat to gain a closer vantage point from the bay of Lake Bemidji and nearly drowned when Van Brocklin turned suddenly near shore, the movement panicking the boaters into capsizing.

On the field, not surprisingly, the rollers were getting sick. And the sicker they got the more penitent they became.

"Coach," one of them said, "take two grand outa my pay but don't make me roll down that field one more time."

"Roll down that field one more time," Van Brocklin bristled.

With the hour approaching 11, Van Brocklin picked his way out of the messy field and left the three flattened and semi-conscious at the 50.

Struggling to their feet, they made their way toward Eason's training room. Exhausted in mid-street, Hayes declined to continue across to the other side although threatened by an approaching semi-trailer. The driver stopped, uncertain about his truck's chances in a collision.

Two of them eventually made it non-stop but Bishop sank onto a curb halfway to the dressing room. He remained there for nearly 30 minutes, and unbeknownst to him, became the subject of a passing art class.

Bishop now hangs in at least one studio in Chanhassen, Minn., alongside the Wreck of the Hesperus and Other Marine Disasters.

There were no further curfew violations in camp.

Van Brocklin, of course, was not always the fulminating ogre.

He had wisecracks and pats on the duffs on the odd days, and every now and then would stroll through the dorm rooms to relive a little of the bonhomie of his old training camp days.

On these occasions he would walk in on a veteran ball player, say a Paul Dickson, and clown a little about the Simon Legree son of a bitch who would run a two-hour scrimmage in the hot sun. Gradually he would move the conversation around to the small talk that is the putty and glue of the football training camp, the hairy-chested professional's version of the Boy Scouts' campfires.

Tommy Mason would put down his guitar a couple of doors away and join in. Eventually there would be more than a half dozen in the room, and the mellowness of the evening drifted toward midnight. Van Brocklin would waive his own barracks regulations and send a runner out for beer—and maybe another shipment a couple of hours later.

They gossiped about the great football players of their time and posturers and the crazies, and they would come back to the Minnesota Vikings. And Van Brocklin would be saying that there was almost nothing that a football team with guts and leadership and willingness to sacrifice couldn't do, even if it was just a couple of years old.

It was not a speech with him, it was a creed. When it was obvious to everybody in the National Football League that his football team did not have the quality, reserves and the three or four great ones it took to be a contender in his early years, Van Brocklin would not believe it.

Because of this he could not bring himself to look at the failures of his first three seasons as the predictable defeats of an inferior football team. If his players developed that outlook, they were going to be devoured. The psychological problem here was pretty fundamental. There are several responses open to it for a coach who is outmanned. One is to take the long view of history, not to regard each game as Armageddon.

Van Brocklin looked on losing somehow as an act of disloyalty by his players, to their coach or the player's code. They did not lose because they weren't good enough but because they were stupid, or they played like a bunch of kwiffies, or they were over-awed by the reputation of people like Alex Karras or Deacon Jones or Gino Marchetti. At one time or other Van Brocklin classified most of the NFL's elite as overrated beach boys.

His football players almost always had two or three minds toward him.

"There is nobody who ever played for Van Brocklin who wasn't impressed or even overwhelmed by his football knowledge," one of his veterans said. "Whatever else you thought about him, you never had the feeling you were going into the game unprepared, or that you might get beat on the sidelines. If the game is played by 12 people—11 out there and the other on the bench, you know you were in pretty good shape on the sideline on Sunday afternoon.

"In film meetings he'd look at the defense you were playing that week and take maybe a linebacker on the other team. He liked to pick on linebackers because up until a few years ago almost everybody played man-to-man defense. He would just sit there and see that this linebacker, when he drops back, crosses over with his left foot. So if we are going to run this particular pass pattern, he'd tell Tarkenton, 'we've got this linebacker off-balance just long enough to get our man out there a step or so before he crosses back over to his right foot.'

"That was the sort of thing he did when he came out in '62 or '63 with all those deep passes to Tommy Mason. Or maybe he'd see that corner back likes to face to the inside and he'd say, 'well, if he's facing that way, he's got to turn to take care of a sideline cut,' and we'd swing a back out short, and all of a sudden he's got the whole defense in a turmoil.

"Tarkenton had a mind that was with him on that stuff. That's why even when the Vikings didn't have enough manpower to take on Rinkydink Normal over a full season, they'd steal one from the Bears or Rams now and then and scare the hell out of the Packers.

"But there's another big part of coaching and that's the way you handle the guys with the hairy rears and the big testicles. Van Brocklin's nature was to bulldoze, everything that got in the way. I know he tried to treat some of the guys on an individual basis, like Flatley, Mason, Hawkins and Tarkenton. But he didn't have much a gift for that. He'd cut down a guy in front of the team in a way that was brutal. Well, sometimes it was brutal. I mean it was always brutal to the guy, and that's why he came to have so many of them hating and fearing him, but it was comical to the rest—although you didn't laugh too damn loud at the time.

"I remember Flatley and John Campbell were rookies in 1963 and they both played in an exhibition game that the Vikings won out at Los Angeles. Campbell got his ribs cracked during the game and Flatley hurt his knee. Now both of these guys later played for years in the NFL so you know they were made of pretty good stuff.

"Anyhow it was after the game and Campbell was getting his ribs taped and Flatley was getting some kind of treatment, and Van Brocklin was sparring with the Los Angeles newspapermen. One of them pointed out the Vikings looked lousy in L.A. the year before but seemed to be strong now and he wanted to know to what did Van Brocklin attribute this new-found tiger attitude.

" 'Well,' Van Brocklin says, turning to Campbell and Flatley, who are in some kind of pain, 'the first thing to do is to go out and draft yourself two Big Ten pussies.'

"He may have meant it as a good-natured needle, but I doubt it, because Van Brocklin was never very good natured about injuries. Like Lombardi, he just didn't believe in them.

"Anyhow, Campbell and Flatley did not join in the general hilarity that the crack seemed to produce among the writers.

"The thing about the players' reaction to Van Brocklin was that he did get you scared enough and mad and reckless enough to fight the world, but after a while the negative part of that reaction would go against him. I say that having defended him against a few people who really thought he was an all-out Nero kind of character. When you played for Van Brocklin, there was always a tenseness in the air that kind of precluded any real camaraderie on the team. Everybody was looking out for himself, and the Dutchman may have been the funniest guy in the world when he was chewing out somebody else, but when he got to you, it was pure misery.

"I remember the day when Bobby Reed, the fast little halfback we had from out in California, came down to the buses as we were about to leave the Bemidji dorm for the West Coast.

"Reed was one of those mod dressers from California, I mean years ahead of the Fourth Galaxy stuff a lot of the football players wear today. He used to like attention. He started out with some one-piece tan job that could have been the model for the first bathing suits. He called it 'my one-piece, continental RE-laxin' suit.' Reed thought it all was a big joke, and loved the kidding, but in his more stylish moments he did see himself as a boulevardier.

"Anyhow, he comes down from his room just before we get on the bus. He's wearing spats, some kind of semi-tux with a boutonniere, a little derby on his head, one glove on and the other in his hand, and an umbrella dangling from his arm.

"Van Brocklin spots him from 150 feet away and just goes crazy. He came at a full charge and gets his nose right up to Reed's and says, 'get those kwiffy clothes off, Reed, or you're not going to be traveling with this football team, nowhere.' There was nothing racial in it. He would have said the same thing to Tingelhoff, which, come to think of it, would have been a spectacular sight.

"But that was Van Brocklin's style. Another guy might have taken the character aside. Or kidded the hell out of him. But Dutch just poured it on, and sooner or later you're going to get a lot of guys with subsurface resentment, even if they do go out and play their tails off.

"But I don't deny that he was the most original guy I ever played for with a put-down or just in sheer talent for blowing up.

"He was at his inventive best with the officials. We played an exhibition out on the coast and he was screaming at one of the guys who wore glasses and·had a tall forehead. Van Brocklin called him 'Cyclops.' He hit us for 15 yards and Van Brocklin called him everything from Mao Tse Tung to last year's hash. The official said Frank Youso or somebody threw an illegal block and Van Brocklin screamed 'go to hell, he couldn't block a hat with a steam iron.'

"Well, they never got along, Youso and Van Brocklin. Van Brocklin thought Youso was dogging it. Youso might have given coaches that impression because he was so strong and had a good mind and quickness and should have been one of the world's great tackles. There were days, incidentally, when he was a very, very good one. Anyhow, they had it out this August day under the trees at practice. And they called each other every name in the book, and it ended up with Van Brocklin and Youso telling each other to go screw yourself. And they went at it that way for five minutes. I though Youso was going to brain him. As a matter of fact Van Brocklin was ready to swing himself. Anyhow, it blew over the next day.

"Van Brocklin fired him."

The Dutchman's frontal-attack style and engulfing ego exerted an effect on certain kinds of players that was almost pathological. It seemed to permanently alter the flow of their body juices.

The author-quarterback Lee Grosscup joined the Vikings in August of 1962, his three-year career with the Giants rarely having emerged beyond the sideline telephone stage. He had a frail, ascetic bearing that gave him the appearance of the poet Wordsworth trying to dodge a pass rush. He did not make friends easily but he was agreeable enough and a regular guy to those who offered friendship; and he drank as well as the next at The Dutchess.

He had a fondness, however, for the breezy language of slick magazines and the Playboy clubs.

Three days after joining the Vikings, Grosscup called his first play in the huddle. "Okay," he said, "4 right 29 A.O. — on the deuce."

Van Brocklin, squatting behind the huddle, erupted to his feet and belted into the huddle.

"What did you say, Grosscup?" Van Brocklin steamed. His face was an inch from Grosscup's, revealing a distinct cast of splotched red.

"29 A.O. — on the deuce," Grosscup confirmed.

"On this team, Grosscup," Van Brocklin shouted, "you learn

to speak English. Around here we go one-two-three-four. We don't want to hear any of that Madison Av. bull. Now call it again, the way all of us peasants can understand."

Grosscup's next call was the essence of wheatbelt orthodoxy. "29 A.O.," he said, loudly but very, very obediently, "on two."

Grosscup lasted only a month. In his heart of hearts, Van Brocklin admitted the longhaired, delicate--looking vagabond had some ability and might have helped for a year or so. But he let him go, ostensibly because he had another sub quarterback, John McCormick, who was alleged to be a punter.

Grosscup played a total of one game plus 5 minutes for Van Brocklin. He worked under him for approximately 20 practice sessions. He had played under Allie Sherman for three years and had been exposed to scores of advisers and king makers over the years. When he left, he told a friend, "It's something. There are three people I'm never going to be able to forget — my father, Sherman and Van Brocklin. And I knew Van Brocklin for one month."

"There are some guys," the friend said, "who figure that's the statute of limitations."

Chapter XIV

"I went up to Jimmy Orr and gave him a forearm. The next thing I knew it was practically a riot."—*Earsell Mackbee, on how to get along in the NFL.*

Nobody flatly accused the Vikings of playing dirty football.

In any case, they did not do so publicly. But there was an undercurrent among NFL coaches that carried the suspicion. The Vikings played football like a gang of runaway dockworkers. There are grounds for maintaining, in fact, that the Minnesota Vikings were actually the decade's first protest against the establishment.

To my knowledge, Van Brocklin conducted no courses in mayhem. He siphoned off most of his violent urges, evicting the lambs from his own rosters.

He did manage to assemble a presentable roll call of rowdies and more civilized rough-housers, these including over a five-year span such as Steve Stonebreaker, Ed Sharockman, Jerry Reichow, Larry Bowie, Paul Dickson, Rip Hawkins, Dale Hackbart, Karl Kassulke, Gary Larsen, Bill Brown and Lonnie Warwick.

Lombardi used to hate to play the Vikings. In his mind it was comparable to sending a symphony orchestra against Spike Jones' band. There was no question how the competition would come out artistically, but what the bumpkins could not achieve esthetically they might make up for in straightforward malice.

The reason Lombardi held this view was that in 1961 against the Vikings Jerry Kramer suffered a leg fracture and in 1962 Paul Hornung was knocked out for the season by a Cliff Livingston tackle. A number of others in Lombardi's distinguished troupe received large knobs about the head and other sensitive regions. Lombardi became convinced the Vikings were out to damage his elite forces. He never said "dirty football" but the difference was so small it usually required a measurement.

There was no question the Vikings colored their football black-and-blue. It was all they really had to qualify for admission in the first few years. The notion that Livingston might deliberately assault a 220-pound back does seem a little far-fetched. Livingston was the most decorated bachelor in pro football at the time, a linebacker who was losing weight alarmingly as he approached the last rungs of his career. Van Brocklin's fierce calisthenics and Livy's accelerated social activities in Minneapolis —a city renowned for the aid and comfort it gave to single men— had sped the shrinking process to the point where Livingston needed wheat germ supplement to say goodnight.

Van Brocklin's blunt dictum was "get yourself a jockstrap," meaning: Hit somebody. Every ball club has some form of this same anti-social philosophy. When your man hits a ball-carrier near the sidelines, you call it aggressive football. When the other guy does it to your man, it's a cheap shot. Neither Van Brocklin nor George Halas nor Lombardi, for that matter, ever seemed to understand why the officials could not comprehend this simple truth.

Nobody, in the consensus judgment of the pro football society of the era, delivered more enthusiastic cheap shots than Bill Pellington, the caveman linebacker of the Colts. Very few people really hated Pelly. Seeing him broadax an unwary halfback as he eased up out of bounds was to watch a man happy in his work.

He did it to Mason one day in Baltimore. "Pelly," Mason recalled, "was a great ballplayer but one of the roughest, meanest characters I ever met on the field, although really a decent one off it. Anyhow, we're playing this game in Baltimore and our fullback carried up the middle and I'm just sort of looking around trying to look alert and WHAM, Pellington bangs me crunch in the mouth with a forearm.

"I just looked at him dazed and then said something goony like 'what the hell did you hit me for?' It was one of the first games I played. When I got to the sidelines, Van Brocklin told me to get back in there and let him have it. We were going to run a sweep and the Dutchman says, 'I want to see you throw a block on Pellington and tear his goddamn legs off at the roots.'

"I was playing out on the flank then. McElhenny started the sweep to my side, and at the snap of the ball I came off the blocks like it's life-or-death. I angled straight for the middle of the field, and there's Pellington giving ground a little trying to fend off Lapham, our center. I was coming full tilt and I had him dead to rights when I came blasting in there. Just as I poured everything I had into the block, Pellington took a little step backward, and I went crashing into Lapham.

"I damned near killed our own center. Lapham was reeling around when I looked up and the play was dead a few yards away. They creamed McElhenny on the sweep. I got back into the huddle and I kind of croaked, 'who made the tackle?'

"McElhenny was rubbing blood from his nose across the back of his hand and he said, 'the meanest, ugliest guy on the field. Pellington. Who the hell do you think'?"

Whatever their multitudinous failures in their first few years, the Vikings were rarely charged with playing finesse football. They had chippy ones, all right. Stonebreaker, a companionable but talkative and rather melodramatic Detroiter, played one season as an offensive tight end. At the time, he caught the ball like a man wearing boxing gloves and ran five minutes behind schedule on all pass routes over five yards.

He played for two reasons: Van Brocklin liked his pushy deportment and, furthermore, he didn't have any other tight ends after Gordie Smith got hurt.

A year later they made a linebacker out of Stonebreaker to exploit his natural belligerence. Stoney responded by decking Dickson in the lockerroom after the growling Texan called him "rook" once too often. He also nearly decapitated two friendly linebackers in scrimmage when he ran the wrong blitz. Fully disenchanted by now, Van Brocklin scornfully traded him to Baltimore, where Stoney promptly made the starting team and picked up a big check for playing in the title game.

Another just short of All-Universe talent was Billy Butler, a runty deputy sheriff from Berlin, Wis., who performed one of the most notable con jobs in the post-war NFL by surviving for six years as a running back and a safetyman. His tenure was spread over half the clubs in the league. He had a little speed, a little cut, a lot of nerve and the shortest wheelbase in the league.

"Butler," Van Brocklin used to bawl, "get the hell out of the grass so I can see you."

But the Dutchman called a squad meeting one Tuesday after a Packer game and handed Billy Butler a bonus check for $500. He had played the full game at safety, run back kickoffs, punts, subbed at offensive half and needled the daylights out of all Green Bays available.

"If he had talent," Van Brocklin said, "he would be unbearable."

As an instructor in gridiron pugilism, Van Brocklin had the virtue of excelling not only on technique but in anticipation.

He demonstrated it most graphically a couple of years later after Earsell Mackbee, the beaming California bon vivant, had made the team at cornerback.

Mackbee was signed on as a free agent after the Viking staff noticed him horning into the scene in Utah State films they had obtained to watch a big tackle named Jim Harris.

Harris was their No. 4 draft choice in 1964, but they never got close to him in the bidding fight.

They did, however, sign Earsell, who was working for a detective agency in San Francisco at the time and had despaired of all pro invitations by then. At Utah State he was a pass receiver, and a reserve at that. At the first squad meetings in Bemidji he was asked—along with the other, longshot free agents—what position he thought offered him the best showcase as a pro prospect in camp. It was the fair thing to do for the unknowns, and Mackbee appreciated the choice.

One of the Viking defensive backs, Lee Calland, advised him to try out for his position. "For receivers they've got guys like Paul Flatley and Reichow and Hal Bedsole and Red Phillips, Tom Hall, people like that," Calland told him. "Your best shot is the secondary."

"So when Van Brocklin came down," Mackbee remembers, "and came to defensive back, I stood up. I never played the position before. I didn't have the faintest idea what I was doing. We had one-on-one drills, which made me tangle with guys like Sharockman and Calland and George Rose and the others. I didn't want to be embarrassed so the next best thing was to be rough. Well, they didn't like a rookie doing that, and I can't say I blame them.

"The first guy who objected was Sharockman. On one series he was supposed to tackle me. Bozo was so mad by now, he just said the hell with tackle and came at me swinging. I ducked, and he missed, but he swung again. I stood in there and swung a little myself. I never saw it as being racial, and I don't think Bozo did. Later, Lee Calland, who is black, came over to me and said I didn't have to take any guff, any time. It wasn't a big deal, but he felt I needed some support.

"Van Brocklin heard about it, and maybe there was a little extra in there for him, because while he chewed me out a lot, he let me stay on, first as a taxi-squadder and then on the big team.

"So in 1965 I got my big chance in the Baltimore game at Met Stadium, and if you remember, that's the one when the Dutchman quit afterward. He was okay with me, I'll say that.

"I was covering Jimmy Orr, who's got all the moves. I played a lot of the game against San Francisco the previous week. George Rose started it on the left corner and Bernie Casey caught three touchdown balls over him. Van Brocklin sent me in there, and Casey caught another touchdown ball.

"The funny thing was, and I'll never forget it, at halftime there was George Rose, a southern white guy whose job I was taking away, coming up and telling me things about how I might play it better.

"We won 42-41, but this was the next week and here was Orr. Van Brocklin told me before the game, 'I know exactly what he is going to do. He is going to try to psyche you out right off the gong. So, the first thing I want you to do when he comes off the line of scrimmage, no matter what the play is, you walk up there and hit him in the mouth.'

"Well, here I am, a rookie, and I just couldn't picture myself going up to this nice guy Jimmy Orr and doing this to him.

"On that particular game, they had an article in the program about me, and both teams read the program in the lockerroom before the game to kill time. Apparently Orr had read the article, so when we line up for the first play, he says very politely, 'pretty nice article about you in the program,' and I say, 'gee, thanks.' And he says, 'how are the wife and kids?' and I tell him, 'fine.' Now you tell me how I'm going to hit this sociable fella in the chops. The game started and he commenced to put the moves on me. The one that really hurt was right near the end of the first half, when Cuozzo threw one 50 or 60 yards and Orr scored on me.

"Van Brocklin wouldn't let me forget it. He didn't say anything about my not following directions, but he remembers, you know.

"We didn't play the Colts again until the following year, in Baltimore. Orr didn't start, but he came in sometime in the first half. I decided now is the time.

"So I went up and gave him a forearm, which is legal. He kicked at me, and I took after him. We started rolling on the ground and big Jim Parker of the Colts came over and took off his helmet, and both benches cleared, and before you know it's a free-for-all and practically a riot.

"Orr and I both got thrown out. He said something as we were leaving, and I don't remember it, but I know sure as hell it wasn't about the wife and kids."

Van Brocklin's football teams caused no tremors in the title race in his transitional years. But, by some primitive order of natural selection, they did uncover and jungle-train enough earnest, young lionhearts to supply Bud Grant with the core of a champion a few years later.

They won only twice in 1962 and five times in 1963. Yet, because of the cavalier style with which Tarkenton quarterbacked and the brawling zest with which they attacked, nobody had the nerve to ignore them.

If there is a personal purgatory in the character of an emerging football team, the Vikings counted theirs as 1962. The ones

who staggered through it numbered some of the later nobility—
Tingelhoff, Marshall, Alderman, Sharockman, Brown, Winston
and Dickson. It was one of those revolving, potluck disasters in
which the victims seemed to compete with each other to see who
could make the most outlandish contributions. The contest was
open to all, Van Brocklin included.

The Vikings lost at least three games in the final 30 seconds
but flavored their weekly mishaps with the spice of the unexpected. This included the collision of one of their flankers with
George Halas' Wrigley Field brass band and the loss of another
one who sprained his leg coming out of the huddle.

By that time the Vikings had divested themselves of most of
their overage dreadnaughts and were in the process of scavenging
a younger and more promising class of NFL culls with which to
defend their innocent draftees.

Successful in his first trade with the Browns, Rose now accepted Paul Brown's benevolence once more. "I will give you,"
Brown declared, "a kicker named Fred Cox, a defensive back
named Tom Franckhauser, a receiver named Charley Ferguson,
and a tackle named Errol Linden. In return, I will ask for your
fourth round draft choice if all of them make your final roster.

"If three of them make it, I will ask for your fifth choice, and
your sixth if one or two of them make it. It nobody makes it,
you owe me nothing."

It was true-hearted charity's last stand in the National Football League. In the light of events of the next eight years, Cox
alone would have been worth half of the liquor tax receipts in
Bloomington.

But Freddie the crackerbarrel sage from Pennsylvania was
headed for improbable grief in the weeks ahead—flesh and blood
proof, if any were needed, that perfection alone was no safeguard
against the firing squad.

Cox was imported as a candidate placement kicker to goad the
jittery Mike Mercer into a high pitch of performance. Daily on
the practice field they would hold field goal kicking contests.
Most of the players, naturally, rooted for the incumbent Mike.
He already had some small status as the club dartboard, the object
of Van Brocklin's most inspired flights of condemnation. "If the

Vikings played in New York," one of his roommates used to say, "Mercer would have gotten the chair."

The competition surged through the better part of two weeks and was still awaiting a verdict heading into the final exhibition against Dallas in Atlanta—where Cox would be tried by combat.

The Vikings had a joyous night. They routed the Cowboys with a bubbly offense and a chesty defense. Tarkenton threw four touchdown passes, but all this dimmed before the exploits of the twangy schoolteacher who was doing their placement kicking under the blade of the guillotine.

Van Brocklin wanted more distance from his kickoff man. Freddie kicked seven straight THROUGH the end zone.

The Dutchman wanted consistency from placement. Freddie kicked all extra points flawlessly.

They tried him one time as a field goal kicker, from 43 yards out. He kicked it through with force and velocity.

The Dutchman shook Freddie's hand appreciatively when he came off the field.

And then he fired him off the squad three days later.

"It's one of those binds," the Dutchman explained, not without embarrassment. "We don't have enough places on the roster to afford to carry a field goal specialist. We're a team that doesn't have enough bench. Mercer will handle both the kicking and punting."

In mid season, the Dutchman fired Mercer.

His punting replacement was McCormick, the determined but pressing rookie quarterback who may have been the only punter in the league worse than Mike in 1962.

His field goal replacement was a linebacker, Jim Christopherson, who never kicked before in the NFL.

Cox was back on the roster in 1963, for field goal kicking AND punting—which he did under protest and about on a par with McCormick and Donald Duck.

Franckhauser stayed on, and so did Linden. Ferguson got hurt just before the start of the 1962 season and was placed on the waiver reserve list as an injury.

Rose dutifully confided to Brown that Ferguson in truth would have made the roster if healthy, and would be restored within a few weeks.

Touched by this rare soul-baring, Brown rose once more to the highest obligations of his pontificate and let Rose get off with a sixth round draft choice, although he could have insisted on the fifth.

"I'll never," said Rose, his voice on the edge of breakdown, "forget the Cleveland Browns for this."

Van Brocklin's emotion-threshold was considerably higher. He managed, in fact, to hide his gratitude completely on viewing films of Linden's first few encounters with Marchetti and Willie Davis.

Chapter XV

*"The worst part is that he hit us right in the brass."—
Bears' band leader amid shambles wrought by on-
charging Viking.*

The happy blush on Rose's cheeks had barely receded when he
received a telephone call from George Allen, then in the employ
of the Chicago Bears. One of Allen's assignments was to try to
market those Bears who were tooth-worn, civilized or otherwise
in disfavor with the head zookeeper.

Among these was a stumpy, bowlegged malcontent named Bill
Brown, a fullback. Brown was pouting because he wasn't playing,
a condition primarily caused by (a) Rick Casares, (b) Joe Mar-
coni and (c) Charlie Bivins.

Allen informed Rose the Bears were oversubscribed with full-
backs and that the Vikings were one team with which the Bears
would like to deal, owing to their longstanding love for the
Dutchman and the fact that the Vikings were the team least
likely to hurt them.

Rose surprised Allen and Van Brocklin by opting for Brown,
surrendering only a fourth round draft choice for 1963 in the
process.

It was one of the most profound strokes of statesmanship in
Minnesota history, ranking with the treaty under which the
state conned the Indians out of bumper-sticker rights at Minne-
haha Falls.

For the better part of the next decade Brown would be the
best all-purpose fullback in pro ball, a reckless, fearless football
bull. He was an unlovely football player, in style and appearance.
At the apex of pro football's years of glamor and photogenic aura,
he was a vestigial reminder of its primeval past. He ran, blocked

and caught the ball without refinement but with a capacity to inflict punishment and — even more — an apparent eagerness to do it.

His natural environment might have been the flying wedge and the days of no time outs or helmets. By instinct and physical behavior he seemed closer to the prize ring than the football field. It would take a genuinely disabling injury, an actual knockout, to get him off the field. He would not give up on a play and he made the slogan "second effort" the badge of his professional conduct.

He was hardly faultless.

"Bill Brown," one of his closest confederates said, "would be Jim Thorpe and Jim Brown combined if they didn't have to kick him in the rear end some of the time to keep his attention."

He did develop tendencies to drift and coast, unaccountable in view of his playing impulses once he was fully aroused. Most of these sins, though, were errors of miscalculation on the practice field and a certain lack of concentration when quarterbacks started calling audibles.

In the stickiest part of it, nobody on the ball club had to worry about Bill Brown's first priorities. More than most players, he seemed untroubled about what happened to No. 1. His attentions stayed on the scoreboard. He was a friend and admirer of Tarkenton, but it was Kapp in whom he found an authentic sidekick, a man with large muscles, short sleeves, and the language of the poker table—plus the same corncob notions about the team that Brown had.

But Bill Brown wrecked no football furniture his first year. The only real damage the Vikings caused all season was absorbed by a bunch of well-oiled musical irregulars sitting in the corner of the Wrigley Field end zone.

The citizens' band had assembled there for years. Alongside the high-powered halftime bands, it was bratwurst alongside filet mignon. It played polkas, pep choruses, a mazurka now and then, and "Nearer My God to Thee" when Halas walked onto the field.

The configuration of the stadium was such that the band had to sit in the first two rows of stands flanking the end zone. On this particular day the band was taxed to the limit of its modest artistic resources. The boys were scoring touchdowns in bushels, both teams. The action was so thick, in fact, the bandsmen were unable to play and keep track of the athletes simultaneously.

Ferguson, the mended recruit from Cleveland, nearly broke up the concert early in the game by dashing through the end zone in pursuit of a Tarkenton pass and just grazing the trombone section before coming to a halt. The only serious damage was transforming "The Stars and Stripes Forever" into a piccolo solo.

Unfortunately for the band, Ferguson was en route to his one great day in football and the trombone section forgot the warning of the first period.

Charley already had scored twice on Tarkenton passes. Now, with the Bears leading by five points and Tarkenton in wild flight behind the line, Ferguson once more angled through the end zone.

This time, he was charging under a forced draft that made him the biblical embodiment of Grim Desperation.

Ferguson was 6 feet 5 inches tall and weighed 235 pounds. His legs covered at least three-fourths of his vertical displacement. At a dead run he was one of the most formidable sights I have ever experienced.

Tarkenton's pass was arching toward the end zone corner, in a tantalizing trajectory. Ferguson seemed too distant to overtake it. But summoning his final reserves of fervor, Charley tore into the corner. He snared the ball just inside the chalkline—and, irresistibly, barreled into the musical irregulars in the stands.

Only the clarinet player saw him coming. He tried to warn the others with an agonized B flat trill, but they were playing The Colonel Bogey March and were in that passage where the whole battalion goes over the bridge.

The trombones, in the front ranks, were defenseless. Ferguson plowed into the unsuspecting bandsmen at maximum velocity. The air was rent with the sounds of splintered brass, busted valves, and the shrapnel of flying tubes. The musicians, not hired for their bravery, betrayed the same impulse to flee that overtakes the faint-hearted infantryman in ambush. Some of them actually threw away their trombones, even tubas.

Through this broken array, Ferguson churned invincibly until the Section H exit ramp allowed him a gradual run-out. Behind him, the band was in virtual carnage, its once-proud horn section decimated.

"The worst part of it," the distraught conductor said later, "was that he hit us right in our brass. The heart and fiber of the band. I was disappointed in the performance of our trombones. I think if they hung in there when Ferguson was going full blast, we at least might have been able to save the trumpet section. But, c'est la guerre, I guess. You learn through adversity. The saddest part was what happened to the clarinet man, who tried to warn us. He was still at his post when Ferguson hit, like Sparks on the Titanic. He didn't have a chance to get the instrument out of his mouth. We had him doing a tight-lipped hum the rest of the season."

The misery of the band, however, was a trifling hangnail beside the sudden asphixiation of the Vikings in the closing moments of the ball game. Emboldened by Ferguson's smashing campaign in the grandstand, they seized the lead in the closing minutes. Doug Mayberry, a muscular young Adonis from Utah State, had barged 12 yards right up to the end zone on a closing drive. The Vikings and Van Brocklin screamed he was IN the end zone. The officials took turns dodging the mortar shots of invective from the Viking bench until Christopherson kicked a field goal a few plays later to put Minnesota into the lead with just a couple of minutes left.

The Bears charged the Viking goal line as time waned. They got to within 30 yards, but Billy Butler intercepted a pass and, with 25 seconds remaining, the young desperadoes seemed secure.

All that was needed here was for Tarkenton to take the ball and fall down at the line of scrimmage at the 20-yard line.

They snapped the ball. "Good old Tark," Van Brocklin was musing, "he will take the ball and fall down at the line of scrimmage."

Tarkenton took the ball and handed off to Mayberry.

In the press box, Rose shrieked numbly, "Oh, no, not a handoff."

Mayberry never got to the line of scrimmage.

In front of him, Frank Youso had flattened the Bears' defensive tackle. Any other time, this would have been the occasion for rejoicing from all sides. Unfortunately, the tackle already had been flattened by two other Viking blockers.

Ed O'Bradovich, the Bears' defensive end, thus happily found himself undisturbed as he bolted into the Viking backfield. He nailed Tarkenton and Mayberry impartially, being careful to sift them out to be sure Mayberry had the ball. The congestion was too much for Mayberry. The ball flopped to the ground and was promptly set upon by the Bears.

Ten seconds later Roger LeCerc kicked a field goal, sinking the Vikings.

Van Brocklin roared across the field to accost the officials before they disappeared into the Wrigley dungeons. He was apoplectic. He was menacing. He wanted satisfaction for the call on Mayberry at the goal line, and he would not mind starting with their heads. He challenged their eyesight, ancestry, the condition of their intestines and the status of their private members. And when the officials disappeared, he continued his tormented oratory in the clubhouse. A witness, Cooper Rollow of the Chicago Tribune, later described it as the definitive work in the pathology of wounded rage. "I never dreamed there were so many synonyms for bastard," he said. "And I say that in all sincere admiration, because I have made a study of it. When I got to some words that completely stopped me, I asked for an interpretation, and Van Brocklin immediately kicked me out.

"He was a big man, and apologized later, but I tell you, I never saw one man so supernaturally mad in all my life."

The reporter I had retained that day to provide me with the weekly post-game communique from the Viking dressing room returned to the Wrigley Field press box an hour later. His face was chalky and his hands noticeably fluttered.

"I can't believe it," he said. "I can't believe it. I have spent 25 years in this business and I can't believe it. Van Brocklin talked for 45 minutes without letup, and there isn't one, publishable syllable that I can give your readers."

Attempting to recoup, I sought an audience with the stricken commander on the flight back to Minneapolis. By now the thunderous wrath had receded and given way to a silent, gaseous incredulity. The Dutchman did not want to talk. He glared and fumed and suffered. I tried again a few minutes later. "Why weren't you there with the rest of them," he yelled, "so all of you could ask your stupid questions at once."

"I didn't make that damn call against Mayberry," I said, "I didn't call the handoff and I didn't blow the block on O'Bradovich. What are you screaming at me for?"

"Go to hell," Van Brocklin said. "The interview is closed."

My telephone rang at 5 o'clock the next morning.

"Thanks a lot, Dutchman," I said. "As a result of your great performance on the plane, the newspaper has got everybody's stupid quotes on the game except yours."

Van Brocklin's pre-dawn telephone calls were not always the chummy gestures of a man willing to bury the ax. The Dutchman was never sure about deadlines. Nor was he ever sure how much of his own nest his grapeshot had splattered the night before. Newspapermen, like coaches, sometimes think vengeful, unadmirable thoughts. The Dutchman had nagging notions, after one of those scattergun diatribes, that he would wake up the next morning to read:

"Van Brocklin Blasts Officials, League Commissioner,"

or—

"Van Brocklin Blasts Owners,"

or—

"Van Brocklin Threatens to Fire 36 Stiffs."

At times like these he had the worried lion's instincts for survival. He offered a tentative paw.

"How about some eggs and Grain Belt for breakfast?" he said.

We lived about a mile apart. I was aware the man hadn't gone to sleep, so I drove over. His performance in this calming, domestic scene was even more remarkable than his eruption in Chicago or his traumatic withdrawal on the plane. Van Brocklin replayed the whole ball game. I don't mean he simply recalled every play. He threw in all the changes at the line, the defensive switches, the audibled blocking, and the commercial timeouts. He had almost total recall and, when it got down to the final summation, there was still one thing he could not forgive.

"That Tarkenton called a handoff?" I asked.

"No, that was stupid, but he's just a kid. I think I will go the grandstand route and very nobly defend his call in public. No, I'll never figure out how we could let O'Bradovich in there, just walk in there. The world is being taken over by stupid football players. But some of those calls—the things Halas gets away with in Wrigley Field. Whatever I said about the officiating, it was worth it."

Rozelle decided, as I remember that what the Dutchman had to say was worth $200.

We concluded breakfast at 9:30, by which time Van Brocklin had finished the Bears and was halfway through his last-minute loss to Pittsburgh the previous week.

That was the way of it. In the matter of blowing games in the last gasps, the Vikings were resourceful, relentless. One might even say they were opportunists. Well before the games, they developed novel approaches. Two days before the Pittsburgh game, for example, Leon Clarke, one of the aging patroons in the business, was struck down innocently at Midway Stadium— a thousand miles from the field of strife.

Clarke was one of the engaging oafs of pro football, a pass receiver of large torso and broomstick legs. He was the Joe Blfstk of the NFL in his prime, a player seemingly marked for luckless events. The Vikings acquired him from Cleveland, where he had aroused some local interest by getting hit by a falling flagpole.

In compensation for this kind of natural abuse, Leon Clarke providentially had acquired the love of a millionaire's daughter, whom he rewarded with marriage. Thus situated, he was not required to play football. But there were good works to be performed, and Clarke decided to devote his energies to the most challenging of these betterment projects, the Minnesota Vikings.

It was an alliance that could have been forged in Disneyland. For maximum effect, Leon postponed his arrival in Viking training camp until most of the strenuous, unworthy stuff was out of the way. He therefore played the first half of the season fat, unmaneuverable, and usually idle.

The Pittsburgh game was to be his formal unveiling as a card-carrying Viking alley-fighter. He steeled himself mentally, punished himself physically. On the final day of light workouts at Midway Stadium, he stood ready, primed.

An hour later Van Brocklin telephoned Thompson in the public relations office. "Better send your releases out in black the rest of the week," he said. "We just lost Leon Clarke for the duration."

"Was it a recurrence of his old shoulder trouble?" Thompson asked.

"No, he sprained his ankle. He was coming out of the huddle. Nobody laid a glove on him."

Whatever his physical infirmities, Clarke nurtured a manly love for his clansmen, a spirit of helpfulness, the essence of the musketeer. It embraced not only his teammates but the traveling journalists.

He was there at my hour of greatest need in five years as a chronicler of professional football. A training camp in pro football is a conclave of the world's most accomplished baiters, needlers and miscellaneous sharpshooters. No one is exempt. In the training camp of so reserved a schoolmaster as Harry Peter (Bud) Grant, for example, a stealthy chorus of the familiar children's hymn, M-I-C . . . K-E-Y . . . M-O-U-S-E, sometimes trailed the dead-panned coach as he walked past the players' quarters. It was a kind of musical salute to Harry Peter's new house rules.

In Van Brocklin's training camps, the practice was lifted beyond commonplace art and brought close to the science of sophisticated warfare.

One of the few accepted ground rules was that newspapermen occupied a gray middle ground between players and coaches. In shooting wars, this area is called no-man's-land. By general consent in camp, the occupants get shot at by everybody.

One of my most persistent hecklers was Walt Yowarsky, the offensive line coach. He was a man of vast chest, insight, devotion to work, a face borrowed from the relief map of the Pamir Mountains, and the only assistant coach I ever knew who could tell off Van Brocklin and stay on the payroll.

Yowarsky decided on a steamy summer day in Bemidji in 1963 that I could not run one mile under seven minutes. On this we held a rare accord. I also did not think I could run a mile under seven minutes. But when Yowarsky tried to establish the point beyond dispute, with a $10 bet, I began making mental computations. I was 35 years old at the time. Years of casual but stubborn dissipation had raised my weight to nearly 200 pounds, gracelessly distributed over a 5 foot 8 inch framework. Years later I would be touched by the wand of rehabilitation, but at this point I was largely a glob.

Still, there was a matter of honor here somewhere. I covered Yowarsky's bet and set the hour of truth for the third day in Portland, Ore., where the team would be billeted for one week on its western pre-season tour.

I began running practice laps at Bemidji by the pale light of the aurora borealis in the early-morning hours. News of the wager circulated around the camp. On one of my practice runs at 6 a.m. I detected the backfield coach, Motormouth Tom Mc-Cormick, taking clandestine stopwatch readings under a distant spruce.

Two hours later a flood of new money from the coaching quarters swelled Yowarsky's war chest. McCormick, Stan West, Darrel Brewster and Harry Gilmer all put down $10. This left me no option but to cover each bet or lose face, irretrievably, with the players.

Van Brocklin and I were not on speaking terms, again, while the tote board was open. Advised of the terms of the wager, he slipped his own ante into the coaches' treasury unannounced. To make certain I understood the implied disdain, however, Van Brocklin later got it into the camp grapevine that he was doubling the individual bets of the other coaches and was considering betting $30 that I would collapse of congested bile before three laps.

The evening before the big run on the University of Portland track I went a final game-condition practice mile and was timed in 7:02. Yowarsky had instigated the bet, but the blood of the Slavic barbarians ran in us both, and he wore a gloomy expression.

"Actually," he said, "it wouldn't hurt my feelings if you win. It might help if you see Clarke. If he doesn't have the pill to cover you, nobody does."

Clarke was the hypochondriac - in - residence at camp. The

players by now had been alerted by Zamberletti, the trainer, who had administered a one-hour whirlpool treatment to me the morning of the showdown. I strolled past Clarke's dormitory room and told him I wanted no pep pills, stimulants or other un-American type medication but simply wanted some kind of pain killer to soothe the lumps in my calves.

With a conspiratorial movement, Clarke summoned me to his infirmary cabinet and opened the door.

It was a remarkable sight. He had four shelves jammed with bottles, vials, boxes and tubes. He could have saved the Russian army at Tannenberg with what he had in the green bottles alone. Opening one small jar of chartreuse pills, he offered me a pair and declared:

"Take one of these 15 minutes before the race and you could give 30 yards to Paavo Nurmi."

"What do I do with the other one?" I asked.

"Give it to Nurmi," Clarke said, "if he's got the guts to enter."

Naturally, I shunned the chartreuse pills but accepted two tablets of Bayer aspirin.

Zamberletti arrived at the track at 10:55 a.m., five minutes before the appointed starting time. By then the curve of the track was lined with t-shirted ballplayers, most of them grudging pals of the worried marathoner. Dr. Donald Lannin was there with his inhalator. Gilmer, West, Yowarsky, McCormick and Brewster were there. Everybody in the traveling troupe was on the field except the grand marshal, who was busy in the dormitory 300 yards away establishing a tone of Distant Indifference.

The trainer walked up to the starting line with a small revolver held in the palm of his hand.

"It looks," Bowie conjectured, "like they're gonna shoot the son of a bitch if he comes up lame at the finish."

Zamberletti fired and I mushed into the first straightaway. I had planned a reasonably brisk first quarter of 80 seconds, after which I would gauge my pace in accordance with the condition of my pulse and my visibility—which got worse as the run progressed, owing to gallons of sweat rolling off the forehead.

I had named Bill Brown as my second, charged with shouting the lap times. As I came up on the finish of the first lap, where the 50 ballplayers had gathered in raucous rooting parties, Brown shouted, "78 seconds and you're dogging it."

Tarkenton had brought a broom out of the dormitory and pretended to be Bill Stern, announcing the progress of the run to a suspenseful world.

"He's one-quarter of the way through, ladies and gentlemen," Tarkenton was announcing, "and he's all over the track. He's the world's first scrambling miler."

The first quarter, I recognized instantly, had been too fast. I throttled down, realizing I had only the thinnest tolerance on stamina and finishing foot.

I came around the second time and Brown crowed, "Three minutes and 10 seconds. Move, man. No frontrunners on this ball club." I was running to mixed catcalls and jeers, about evenly divided, I thought. The sun was bouncing radiation waves above the parking lot asphalt next to the field end and, as I rounded the end zone turn for the third time, Brown seemed miles away through the film of perspiration smudging my eyes. He looked stricken.

"You're three seconds behind," he yelled. "You got to make up three seconds. Dig man. Nobody talks to you on this ball club if you don't make it."

They were running alongside the track now, acting fevered. Tarkenton reverted to instinct in time of stress and appeared to be looking for Reichow downfield. I tried to pour it on, but my legs were getting mealy. I was in the backstretch now, 120 yards away, and I could hear Brown hollering, "One second, you still got one second to make up." Tarkenton had his broom up by the neck and looked like the guy who did the on-the-scene broadcast of the burning of the Hindenburg zeppelin at Lakehurst.

Glancing far out over the field, I noticed the curtains in Van Brocklin's office twitch a little. The ballplayers were waving their arms at the finish, exhorting and making gestures here and then, some of them memorable. I staggered over the line and started to go down, but there was no way I was going to flop in front of that boisterous mob. Brown came over into the middle of the track and showed me the actual time. His cheeks were popped out like a burping squirrel, and he seemed ready to explode in giggles.

It said 6:42.

I had 18 seconds to spare.

"Brown," I said, "you count time like you pick up Tarkenton's audibles, 20 seconds late."

The bitterness was lost on my bow-legged second. He was now rolling on the field hysterically. Tarkenton came up with his broom. "No interviews," I said reluctantly, "give the athletes 15 minutes to cool off."

They gave me one of those triumphant shoulder rides to the dorm, where I collapsed without further provocation.

So I collected from all the coaches three days later when we flew to Los Angeles. The money lasted 30 minutes, time for four rounds of beer for the staff and all the subalterns.

The Dutchman paid along with the rest. With the smile of conciliation, he reached into his wallet for the $20. Unaccountably, it fluttered to the floor on the Sheraton-West bar, where it waited to be plucked, either by the donor or the beneficiary. The Dutchman and I peered at each other with rich understanding of the situation.

As far as I know, the $20 is still there on the floor.

Chapter XVI

"If you want to and can, I think you should accept the Eagles offer."—Viking owner Bernie Ridder to Norm Van Brocklin.

The romantic buccaneer Jean LaFitte would have understood Jim Marshall, football player and restless seeker of broad horizons.

In another era Jim Marshall might have shared the peril and the frostbitten valor of the mountaineer George Leigh-Mallory, inching toward the summit of Everest in the snowfields and mists at 28,000 feet.

Over a glass of pernod the immortal French fighter pilot Nungesser would have drawn straws with Eddie Rickenbacker of the Lafayette Escadrille for the right to choose the next wingmate. Winning, Nungesser would turn to Rickenbacker, fling his scarf over his shoulder and say: "Ah, Eddie, zat Jeems Marshall, he eez one of us, no?"

The answer, of course, was incontestably yes. Intimates of Jim Marshall often argued that the theory of reincarnation needed no further evidence than Marshall himself to squelch also reasonable doubt of its validity. Vigorous arguments would break out in the dormitory debating circles on the question of which corporeal form Jim Marshall had occupied in a previous life, that of LaFitte, Paul Revere, the general Hannibal, the explorer Fernando Magellan, the entrepreneur Prof. Harold Hill, the daredevil Montgolfier—or all of them.

For the most part, Jim Marshall would view these recurring controversies with a tolerant aloofness. He was never sure about

Revere and Montgolfier. But he had small doubt that his own exploits in the 1960s would at least match and probably outlive the over-publicized feats of those other cats.

For this reason, his associates were not surprised that if anybody on the squad had been handpicked by fate to propel the Vikings out of the want ads and into the nation's consciousness, Jim Marshall would be this instrument of deliverance.

It ought to be understood that the Vikings had sprouted dense thickets of internal disorder that made the whole thing a hard challenge for any Moses-designate.

By the barometer of the scoreboard, the Vikings in their first three years had made encouraging progress. But they now aspired to a larger status in which the perplexity they might spread around the league would equal the disruption they had achieved in their own organization.

Their original crisis centered on their debacles at the draft table. More precisely, their debacles in the market. Successful in their first draft (the one that harvested Mason, Tarkenton, Hawkins and Sharockman), they were virtually blanked the second time around. The consolations were Winston and Bowie.

It was at about this point that the club's ranking table-pounder, H. P. Skoglund, convened the owners and declared: "Gentlemen, it looks as though getting this Bill Miller from Miami—our top draft choice this year—is going to begin a contract war that will last for several years and will really come down to an old-fashioned urinating contest among the bidders."

Miller was lost to the AFL's Lamar Hunt. Several conclusions were drawn from this in light of Skoglund's colorful definition of the rules of war. One hypothesis was that the Vikings did not want to lose any more draft choices by getting out-kidneyed.

Shaken, Skoglund called a morale meeting on the eve of the bidding for Minnesota's Bobby Bell and Mississippi's Jim Dunaway the next year. "Remember," he was understood to have told his colleagues, "we're never going into another bidding battle crosslegged."

Whether it was overconfidence or a sudden shift in wind, the Vikings lost not only Dunaway but Bell, their first and second draft choices and quite probably the two best college linemen in the country.

Bell was an authentic football prodigy, a 220-pounder with a speed, range and instinctiveness that qualified him for any position on the football team. He was a stranger from the south and a Negro. Yet he needed only a year to get himself installed as the people's Merriwell on a University of Minnesota football team which was then at the zenith of its Rose Bowl prestige.

The Vikings in those years were earnestly grubbing for crumbs of popularity around town. Toward university football they were elaborately courteous. Weekly on their scoreboard at the Met, Thompson and Rose—not without some pain—would hang up congratulatory messages announcing the Vikings' joy in the Gophers' 42-7 demolition of Northwestern.

In the face of these overtures, the Minnesota athletic department impressarios maintained a frosty distance. Once in a while the Vikings would openly ask a favor, in the use of a practice facility or the university stadium itself, and be met either with 45 bylawed reasons why it was impossible, or by editorial silence.

None of this made the university's hasty and groveling turnaround any more graceful five years later. This was when it publicly began campaigning for a pro football franchise by offering the unrestricted use of Memorial Stadium for Viking football games.

From the very beginning, however, the two coaches, Van Brocklin and Murray Warmath, hit it off supremely well and with mutual trust. For these and other reasons, it was generally assumed that Bobby Bell could safely be measured for a purple helmet.

Almost frivolously, Lamar Hunt's procurement agent, Don Klosterman, called on Bell in the Twin Cities in late November. There were few talent prospectors in the business who could match Klosterman's reputation for craft and zeal and, as long as he was toting Hunt's contracts, for bucks per square inch of small print.

Still, the only thing that brought him to Minneapolis was the longshot bettor's fascination for hopeless causes.

So Klosterman telephoned Bell. First surprise, he wasn't signed. Second surprise, he wasn't crazy about the Viking terms. Third surprise, he would listen to Klosterman.

"I will be there," Klosterman told Bell, as sedately as a man can when he has two feet out of the door and his hand on the hotel elevator button, "in five minutes."

Klosterman first informed Hunt. The decision now was to go after Bobby Bell with a sincerity that could not be misunderstood. This took the form of large bills and longevity.

It came out to something like five years, $150,000, no cuts and fringe business opportunities.

The Vikings had put together a bonus and salary package amounting to something between $25,000 and $30,000 for one year.

Philosophically, the Vikings told Bobby Bell, they were opposed to giving a player a no-cut contract, arguing it wasn't fair to those not given such contracts. Further, it had been their experience that no great college football player had any reason to doubt his ability to make it with the pros.

Bobby was impressed with the Viking presentation as a student of philosophy. As a 21-year-old college student with bills to pay, however, he found something stubbornly eloquent in Klosterman's offer. He took his time, and it must have been at least a minute or two, weighing the respective merits of the two proposals.

Warmath was asked to intervene but could not find it in his heart to ask a kid four years out of poverty to turn down $150,000.

At this moment, the rest of the Viking owners felt obliged to question Skoglund's choice of weapons. The organization decided to advance with its most expensive gunners, dispatching both Van Brocklin and Rose into the field for Dunaway's signature.

Dunaway was a 260-pound baby rhino, a one-eyed athletic marvel of enormous strength and pro football promise. He had been drafted by the Buffalo organization of the AFL in addition to the Vikings. For several days Van Brocklin and Rose reconnoitered the battleground in New Orleans, in advance of the Sugar Bowl game in which Dunaway was playing.

A few hours after the game, Dunaway appeared in the Rose-Van Brocklin suite and viewed admiringly the terms of the Viking offer—$15,000 bonus and $15,000 for each of his first two years.

But he declined to sign it. Dunaway explained he thought the offer fair and more than ample to cover his expected grocery bills the next two years. He owed a courtesy call, however, to his other suitors.

This news set off immediate alarm bells for Rose and Van Brocklin. In the contract wars of those days, the principal element of strategy was to be able to euchre the enemy before the contest was actually under way.

Rose brooded because the Viking reconnaisance so far had not turned up a trace of the enemy. This was a notable achievement inasmuch as the enemy was 50 feet away all the time, in another room of the same hotel on the same floor.

It had escaped the attention of the Viking G2 planners that Dunaway's line coach at Mississippi, Bruiser Kinnard, had spent some of his merriest years in pro football as a roommate of one Harvey Johnson.

Normally, this would have merited only passing notice in the social pages. It was pertinent in New Orleans, however, because Harvey Johnson was on the staff of the Buffalo Bills. His pal, Kinnard, turned out to be Dunaway's chief negotiator at Mississippi.

This snug arrangement had the effect of putting all Viking contract offers in the hands of their rivals for prompt attention and improvement. The situation was comparable to the Czar of Russia negotiating with Lenin through the intermediate offices of Leon Trotsky.

Rose's misgivings when Dunaway asked to be excused were well founded. For 20 minutes Van Brocklin and Rose filled the awkward silence in their hotel room with spasmodic clicking of their ballpoint pens.

When another ten minutes went by, Rose was convinced of the dismal truth and walked dumbly out of the room on the one-in-a-thousand chance that Dunaway had lost his way and was roaming the corridor aimlessly.

Bert had advanced 10 or 15 yards when he heard the slow, hesitant clack of typewriter keys, as though made by large, fleshy fingers unaccustomed to a keyboard.

It was the kind of typing rhythm Rose had heard before, in a hundred football coaches' offices.

Magnetized by the stuttering Smith-Corona, Rose nudged up near the door of the room from which the sounds came. He now heard not only typewriter keys but a new sound, which he identified as sort of gutteral twitter.

Bert Rose rapped on the door, impelled by an overwhelming professional curiosity. The typing stopped and the door opened, to reveal the large forms of Jim Dunaway, Bruiser Kinnard, Harvey Johnson and the balance of the Buffalo organization. Most of them were still hunched over the well-pecked typewriter.

Bert Rose struggled manfully to observe the amenities, in the fashion of the professor who has just launched the lecture by discovering his fly is open.

"Hiya," Bert said courteously, "just throught I'd say hello. I see you're, er, signing him up, huh? Well, that's the business. No hard feelings."

It was not the most moving concession speech, but it certainly was one of the shortest.

Shorn of Dunaway and Bell, the Vikings counted only Paul Flatley and John Campbell as productive salvage from this latest draft. The next decision was to change ammunition once more. They would throw into the bidding war the one weapon whose use until now had been carefully conserved, namely money.

The following year the Dutchman took personal command of the Vikings' operations and intelligence divisions, leaving Bert pretty much with the task of hauling around the footlockers. It worked splendidly in 1964, after which the Dutchman's performance as the company selective service officer fell off drastically.

With all high draft choices available, the Vikings decided they would offer their premium recruits a minimum of philosophy and a maximum of cash.

The old distaste for no-cut agreements vanished in favor of a more practical attitude toward such contracts, which meant the Vikings decided to give them.

At the same time, their agents in the field were given blunt instructions that the days of wine and roses were gone in recruiting, and had now given way to an era of groin-butting, heavy security and light extortion.

The priority ballplayers for the Vikings this time were Carl Eller, the huge and mobile tackle at Minnesota; Dick Evey, a lineman from Tennessee; and Hal Bedsole, a Southern California receiver with the gifts of a large Don Hutson and the temperament of Dennis the Menace.

Eller they drafted on the first round in Chicago. They did it without fretting, inasmuch as The Moose was grazingly contentedly back in the Twin Cities. He had already agreed to their offer and was virtually under contract before being drafted.

Bedsole, meanwhile, had been smuggled into a Chicago hotel and was kept under a modified form of house arrest. In these conditions he was protected not only from the rival AFL but potential buyers in the Vikings' own NFL. The logic here was that nobody was going to draft Bedsole if they didn't know where he stood contractually.

Not surprisingly, he was available on the second round and duly drafted by the Vikings.

Thus heartened, the Vikings' strongarm squad stashed away Evey in the same style. Rather grandly, he was turned over to the Bears that evening when Halas' people humbly asked permission to speak to the man they had just drafted on the first round.

Not long afterward in Miami, Thomas, the scouting chief, signed linebacker John Kirby of Nebraska by delivering a right cross to a rival scout on the 30-yard line of the Orange Bowl, moments after Kirby became eligible.

With this flaming new spirit of pugnacity in the marketplace, the Vikings also signed defensive back George Rose of Auburn, the third round choice. With the exception of a first-rate lineman named Tom Keating of Michigan, they also signed practically everybody else on the draft list. Among them was a stubborn blond lineman allegedly drafted as a sentimental gesture but destined to outlast almost all of them. His name was Milt Sunde of Minnesota.

By now the Dutchman had collected a lively clutch of young football players. Some day, by themselves or trade, playing for Van Brocklin or somebody else, they would barge into the social registry of championship football. Among these were Tarkenton, Marshall, Eller, Mason, Alderman, Tingelhoff, Sunde, Brown, Flatley, Campbell, Bowie, Sharockman, Kassulke, Hawkins, Cox, the punter Bobbie Walden and a few more. He had others, veteran pluggers, and he continued to traffic briskly in cronies from his old playing days; he had nomads like Tommy Wilson, Charley Britt, Mike Bundra, Bill Jobko and L. Vargo, another Dutchman quarterback named Ron VanderKelen, and a quiet young Minnesotan of high character and surprising first-year ability as a defensive back.

The last was Terry Dillon, a mannerly kid who had played his college football in Montana and who kept reminding Van Brocklin of the great Lions' defensive back, Yale Lary.

They activated Terry Dillon from the taxi squad in mid-season of 1963. He played uncommonly well for a first-year man. And he might have been playing today. But he returned to Montana in the off-season in 1964. While working on a construction project on the Clark's Fork of the Yellowstone River, he fell from a bridge, and drowned.

As early as the spring of 1964 Van Brocklin had considered trading Tarkenton. There was no serious enmity between them then, although there had been random clashes in club meetings and once on a plane. But Francis' style had now annoyed the Dutchman to the point where, in Van Brocklin's mind, the squiggly quarterback had assumed the role of a preening coloratura. The Vikings had won a highly acceptable five games and tied one in their third season. Yet Van Brocklin clearly relished the final game of the season. In this he played VanderKelen the whole route with what amounted to his second team offense and he butchered his old employers, the Eagles.

So the Dutchman weighed the proposition when the new owner of the Eagles, Jerry Wolman, offered Sonny Jurgensen even-up for Tarkenton. He turned it down, despite what he later said was a 5-0 vote by his assistants in favor of the trade.

Wolman's interest in the Vikings went beyond .Tarkenton and focused on the grand marshal himself. The Vikings' season-closing destruction of the Eagles sealed the execution of the head coach, Nick Skorich. The Dutchman stood confirmed as an oracle. The Eagles were nothing when he got there in 1958 and were nothing now in 1964. Van Brocklin's popularity remained strong in Philadelphia. Wolman wanted him to come back as the coach and general manager. The idea appealed to Van Brocklin's sense of vindication, and it wouldn't have offended his sense of economics, either.

At this point, Rozelle entered the negotiations. The league, he conceded, could not stand in the way of a man's professional advancement and technically Van Brocklin was being offered an advancement from coach to general manager.

Between us boys, though, Rozelle reasoned, "what the Eagles really want is Van Brocklin the coach, and we can't have one club going around prying loose another club's coach."

We can't, he might have added, unless the coach is Vince Lombardi; and enough time has elapsed between his abdication in Green Bay and re-coronation in Washington to meet the requirements of form, order, decency and football fans in the Senate. Nobody objected. Vince deserved the courtesy.

By this time Van Brocklin was experiencing pangs of impatience with the bureaucracy. In conversation with friends, owners and sometimes within earshot of strangers, he made no special effort to conceal his lack of esteem for Rose or general managers of any description who had not spent time in the huddle.

In addition, he seemed to harbor vague, mysterious feelings of being unappreciated. Thus he welcomed the enthusiasm with which Wolman pursued his services. Eventually they thrashed it out—Dutch and the owners—in Fairview Hospital where Skoglund was recovering from an operation. Ridder, as much an admirer of Van Brocklin's field achievements as the others, nevertheless took the position that if the Dutchman wanted to go, he should go. Ridder never insisted on ceremony in his business or social dealing, but he had the aristocrat's fondness for order and some semblance of peace within the corporate family.

Rose was sulking and in the process of being overpowered in the office. The Dutchman had offers from Philadelphia. The Dutchman also was unhappy about being denied additional stock in the Vikings and there was strife within the board and office over the Rose-Van Brocklin split.

"If you want to and can," Ridder told Van Brocklin, "I think you should accept the Eagles' offer."

Rozelle ended the whole awkward diplomacy by telling Wolman the deal looked very unattractive to the commissioner.

Van Brocklin withdrew, and the Vikings owners gratefully gave him a new three-year contract, with salary increases. Nobody had to prompt them. The team had performed exceptionally well, and the owners felt doubly indebted because Van Brocklin had just been maneuverd out of another job offering wider vistas, and heavier bank balances.

For Bert Rose, these new and unanimous endorsements of Van Brocklin all but clinched an early departure from the general manager's office.

Bert's admiration for the symbols of his command — large, board chairman-type offices wherever possible, his role in the draft, his press conferences, and his fetish for procedure—struck Van Brocklin from the very beginning as the essence of the football desk-jockey's memo pad mentality.

The two were not constantly at war. They got along well enough socially much of the time. But the Dutchman never really accepted Bert Rose as the fountain of decision in the Viking office.

Within a couple of years the general manager had lost any real influence over the operation of Joe Thomas' scouting system and in the selection process of the draft.

Lacking leverage among the owners, he was powerless to resist this systematic disrobing—and it got to be pretty public— of his administrative control. But he could never really understand it.

"The dispute between us," he would say later, "was more

one-sided, I'd guess. I suppose scouting was the first point of friction. I always looked on it as a department of management. The career of coaching is not necessarily permanent. Management tends to have more permanency. It has something to do with the Ws and Ls in the standings. This is not necessarily right, but that is the way it is. Let's say a coach wants to have his scouting set up a certain way. So we set it up. But now a new coach comes in and says he doesn't like it. So now we have to tear up the whole department. The ideal scouting system ought to look toward the long-range interests of the team. In addition, most coaches are simply too busy to devote any meaningful time to scouting.

"I think the most successful systems will be those in which a full-time professional staff sifts and sorts and makes its judgments and lays its findings before the coach and says 'this is what we think.' "

As a practical matter, however, Joe Thomas began reporting directly to Van Brocklin. If and when he made a side report to the newspapers, he got his tail kicked—publicly.

Among the owners Skoglund, especially, was energetic in the campaign to shove Bert closer to the exit ramp. Winter, too, could see no logic in Rose presiding over a squabbling front office with most of his functions already being performed by the head coach.

Ridder's sense of decorum was offended by the enlarging mess, but it bothered him to see the general manager being ganged by his detractors. Even Ridder understood, however, that the Viking front office performance by now was a burlesque of the most comical double-agentry in the gunshot republics of Latin America. It was laced with small conspiracies, cabals and wary footwork.

It reached the cracking point when Ridder discovered his own general manager under surveillance by the Swedish Underground on a trip to Ridder's St. Paul newspaper plant. And it produced a final stroke of bathos when Rose fired one of the office secretaries whom he suspected of spreading his confidential telephone conversations to Van Brocklin and others alleged to be disloyal to the general manager.

The only stagecraft the whole plot lacked was invisible ink and a fizzing bomb.

In the end the decision was not Rose's nor Van Brocklin's but Ridder's. The situation's only solution, he concluded, was the removal of one of the two. Bert's ratings in the polls at this point were not much higher than Harold Stassen's.

"Bert," Ridder said, "it looks like the end. I'm sorry. You've done one great job for us in a lot of ways, but this can't go on; you know it and I know it. If I thought there was a way out of it, I'd stick with you. All this is going to lead to is more turmoil in the front office and a reaction on the field."

And in the appropriate board meeting, it was Ridder who had to perform the ceremonial act of cashiering Bert Rose, audacious general manager. Bert put out a one-line statement, explaining he was resigning for the good of all concerned.

If he could have stretched out the Lenten season a couple of months, he might still be there.

It was against this backdrop, then, that Jim Marshall moth-balled his orange-and-silver parachute for another summer after a flawless leap of 10,000 feet, and headed for a journey even more exotic.

Chapter XVII

"I don't even remember picking up the ball. It didn't dawn on me that something was wrong until Bosley ran up to me in the end zone."—Jim Marshall.

Thirty years separated the Gas House Gang of the St. Louis Cardinals and the Minnesota Vikings of 1964. But there was a brotherhood of the bizarre that linked them across the generations, made them kindred souls in the pursuit of daffy joys. Both of them —for one season at least—were teams for none but the flaky hearts.

The Cardinals won a World Series and therefore consigned a few more to legend than the Vikings, namely Pepper Martin, Dizzy Dean, Daffy Dean, Joe Medwick and Leo Durocher.

But aficionadoes who treasure a certain style and grace in their athletic oddballs and revolutionaries will have no trouble ignoring the Vikings' lack of championship class in 1964. The team did win 8, lost only 5, and tied 1. Anything better than that would have made them suspect.

Even their most resolute partisans of the time, however, may have been unaware that the real unsung giant of the cast was one Palmer Pyle, a chubby offensive lineman acquired from Baltimore in a trade for Stonebreaker before the 1963 season.

He had a brother playing center for the Chicago Bars, Mike, a Yale man and therefore a pillar of orthodoxy in the huddle and the drawing room.

Palmer, however, played at Michigan State, where the ongoing society is viewed with slightly less rigidity. Palmer, in short, was something of a screwball, although a good man with a forearm and a fold block in his prime.

He brought an early celebrity to the league with his marriage to the very attractive and popular daughter of Anthony (Tough Tony) Accardo, who in all the journals of the time was certified as the No. 2 man of the Chicago Mafia.

The newlyweds were headstrong young people, individually and in concert. Palmer's fondness for marathon tippling and unconventional hours did nothing to change the disposition of his bride.

Your average pro football team is going to have a dozen people who will qualify as authentic swingers, subdivided into those who are out-and-out-bounders, those who are latent bounders, and those who have the will but lack the charisma.

There will be two or three others who, through diligent day-in and day-out plugging, have earned the more distinguished rating of roisterer.

There were these on the Vikings, and then there was Pyle.

One of his running mates remembers him with complete wonderment.

"He was one of the all-timers all right. He came with great credentials. While he was with Baltimore, he once hid a turtle in the foot of Big Jim Parker's bed. Parker was the gentlest guy but he was the toughest, strongest offensive lineman you ever saw and maybe the greatest in pro history. On this night he was reading in a newspaper by the goofiest coincidence about some guy getting killed by a snake down South. And he's reading it aloud to his roomie and Pyle is next door. Just as Big Jim gets to the climax of the newspaper story, the turtle down under the cover moves and nudges up to Parker's foot.

"Well, he came out of that bed like Vesuvius at Pompeii. If the door hadn't been open, he would have taken out the whole wall. If he knew Pyle was the guy, I actually believe Parker would have squashed him to death.

"When Palmer came to the Vikings, his reputation for being one of the league's great ding-a-lings sort of preceded him. He was a big-shouldered, kind of squat guy with a little puff to his cheeks and a deep, nasal voice perfect for telling stories. Nothing shook the guy—coaches, general managers, defensive tackles, cops, his wife, nobody. He did his thing, wherever it or he happened to be. He sort of set the stage at the Viking welcome home luncheon. We had won big in the exhibition season and somebody asked to what he attributed the team's success. And he said, 'I like to believe it's the shrewdness of their off-season trades.'

"There was a story going around in camp that the reason Palmer got in bad with the Colts before being traded was that he talked back to Carroll Rosenbloom (the owner) and Don Shula (the coach). Palmer was a guard. He said, 'If you switch Jim Parker from tackle to guard, I'm going to have my father-in-law come down and outfit you two with cement vests.'

"The guy was one of the all-time roamers. He would take off and go and have a few schnapps and you didn't know if you'd see him again. He invited a lot of people over one Thanksgiving and was the only one who didn't show up. He went out to get the cranberries and just didn't come back—for two days.

"I'll never forget the time Bill and Katie Jobko were going to have some of the people over for a lasagna party. It was right after the game and everybody was supposed to go home and change into something casual. Well, Palmer was the only one in the group who forgot to go home and pick up his wife, Marie, who was a peach, as I say, but with a temper.

"Marie went home and got herself all prepared and was waiting for Palmer to come over and pick her up to take her to the Jobkos' place.

"Well, my wife and I were about the last to leave, and that was the last I saw of Palmer that night. He seemed to have a great time. He liked the lasagna so well he took a whole tray that was left over and made himself a big martini, and headed out of the Jobkos' apartment to his own. We saw him sort of stumbling through this vacant lot.

"So he got home and knocked on the door and she opened up. Palmer said, 'You should have been at the party, hon.'

"This teed her off something fierce, as you can probably imagine. So Palmer goes into the kitchen and puts the lasagna in the oven and turns it up piping hot. He then goes into the bedroom and strips down and is lying there like King Tut and he yells, 'Hey, Marie, when that lasagna is done, bring it over here.'

"He's still sipping on his martini awaiting the arrival of his devoted wife with the lasagna, but she's out there waiting for the mess to get really steaming hot.

"After 15 more minutes she takes it out and brings it into the bedroom and says, 'Palmer, honey'—and dumps the whole thing on his chest. The guy nearly burned to death. He roars out of bed and starts throwing that hot cheese and goop in her hair, and I guess it was the wildest scene in the history of the suburbs. We got the story more or less that way direct from the returning hero. Everybody in the lockerroom used to rush the door when Palmer came in to get the latest news from the arena, like you call the newspaper office to get the wrestling results.

"He was with us for just one year, but I kid you not, with the ones that are still left, he's one of those intramural legends. A couple of guys wanted to vote him a quarter share from the Super Bowl, to keep him in lasagna if nothing else.

"He used to drive Van Brocklin up the wall. Like the time the Dutchman got on Mick Tingelhoff. This was just about the time Mick was replacing Jim Ringo of Green Bay as the all-pro center. Van Brocklin used to say a lot of rah-rah things about Mick in public to puff up his morale when he was just getting started, because he was a free agent, after all, and pretty much awed by the whole thing.

"But it's Mick's third year now and he's been around. So we're looking at the films and there's Mick blowing a block on Ray Nitschke of the Packers big as life, and Nitschke just hammered Mason.

"It kind of annoyed Van Brocklin, you could see that. So he runs it again. And then again. And each time he runs it, Nitschke seems to be hammering Mason a little harder, and Van Brocklin is getting a little more irritated each time. He keeps re-running that play, flicking that little projector button in his hand, and Tingelhoff is looking for a hole back in the audience.

"VAN BROCKLIN RAN THAT PLAY 13 TIMES, I swear. The last time he just gets up and explodes. He flips off the projector, turns on the lights, and starts eating out Tingelhoff. A real grand-tour chewing.

" 'Tingelhoff,' he says, 'for three years I've been telling everybody you're going to be all-pro, all-this, all-that. You're a diamond in the rough, a free agent that's going to really make his mark in this league. For three years I've been telling people. All-pro, my foot. You make any more of those blocks on Nitschke and you couldn't make All-Barnyard Crap.'

"Well, everybody in the room damned near went through the roof trying to keep from laughing, but Palmer couldn't keep his face straight. He was sitting next to Tingelhoff who, incidentally, was looking pretty miserable—and he starts nudging Mick with his elbow.

" 'Hey, did you hear what the Dutchman said? All-Barnyard what?' he asks Tingelhoff. And Van Brocklin hears him and now the Dutchman turns his artillery on Pyle, which must have been a great relief to Tingelhoff. Van Brocklin yells at Pyle, 'What are you laughing at, you fat ass?'

"It didn't shock anybody very much that Palmer was among the missing when they put out the roster for 1965.

"But the guy really was unbelievable. I remember him telling me about another spat he had with his wife in the off-season, when he had a projectionist's job but preferred to lounge and rest up for the great adventures of training camp. They lived in one of the northern Chicago suburbs. Palmer sometimes occupied the winter hours feeding the birds and protecting the home from squirrels with his B-B gun. So she got a little weary of that and hid the B-B gun. He came home one night, and couldn't find the gun. He finally located it and stationed himself in one of the easy chairs. Using his best sharpshooting form with the B-B gun, he picked off every one of her family portraits on the wall, ping-ping-ping, one glass-covered relative at a time.

"He usually came to play and he had some very good days. But in practice he usually had a pale green color. Palmer often showed up a little bent out of shape. The Dutchman and Yowarsky used to run the daylights out of the guards. And Palmer would get so bushed, the quarterback didn't know whether to call a play or the rescue squad. The guards had to run interference on the end sweeps, of course. It went play after play, Palmer pulling out of the line and running. In the huddle he would just kind of bob and wheeze. They'd stand up a dummy out on the flank to simulate a defensive man, and the guard was supposed to knock the dummy down. Poor Palmer would come charging off the line and never see the dummy. He'd just turn the corner and go snorting upfield. It took him a very long time to get out of the shower on days like that.

"He decided not to bother showing up for the last day of practice. Palmer had a suspicion he was getting traded. It might have gone back to the week before when we played the Giants. The Vikings were having a big day at Yankee Stadium in December and some of the guys on the bench got into a yule-log mood. It was really cold. Everybody was wearing those big Afghanistan warmup coats, but it wasn't enough for Pyle. He talked Reichow into helping him build a little tent out of their warmup coats behind the benches and and the next thing we knew somebody on the bench yelled, 'Migawd, Palmer's on fire.'

"Which he was. Palmer had built a little fire in the tent and was kind of warming himself around the hearth when the flames started running up his coat. It took three guys to prevent Pyle from becoming the first NFL ballplayer to get cremated wearing hip pads and a bird cage.

"He was gone the next year. I can't say I especially blame the Vikings. But they would have shown me a little more class if they retired the guy's number."

It began to take on the look of one of those landmark seasons when Reichow, Flatley and Winston rented a boat for a reflective Sunday afternoon's fishing on the Mississippi in summer camp. They had returned that morning from Atlanta, Ga., where the humidity set off rare turbulences in Reichow's cornfed respiratory system. He sneezed all the way back and still had not completely recovered when they boarded the boat.

In midstream Reichow sneezed again. The outburst was followed by a gentle distinctive "plop" in the water a few feet from the boat.

"It's a walleye," exclaimed Flatley.

"Walleye nuts" Reichow muttered through pursed lips. "It's my teeth. They went over the side when I sneezed."

Fearing the possible effects of bends, none of the nimrods chose to dive for the submerged dentures. Richow spent the next four days, "gumming around," in the quaint lexicon of the clubhouse, until a replacement plate arrived from the family homestead in Iowa.

Flatley had long since established his own enviable distinction with the Vikings as the ranking swain in the organization. He did not have the national acclaim in this league to match the lavishly publicized Paul Hornung and Bo Belinsky, whose names usually led all the rest among the great boulevardiers of the 1960s.

The testimony on this came to me from an airline stewardess who was one of at least 50 who thought seriously of enlisting in the Tanganyika Peace Corps when Flatley finally renounced bachelorhood in 1965.

"The truth is," the young lady said, "They never made another guy like Paul Flatley, which may be a bad figure of speech but is the absolute truth. Compared with Paul Flatley, Hornung and Belinsky had to be Hairless Joes in the vestibule, and I do not speak from hearsay."

About his accomplishments in this field, Flatley maintained a calm, masculine restraint that he relaxed only at the Bemidji training camp for the benefit of Tarkenton.

Among the Vikings, Francis was regarded as a social conservative. But he was a man of spirit, after all, and he did enjoy a good story. Flatley's accounts of his off-season hell-raising invariably left the preacher's son agape and dazzled, his eyes gradually assuming the size of billiard balls.

It was contended by some of their buddies that Tarkenton passed so often to Flatley not so much out of necessity as awe.

He came into the league with a jaw-up jauntiness and a notable lack of the standard first-year hangups. Van Brocklin saw some of himself in this yeasty kid from Northwestern and liked him instantly. It was not an offensive bravado. Flatley understood his limitations of speed and size, and knew he had to compensate with moves, savvy and a little consmanship. If everybody played scrambling football, he would have made All-Pro every year. The impromptu stuff was his metier. For two or three years he flourished in it, and then faded with the Vikings—not only because the quarterbacking had changed but because the coach had changed.

Flatley was a frank epicurean, a pleasure-seeker. Getting domesticated did not expunge his fondness for some good after-hours clubbiness with a few of the boys. He didn't necessarily scoff at curfews but he did outflank a few now and then. They nailed him only once, and it almost cost him two grand.

Flatley, Brown and Dickson missed a cab back to the Sheraton-Cadillac the night before a game with the Lions in 1965 and came skulking into the hotel nearly an hour after curfew. Entering the hotel, they counseled briefly and decided to split the landing party in hopes of dividing Van Brocklin's midnight patrol. Dickson and Brown entered on the basement floor, Flatley taking the stairway to the main lobby. Dickson and Brown captured an elevator in the basement and went up past the first floor. This had the effect of stranding Flatley, who was hotly arguing with an attendant to get him an elevator because of a personal emergency—the emergency being that he was on the verge of getting nabbed.

Dickson and Brown made it to the upper floor but were overtaken abruptly by Lew Carpenter, the end coach. Carpenter then boarded the elevator, descended to the main floor, walked out when the door opened and virtually collided with Flatley.

The flames of compassion burned deeply in Lew Carpenter, however. They were nourished by recollections of the few dozen times he blew curfew himself as a ballplayer. None of the coaching assistants reported the incident to Van Brocklin, therefore, although they did deliver an ultimatum to the wrongdoers. "If you don't play your best game of the year," one of them announced bluntly, "I'm telling Van Brocklin."

The parolees almost escaped. Flatley played with the kind of aroused desperation he had not felt since the day in San Francisco when he never did get to sleep and, conscience-stricken, caught eight passes for more than 200 yards. In Detroit he was a whirlwind of moves, cuts, fakes and diving catches. As an act of contrition, it was one of the most devout performances of his career.

Dickson, too, reached new levels of inspired malice.

He was a strange one, Paul Dickson, a man marked for the 19th century but unaccountably delivered into the clutches of the machine age. He would have been happier and occasionally more valuable riding point for the covered wagons on the Oregon Trail or shooting wild turkeys on the Pecos.

If Mason was the club's Glen Campbell, Dickson was its Schopenhauer, its brooding philosopher.

Dickson's avocation was hunting for True Identity. This he has sought in books poetry, exotic Eastern mind disciplines, and on the line of scrimmage of 11 seasons of football brawling. His creed was the creed of the western mountain man, the hymn of the individualist. Occasionally it seemed to be a philosophical standoff in the clubhouse mind-stretching debates to see who could conform least—Dickson or Marshall.

At one time or other both hauled private gun arsenals to Bemidji big enough to hold off a regiment of avenging Chippewa. To Dickson, the unreformed Texan, guns were symbols of a man's self-reliance and his faith in the hair trigger. He used one once in hot pursuit of a suspected trespasser at his suburban apartment. He went charging enormously across a parking lot in a style that terrified the intruder into superhuman speeds and mercurial shifts in directions. Dickson never did get off a warning shot.

These encounters with the seamier elements of humanity convinced Paul Dickson that a sizeable part of the world's population is made up of dry-gulchers, cutpurses and other unworthy characters. At an early point, therefore, he developed attitude characterized by a wary scowl, suspicious glands and the nickname of "The Growler."

It was manifested one morning in Bemidji when his roommate awoke at 6:30 to the splendor of a northwoods morning, the sun's nourishing rays piercing the thick rich leaves of the elms outside the dormitory and washing their room with the amber light of a perfect new day.

"Wake up, Paul, it's a great day," the roomie exuded.

Dickson lifted himself silently, threw open the window, was struck with the small sounds of pristine summer, and closed the window again.

"Those goddamned birds," he said. "They try a man when he needs sleep."

As an athlete, he was a geyser of emotion and passions, driven by the obsession of playing for a champion. When he finally did, he bawled for five minutes.

Rookies always typed Paul Dickson as a man to avoid, partly because of his fierce belief in the seniority system and partly because of his .38 magnum. Despite his aversion to early-morning birdcalls, however, he admired animals devotedly. This attachment nearly cost Hackbart his head one year in Mankato when the devious Badger got involved in a feud with John Kirby, the prairie linebacker, over a dormitory water fight. Hackbart threatened to wring the neck of a wild rabbit Kirby had apprehended on the practice field and was keeping in his room.

Dickson overheard the dialogue. In fact he was tenderly holding and cuddling the rabbit at that very moment. "You lay a hand on this rabbit, you S.O.B." Dickson shouted, "and I'll break your neck."

This made two necks in peril almost simultaneously. Kirby rescued the situation by guaranteeing the care and treatment of the rabbit for the rest of the training season, leaving Hackbart to look after himself.

The rabbit, Harvey, eventually made its way to Minneapolis aboard the team bus. It was finally released in some suitable wildwood, qualifying its principal champions—Kirby, Dickson, Warwick and Winston—for an Izaak Walton chapter at Metropolitan Stadium.

And so Dickson quite plainly had the kind of disposition to drive him to the highest competitive levels where self-preservation was involved, as it was in the Detroit incident.

Paul was predictably great and so was Flatley. Unfortunately, Brown screwed up.

It was not a matter of Bill Brown being unready to play. It should be remembered he goes through cycles where he has trouble overtaking the football. In this game he fumbled a couple of times. The Vikings won, nevertheless, and the transgressors congratulated themselves for emerging free and clear.

At the Tuesday film session, however, each of Brown's several blunders set off an audible grinding of teeth by one of the coaching aides, followed by a mysterious litany: "that lousy Brown, that lousy Flatley, that lousy Dickson."

Puzzled, Van Brocklin finally interrupted the screening and demanded to know what the hell the lieutenant was talking about. "Do you want me to talk to you as a man or coach?" the addled lieutenant asked.

Van Brocklin never split the hairs too cautiously when the hackles started climbing. He advised the coach at this point he wasn't interested in any identity crisis on his staff but did order him to make some sense out of his mumblings.

They repaired to the office, where Van Brocklin was informed of the events of Saturday night.

The next summons went to Brown, Flatley, and Dickson.

Van Brocklin greeted them in the office with a minimum of ceremony. For opening remarks he chose:

"That'll be two grand apiece."

This disclosure wrought havoc among the assembled penitents. Lesser men, however, might have accepted the verdict with a hangdog departure and a telephone call to the bank.

Dickson, Brown and Flatley are eminently practical men. They decided to negotiate, as a matter of fiscal responsibility.

Eventually they got it down to $500. At least this was the figure Van Brocklin deducted from their next payroll installment. In the field of club fines, it was not a record, but it did serve to keep the average up.

The whole episode offended Flatley's pride in his ability to maintain an active social life without interference from the club accountants. Although popular with his buddies, he normally did not divulge his modus operandi, preferring to profit from the bungling of less systematic carousers.

In his second year in Bemidji, for example, Flatley was jarred to discover a 11 p.m. curfew had been imposed on a night he had already committed for some off-campus socializing with a girl friend from Minneapolis.

Others in the dorm were similarly jarred. Several chose to party, nevertheless. Flatley stayed behind, retiring at an unbecoming early hour. The others would wake him up on their guilt-ridden return, he reasoned, a few hours later.

They did, at 3:15. All of them were nailed in the bedcheck. Flatley smoothly set his alarm for 3:30 and glided out of his quarters past the sleeping sentinels. He spent the next two hours in a happy reunion—undoubtedly skipping stones across the lake, the favorite after-hour diversion—and returned at 5:30.

As indicated, he is well domesticated now and regards his rakish youth with occasional dim regrets. This remorse he seasons with a certain amount of gratitude for all the good luck.

Looming above these very formidable personalities, colossus-like, stood Jim Marshall.

Van Brocklin used to draw on the imagery of the jungle to portray Jim Marshall. By his second season he was calling Marshall, "a panther, just about the fastest animal of his size I ever saw." He called him a cat and a tiger, and for a while it was not quite clear whether the Dutchman was going to use Marshall at defensive end or trade him to Barnum and Bailey.

He played some very good football for Van Brocklin and always he played very earnest football. He may not have had the one great year Van Brocklin envisioned for him, but he did have at least one of those with Grant. The Dutchman and Marshall got along rosily. This was true partly because Van Brocklin respected the virtuoso levels of his physical skills and partly because Marshall had the jester's talent for spontaneity, laughter and gentle mockery that permitted him easily to deflect the Dutchman's noisiest lightning bolts.

He brought to football a first-rate mind and instinct for the game plus the sandlotter's supreme delight in playing it. More than any player in the NFL, he shot holes in the popular conception of the pro footballer of the 1960s as a cool, bankrolling operator introducing a new economics to the game. Football is still fox-and-hounds to Jim Marshall, the old hit-the-can of the street corner and small town sandpit.

Yet, because he went through an improverished childhood and because the poor renegade black kid would take refuge in his dreams in those days, Jim Marshall could not find enough lives to lead once he discovered he had the money and nerve to go where his dreams and whims carried him. He could feel the wind now and touch the heights, experiences that were once the treasures of his imagination.

He became a parachutist, a skier, an investment man, a capitalist, a scuba diver, a marksman. He used to pester me to enlist him on some of my mountain climbing ventures. I would have, except that the football and the climbing seasons collided. I can only speculate now in which direction he might have hammered the pitons. But he would have been a great companion. He looked on himself as a globetrotter, an adventurer in the great tradition of the Richard Halliburtons and the Edmund Hillarys.

His lightness of heart and fondness for mimicry often concealed from the outsider an introspective, sensitive side. It might immerse him for an entire evening in what the dormitory needlers of Dickson and Marshall would call The Meaning of Life Hour.

He was not an activist in the racial confrontations of the 1960s, and perhaps it bothered him. There was no question of his pride in his blackness. He simply lacked the anger of a John Carlos or Jim Brown. He liked fellowship and good times and large, arch guffaws, and in this there was a brotherhood in the football lockerroom that cut across colors and accents.

In a fashion he aspired to be a Renaissance Man of pro football, which is to say he sampled life in its variegated forms. Because of his bedrock optimism, he could not understand why it should take so long — some predicted as much as a month — for Jim Marshall, Private Enterpriser, or Jim Marshall, Daredevil Skydiver, to master his latest undertaking and move on to something even more taxing.

He found audiences everywhere, in the football arena or in the neighborhood party. The most stimulating part of life for Marshall was the forum it gave him to mix reality with his effervescing urges for role-playing — the voyageur, gunfighter, comic or Itinerant Commentator on Life.

But at the times in life when Jim Marshall had just about assured himself he was in calm control of all his destinies, somebody would drop a banana peel on his doorstep.

He was touched by a magnetic lure for small calamities. It was as though someone in the zodiac were saying nobody ought to have that much fun without getting his astral projections jabbed now and then.

His fascination for guns got him in trouble and nearly killed him early in his career. Removing a revolver from the glove compartment of his car in Cleveland shortly after being traded to the Vikings, Marshall blithely flipped the cylinder. He awoke in a hospital to discover himself shot. The bullet had passed through some non-critical area below the rib cage, however, and Marshall healed without incident.

The police report on the case included a statement by the victim that he carried a gun because he frequently had large sums of money on his person—which must have greatly surprised a number of his early creditors in Minneapolis.

Later he experienced such novel setbacks as failing in a women's wig sales enterprise and, back in camp, being confined to hospital for a week when a grape lodged in the wrong channel.

And yet it is entirely possible that the nation as a whole had not been prepared psychologically for the truly spellbinding events of Oct. 26, 1964, in San Francisco.

The Vikings led the 49ers 27-17 in the fourth period. For this they were indebted chiefly to naked luck, the aching arm of San Francisco's John Brodie, and the vigor of the Viking defense, featuring the exuberant deeds of Jim Marshall.

He stymied the 49ers a dozen times, with tackles, pass rushes, a fumble recovery on Brodie here, and an open-field tackle on Bill Kilmer there.

Unquestionably Jim Marshall was en route to one of his four or five best games as a professional. In the third period he eluded three aspiring blockers to maul reserve quarterback George Mira, forced a fumble, and then cheered mightily as Eller seized the ball on the second dribble and rushed into the end zone 45 yards away for a touchdown.

And so none of the 31,845 catcalling customers in Kezar Stadium, nor the televiewers back on the prairie, were notably surprised when Kilmer caught a pass from Mira, made two strides and fumbled into the path of the omnipresent Marshall at the 49er 34-yard line.

The 49ers at the time were moving south. Marshall's momentum when he overtook the bobbling football was generally southward. So it would take him a stride or two to rearrange his heading and begin making the expected large and hasty tracks for the 49er goal line to the north.

By the time he reached the San Francisco 45, however, the first intimations of panic began to seize the Viking bench. Marshall was in full stride now. Without provocation, explanation and—most terrifying of all—without resistance, he was running the wrong way.

On the bench, Tarkenton was the first to see the enormity of the situation. "Jim, Jim," he shrieked, "the other way, the other way." Soon he was joined by anguished teammates, sprinting down the sidelines paralleling Jim Marshall's route, their arms pointed northward.

In the center of the field, Jim Marshall could not see them, could not hear them. He ran majestically, obliviously. One swift glance over his shoulder at midfield had assured him all remaining obstacles had been removed or outrun. No one would overtake him, he vowed inwardly, because there just were not many people in the National Football League above 200 pounds who could beat Jim Marshall in a race to the goal line. It was a rare, intoxicating sensation for a lineman. Running free and unbridled at the 10, he thought momentarily about swinging into that newsreel gallop that the halfbacks staged when home free on the end of a long run. But he restrained this impulse as unworthy for the occasion.

He crossed the goal line and then, overwhelmed by the ecstasy of it, flung the football high in the air and out of the end zone. Turning, he thrust out his right arm to receive the jubilation of his converging teammates.

The first uniformed man who got there was Bruce Bosley, the center of the 49ers. Bosley engulfed the panting ball-carrier in an embrace of make-believe gratitude. The crowd reacted schizophrenically. Thousands of them were hooting uproariously but just as many were booing the 49ers in the utter belief that their favorite clowns had given away another cheap touchdown.

Marshall shoved Bosley away, annoyed at the intrusion. And then, from teammates who had tried to pursue him down the sidelines, he got the crushing truth. It was no touchdown for Jim Marshall. It was a safety for San Francisco.

He walked back toward the bench, shrinking with disgrace. He was a joker in the clubhouse but he was proud of his football reputation. He knelt near the bench while the donkey-braying from the stands rolled down on his head, and he cried.

This was the multimillion-dollar world of bigtime football. But he was the little boy who had leaped for joy when the judges gave his name for the blue ribbon; and now he learned they had given him the dunce hat. He closed his eyes, and the ignominy whirled and pealed in his head.

He wanted, literally, to die right there in Kezar Stadium.

In the lockerroom after they had won, the Vikings came up to him and told him, with the gruff tenderness football players give to one of their own in distress, that he would forget it, and he played a great game, and the fans would forget it.

They didn't really believe what they were saying, because the whole thing had those grand and simple designs of the classic blunder—with just a sprig of temporary tragedy to ennoble its boomerang futility.

They did forget, of course. Much sooner than Marshall had the nerve to hope for and certainly a lot sooner than Bosley would have predicted. Jim survived because his natural craving for the sunlight very quickly nudged him out of the shadows of his private sanctuaries from ridicule. Within three or four days he was laughing with the gagsters. Because he was, he suddenly became a very human being to thousands in Minnesota who had not known him before or laughed at his epic pratfall on television.

But in the clubhouse afterward, his defeat was total.

In defense, he clothed himself in his playroles. He conducted at first a very straightforward press conference, as though he were the power company president announcing an outage.

"I just got mixed up," he said. "I can't even remember picking up the ball, the thing was that confused.

"I couldn't hear our guys yelling that I was going the wrong way. I saw my teammates running down the sidelines. I thought they were cheering for me. I don't think it really dawned on me that something was wrong until after I flipped the ball away and Bosley ran up to me in the end zone and I could hear what my guys from the bench were saying."

Van Brocklin came up, put an arm on his shoulder, and told him he would forget and that he had played one of his greatest football games. "You know," he said, grinning, "I actually thought you were kidding, the way you ham around in practice."

Jim Marshall, Jester, tried to gag. "You know," he said, "I think I'll hang around here and try to collect some of the 49ers game money. It isn't everybody who can make them forget that other guy who went the wrong way (Roy Riegels of California in the Rose Bowl)."

They laughed around him, but Marshall's was shallow. He sat down in front of his locker. "I never did anything," he said, "that hurt so much in all my life."

I telephoned him the next morning to remind him of his promise to appear with me at the Minneapolis Tribune's weekly quarterback club meeting. "Come on, Klobey," he said, "let me back out of it. Any other time. It would kill me to go out in public right now. I feel so damn bad."

Without much insistence, I suggested it might be the best tonic of all, a chance to meet the comics right off and to get it over with. "You'll find more friends than you thought you had," I said.

Marshall didn't really believe me, but he may have needed a friend. We walked into the Pick-Nicollet ballroom, and he got a standing ovation. We talked for five or ten minutes, and the warm, affectionate rapport of the audience and its gleeful response to his pained humor revived the mischief in his nature and the lightness in his heart.

So he was mended in a couple of days, and when all the

jokes were exhausted, the National Football League forgot about Jim Marshall's unforgettable adventure.

He was so open-handed about it, in fact, that he accepted a Texas club's invitation to receive their Bonehead of the Year award. He arrived an hour late for the presentation. He mistook the flight number of his plane for Dallas, and boarded a plane for Chicago.

Chapter XVIII

"At midnight the Dutchman called his first and last press conference."

Norm Van Brocklin, the Civil War scholar, had a fascination for the mileposts of military history, turning points on which hinged the climactic shifts in momentum of the armies and their wills.

It is not hard to make an argument that the ultimate fulfillment of Van Brocklin's nature and urges would have put him in a command post at the head of an army.

I have no doubt Van Brocklin would have been a good army commander, as long as they kept him out of the toils of the inspector general. It was natural for him to transmit to football his absorption in the psychology and impact of the Vicksburgs, Verduns and Gettysburgs.

He motivated his teams and himself by using "now-or-never" games as recurring points of reference—the games that would determine the Vikings' fitness to be listed among the respectable and the feared. He invested these with medieval tones of trial-by-combat and tests of virility.

From 1961 to 1965 he brought his football team to certain symbolic moments that would determine, he told them, "whether we're man enough."

Invariably, by the Dutchman's ground rules, they weren't.

The detached viewer was inclined to a less Freudian judgment. It wasn't that the Vikings weren't man enough. They simply did not have enough men. The Dutchman could never make this admission. According to the Van Brocklin dogma, any team

could win if it paid a price high enough in sweat, guts, preparation and sacrifice. Every coach has the same dogma, but will
make private concessions now and then to the physical limitations
of the people wearing his uniform. Van Brocklin rarely made any.

But those hallmark days when his team would win its final
accreditation, the times of redemption, kept coming and going.
Neither players nor customers had any reason to believe it would
change appreciably in the next few years.

And there was no cause for anybody—even those intimately
acquainted with Van Brocklin's mercurial behavior—to foresee
the game of Nov. 14, 1965, as some kind of jock-strapped
Stalingrad.

On the surface, the squad and the organization had settled
into a comforting and largely unprecedented atmosphere of calm
and stability by the eve of the Viking-Baltimore Colt game of
Nov. 14.

Van Brocklin's team had survived a demoralizing near-fatal
accident in the summer of 1964 to excite its growing crowds and
the National Football League with a first-rate football team
in its fourth year at large.

It was not only the 8-5-1 record, matching Green Bay in the
Western Division for second place. It was the reckless-moppet
character of the team that captivated the audiences. Their style
reached the rollicking level of improvisation where Tarkenton
and Flatley actually created new plays on the sidelines during
the commercials, and sometimes between downs. Even the punter,
Bobby Walden from Georgia, scrambled. He had a 46-yard
kicking average but seemed obsessed with surpassing this on
unscripted end runs on fourth down.

The team, both in 1964 and heading into 1965, had the
fraternity of impatient youth, matured by its distress of August
1964 when Tom Franckhauser nearly died of a practice field
injury.

Franckhauser was an urbane, happy young man from Purdue
who played on the fringes in the NFL, good enough to make

somebody's roster as a defensive back but not consistently good enough to establish tenure. He went from Dallas to Cleveland to Minnesota and appeared reasonably secure with the Vikings until late one afternoon, in the final minutes of a long, ennervating scrimmage.

Darrell Lester, a young 240-pound fullback, broke open on a line buck and headed upfield. John Campbell, who hit him simultaneously with Franckhauser, remembers each detail of the play.

"I moved in on Lester from my outside linebacker spot and Franckhauser came up from safety. I didn't see him until just before all three of us hit. I put my head down on Lester and just smacked into him. But I also hit Tommy. So did Lester, with his thigh. Tommy couldn't have seen me, because he just put his head in there and took up most of the area I had to hit. I saw him coming right before the collision and figured that he would take Darrell on one shoulder and I would take him on the other.

"The three of us came together with a helluva crack. I got up and was a little dizzy. Tommy just stood there. After a while Tommy went over to Harry Gilmer and said he had a terrible headache. A few seconds later he dropped on the field. God, I remember that so well. Freddie (Zamberletti, the trainer) started helping him off and all of a sudden the whole one side of his body went limp. And Fred could feel that.

"They had that equipment truck parked on the side of the field just in case of an emergency like that. It saved Tommy's life. Freddie and Jimmy Eason put him in the truck and tore to the hospital."

Another few minutes' delay in the required surgery, for the blood clot that formed on the brain, undoubtedly would have killed the young football player.

The experience jarred Van Brocklin as none had in football. But in the shared grief of the night and in the subsequent jubilance in Franckhauser's recovery, the team acquired a sense of the corps that had eluded it in the earlier years. The men took turns at the doorside vigil for Franckhauser; and the captains, Hawkins and Tarkenton, brought them together. They beat the ultimate division champions, Baltimore, one out of two, and they did the same to Green Bay. In the final three games they crushed Los Angeles, New York and Chicago. And quite suddenly, Van Brocklin was looking once more to "the hump we have to get over"—this time to a championship.

The ownership felt no urgency in picking a successor to the deposed Bert Rose. Van Brocklin was perfectly capable of making player personnel decisions. As a matter of fact, he insisted on it, which was why the owners were short one general manager in the first place. As for the purely administrative side of the general manager's work, the directors were capable of making all the money decisions that Pete Rozelle didn't make for them in New York. Beyond all this, there was Ed Martini.

Ed was the Duluth lawyer who was a charter member of the organization as counsellor to Ole Haugsrud. He was also the Vikings attorney. He cut a distinguished figure as a barrister of the old stripe—tall, formidable, and flawlessly dressed with just an agreeable hint of patrician air. His accent was a good deal closer to Nantucket than it was to Park Point in Duluth. He was intrigued by the many untapped but still promising objects of oratory—so that Ed would frequently convert a simple 'good morning' into a 10-minute discourse on the gas output of the rising sun.

Clearly, in the Vikings' corporate scheme, he was a man who could be trusted. Somewhat to his surprise he discovered in mid-1964 that he would not at all object to the extra duties of general managing.

The same thought was entertained by one William (Bill) Williams, the manager of Metropolitan Stadium and a former FBI agent.

Martini handled the general manager's administrative chores in the interregnum after Rose's ouster. He handled them well, and with some enjoyment in this new and stimulating role of athletic impressario. He talked contract with many of the players, supervised training camp details, and successfully avoided conflicts with Van Brocklin.

He did not exactly campaign for the general manager's job but he would not have rejected it. Respecting him, Ridder nonetheless decided the organization had to have a fulltime, football-tempered director.

After the Rose hassle, Van Brocklin was not about to step into the general manager's job to please those who said he lobbied Bert out of it to serve his own ambitions. Van Brocklin didn't need or want the title. He had all the required authority.

The chief scout, Joe Thomas, released a few balloons of candidacy on his own, and so did Billy Bye of the office business staff.

The candidate of Skoglund and Winter, however, was Williams of the stadium commission.

Ridder suspected what he sensed was the buildup of a new power center here involving Skoglund, Winter and Van Brocklin, a novel three-man general managership operating in the name of Bill Williams.

At about this time Ole Haugsrud, the friendly football antiquarian whose advice usually disappeared in the footnotes of the minutes, decided a very good general manager of the Minnesota Vikings would be a man named Jim Finks.

The revelation failed to ignite Skoglund and Winter, and did not stir Ridder and Boyer much more. Haugsrud, however, went ahead with a telephone call to Calgary, Alta., where Jim Finks was managing the Calgary Stampeders.

The two men were linked casually by a mutual acquaintance with Steve Owen, the former New York Giant coach who had served briefly as a coach of one of Finks' Calgary team.

Ole looked on Jim Finks as the ideal solution to the Vikings' internal disarray. He was a football diplomat, a man of wit, reasonableness and judgment. He had been a quarterback in the National Football League, an assistant coach at North Dame, and had an excellent track record as a general manager at Calgary. Above all this, he had a high quotient in the quiet art of survival. Among the professionals, he made friends at all of his points of call. Among the media people he registered high grades with his decency and a gift—when needed—for the very earnest blarney that almost always disarms the skeptical journalist.

On Ole's invitation, Finks visited for two hours with Ridder, Boyer, Winter and Haugsrud shortly before the All-Star game in Chicago. When he continued to Montreal, where Calgary was playing an exhibition, Finks was overtaken by another phone call, this one from Ridder inviting him back to Minnesota for a more specific talk looking toward his possible appointment as general manager—and a conference with Van Brocklin.

Finks and the Dutchman talked for an hour at the Bemidji airport. They had met as rival quarterbacks once or twice, but had no connections socially. Finks by now had told the Vikings he was interested in the job. But he was also aware of the intramural axwork and jostling in the organization. He assessed no blame and made no judgment, but quite clearly he was not going to walk into a recessed civil war.

His first question at Bemidji was, "Norm, do you want the general manager's job? Because if you do, I don't want any part of it. I've got a fine job in Calgary and I'm completely happy. I'm even considering becoming a Canadian citizen. I know football is a tough game at best, and if you have internal stress it's just impossible. I just want to lay all the cards on the table."

This struck Van Brocklin as not only a fair question but practically a testament.

"No," he said, "I have no ambitions whatsoever to be general manager of the Vikings."

They talked generally thereafter, striking most of the right chords. Finks went back to Canada and heard no further word for several weeks.

The ballot on the Viking board was 3 to 2 in favor of Finks as the next general manager, Skoglund and Winter preferring Williams. Technically it was sufficient to elect Finks, but Ridder declined to bring in a new general manager to administer for a divided board—an open manhole if there ever was one.

He sought unanimity. Skog and Winter resisted. Martini volunteered as a compromise choice. Ridder now decided to invoke the possibility of intervention by Rozelle, who was coming west for his annual pre-session visit. The question was resubmitted to the board, and Jim Finks cleared unanimously.

He needed a year before he really understood the terrain of the organization, its random power pockets, its football problems, and the market. But with these in hand, Finks was the drawing board model of the successful general manager—casting a generally low profile to the public but effective internally and respected by both coaches with whom he worked, the owners and especially the players at contract time.

He was chiefly responsible for the two pivotal trades of 1966 that pointed the club in the direction of a championship. Still, he regarded as cardinal his operating rule of letting the head coach "front" for the organization, to be the answer man on virtually all football matters not related to the ticket box, the television box or the soap box.

For these and other favors, the very-much-impressed owners voted him a vice presidency in 1969. His strength as a general manager traces largely to his backdrop as a professional player and his unshowy willingness to grasp the coach's problems. On the larger canvas of his public performance Finks has, like all successful general managers, perfected the diplomacy of evasion.

His skills are considerable in the important art of clouding up the unflattering details of pro football's monopoly operation. In dealing with the news media, for example, Jim can deliver a curveball that may break even faster than Rose's but simply is not as noticeable.

Football managers, like presidents and corporation chairmen, often regard the absolute truth as an encroachment on their craft and higher duties. The typical journalist will take today's public announcement from the front office, divide by two, and expect to come reasonably close to the unquilted truth. This equation hardly applies to all public statements, but it is a pretty reasonable formula to apply to (a) public explanations for ticket increases, (b) trades, (c) stadium politics, (d) board meetings and (e) board meetings.

The public's innocence may then be further exploited by (a) speculating reporters, (b) opinionated columnists, and (c) a leak to one of the club's writing or broadcasting shills. The result may be a flourishing credibility gap all around. This is why the public's attention span on the subject of sports-politics is so short. The fan may be diverted by it momentarily but he pines to get back to the game itself, which is something he can see and believe.

Finks' own credibility, it should be added, is better than most among the football prime ministers. It may be that it is hard for him to forget his traumatic start. He arrived in Bloomington on Sept. 19, the day before the Vikings-Bears game. In the next 24 hours:

1. Burglars ransacked the Vikings office and departed with $3,000 from the company safe.

2. It rained a cloudburst, round the clock.

3. The Vikings lost to the Chicago Bears.

4. Tommy Mason suffered an injury that immobilized him for half the season.

Groggy, Finks headed for the airport to return to Calgary, where he needed a few more days to wind up his affairs. "What else," mused the general manager-designate, "could possibly happen to this organization that already hasn't happened this weekend? Not even an albatross could bring this much bad luck."

A few minutes after Finks left a car in which Ted Dean, the Vikings' newly-acquired halfback was riding, plowed into a tree in south Minneapolis on a rain-drenched parkway.

The other occupant, former University of Minnesota quarterback Sandy Stephens, escaped serious injury.

Dean's hip was mangled. He was hospitalized for four weeks and never played football again. He had come to the Vikings in a trade for a defensive end, Don Hultz, the flanker Ray Poage, and defensive back Terry Kosens. Van Brocklin made the trade not only for an ex-teammate from the title year at Philadelphia but for the rights to Bob Berry, the squatly pugnacious Oregon quarterback whom Van Brocklin envisioned as a likely star in the National Football League.

With just two games gone he had neither Berry, then in his final season with Oregon, nor Dean.

"It was not the most thrilling omen for a happy new relationship between the general manager and coach," Finks acknowledged. "But Norm and I did work well together, as it turned out."

The Dutchman plainly had no stomach for any renewed

haggling over professional prerogatives. And Finks, being a stranger, had no reason to resent Van Brocklin's advice or decisions on personnel matters.

Finks' functioning code as a general manager is nothing more than an application of the 'live and let live' principle carried out in a bare-chested environment where the jurisdiction lines are never tightly drawn. The practitioners are almost always willful, ambitious people. It is not an easy relationship to maintain, especially when the L's in the small-type columns start outnumbering the W's.

Finks reflected on its hazards some time after going to football's summit, the Super Bowl, in his sixth year on the job.

"I find that when you have to reduce things to writing and say 'this is my responsibility and this is my authority, and you have to answer to me on this stuff and I won't ever interfere on this'—well, I think you weaken the whole structure of the thing. There is going to be mistrust there. If the two men involved don't have mutual respect from the beginning, it might as well come right out in the open and let somebody decide which one should go, because it just isn't going to work out.

"When you get into a situation and when one guy says, 'by God, my contract says this and that', you've got a basic weakness that is pretty prevalent in the front office power struggles in big time sports.

"I've always believed that the coach has to be the spokesman when it comes to setting up policy for players, to have complete freedom to cut whom he chooses, keep whom he chooses, to recommend getting rid of people in trades, or just getting rid of them.

"Now, there are going to be times when management says, 'I think that has merit but—'

"It's fundamental that there is such a thing as the club's long-range interest and that a coach in an insecure position may not have the wisdom or the time or the votes to see it. You can't blame him.

"But it comes down to the individuals involved. At no time in the three years we were together can I recall Norm Van Brocklin doing anything of consequence that I thought was circumventing my authority or embarrassing me before the owners or the public. Grant, of course, is the kind of coach who wears so well he's likely to be around forever.

"So, let's say Bud Grant has an idea and he wants to do something, and if in my opinion it's sound—or maybe in my opinion it's not completely sound but it's not going to have a life-and-death effect on the future one way or another—why, hell, we'll do it."

Thus did sweet amity break out in the Viking front office. Chief scout Joe Thomas, a very capable man but one of the last of the disgruntled, left in the fall of 1965 to take a personnel job with Miami of the AFL. His successor was Jerry Reichow, a man of remarkably few enemies in the trade despite his impressive record of assault as a player.

Van Brocklin adjudged his purple platoons finally ready for a charge to the championship. In his heart, he may have known only the most charitable kind of luck would take them there. He had a handful of prime players in Tarkenton, Mason, Marshall, Tingelhoff, Brown, Alderman, Hawkins and Flatley. Only one or two of these were great in the accepted usage, and the team was still inadequate in reserve strength and shy on important help from its most recent draft.

Its best young players were reputed to be Eller; Bedsole, the eccentric pass receiver; and Lance Rentzel, freshly acquired in the draft. Eller's performance as a young football player was uneven, devastating this week, bungling the next. He would need two or three years to become what he was in 1969—the best defensive end in professional football.

Bedsole was one of those textbook cases of the athletic wunderkind who never got past adolescence in pro football. Physically he had something very close to Superman dimensions. He had extraordinary speed for a man 6 feet 5 and 235 pounds, the strength of a linebacker, and the mobility of a halfback. Psychologically, he was an organization dropout. He infuriated John McKay at South Cal to the point where the coach fired him temporarily, in his senior year. But aimless, friendless Hal never doubted that his physical gifts were exceptional enough to redeem his practice field derelictions and his reluctance to knock down walls for The Team.

Partly because of a difficult childhood, he had complexes and over-reactions. He was essentially a loner with an ironic outlook on humanity. He wanted to be popular with teammates but had small talent for the technique. Veterans in the Viking training camp roasted him ruthlessly when they saw his pouting reaction to the hazing rituals all rookies have to endure.

The most common of these is to require the apprentice to stand on his chair at the training table, place his hand over his heart in make-believe devotion, and sing the hymn of his alma mater.

When Bedsole objected to being called more than twice a session, they turned him into a seven-act vaudeville. He sang "Fight On for USC" so many times a cook who had attended UCLA threatened to quit.

These performances were supposed to be accompanied by harmless jeers from the audience, but when the singer was Hal Bedsole, the jeers had sting and mockery.

Observing this, Van Brocklin was still determined to preside over the rejuvenation of Hal Bedsole, the scenario informally entitled The Making of a Man. And Bedsole tried. He would have streaks of glitter. At times he would harmonize his gifts and strengths, and he would be lifted by a fleeting exuberance that came with belonging. On these days, he had the appearance of a potentially great player who would last for a decade.

But the next week he would lapse, or get himself hurt. Van Brocklin mistrusted injuries. Most coaches do. They respond differently. Van Brocklin's patience as a nurse-in-waiting was shorter than most. He could watch a limping athlete just so long without convincing himself there was as much imagination as pain bedeviling the wounded warrior. In time, he would say so, sometimes publicly. Pure percentages dictated that the Dutchman's medical analysis was sometimes in error. The player's reaction very often determined whether he made it in pro ball or was chewed up in the attrition mills of waiver lists, injured reserve lists, and cutdown deadlines.

It was a special kind of examination of fitness, the test of the kid's ability to withstand a bum rap. Everybody in pro ball is subjected to it—and some frequently.

A veteran who had been stung by Van Brocklin as often as the others, but bore no rancor, saw the alienation of Bedsole and Rentzel this way:

"Neither of them were able to cope with Van Brocklin's emotionalism in a way that, let's say, Mason or Flatley could. I don't think Van Brocklin deliberately put people to the test in a thought-out way. He was a hipshooter. He has to know some of his bitching and name-calling isn't deserved. But when he saw moody guys like Bedsole and Rentzel getting defensive about it and eating themselves out, it stirred him up even more.

"I mentioned Mason and Flatley, because you have a good example there of how two sets of guys—both coming in with the same advantages—reacted exactly the opposite to Van Brocklin's sarcasm.

"The Dutchman liked Mason and Flatley. They were happy-go-lucky guys who rolled with the punches. He may not have loved Bedsole, but he made a reclamation project out of him. He was damned if he wasn't going to show the skeptics in college and pro ball both that it could be done. Rentzel was the kid who got a high recommendation from the Dutchman's friends in the Southwest. He came in as a finger-snapper, played the organ, and was dingy enough to present a challenge to Van Brocklin.

"Well, the Dutchman never did bug Flatley much. I don't think anything could. He did bother Mason, but Tommy really liked the guy and played his guts out for him. Years later when not too many of the old Vikings had a good word for Van Brocklin, Mason would tell you that Van Brocklin didn't really mean it when he was cutting up a ballplayer, that this was his way of trying to goad the guy. Well, that was a pretty mild way to describe the Dutchman, but it tells you something about Mason. And let me tell you. Van Brocklin said a few lousy things to Tommy.

"But the wildest was the line Van Brocklin got off in one of the film sessions. Tommy loved the Cadillac cars, you know. He was a little dingy himself, with that monkey he kept for awhile, and the rock band he played with and all.

"So we're playing the Packers, and Van Brocklin is showing it on film. The Packers never blitzed much when they were great, but on this play Bill Forrester, the linebacker, came blowing in and Mase is supposed to pick him up. The field was wet and Tommy's foot slipped as he lunged to make the block. Forrester went over him easy and just blasted Tarkenton to pieces.

"Van Brocklin turned on the lights—he was great for that stuff—and said very deliberately: 'Mason, take that Cadillac and stick it in your rear end.'

"I thought the whole squadroom was going to choke. It's amazing how fast the intramural stuff gets around the league. Ballplayers recognize true eloquence, and they have a habit of noising it to their old buddies in other towns, by telephone sometimes.

"So the next week the Colts came in to play and Mason went to his old buddy Tom Matte, the Colt halfback. Just as he gets into the elevator, he runs into Brutal Bill Hisself, Pellington.

"Pellington gives him that side of the lip mumble like the bouncer in the speakeasy. 'Hey, Tommy,' he says, 'tell me where the Dutchman told you to park the Cadillac.'

"The point is that nobody got a bigger kick out of it, after the first day, I mean, than Mason. His idea was that when Van Brocklin called you a son of a bitch, or said something about your social life or just blistered the hell out of you in front of your buddies on general principles, he didn't mean anything by the words; it was just his way of talking. My answer to that—even though I was in Van Brocklin's corner most of the time—was how do you expect a football player to be a mindreader when somebody is calling him a bastard.

"Tarkenton didn't get much of that, but he used to hate some of the things Dutch called his teammates.

"I don't know. Maybe Mason was right. If you excused Van Brocklin's nastiness and took him for his football, you would go to the moon with him; he knew that much football and he gave that much to a team. His fundamental weakness was that he was just so damned erratic in his approach to the players. On days when he was sunshine and blue sky, you could have played all day for him. Then he would switch faces. When he was Caesar on the field, the league didn't make them any worse.

"Face to face he was all right. He really tried to get into a guy's problems sometimes. When he felt the guy was really sincere about something deep that was bothering him, I've seen him close to tears.

"But he couldn't reach a player like Bedsole. When the kid really started hurting with leg troubles, the whole thing blew up. In the end the Vikings got practically nothing out of Hal.

"Rentzel was even stranger. The Dutchman wanted to make a runner out of him and it was pretty apparent Lance wasn't going to be a heavy duty runner. The Dutchman put him on the flank and the kid got all confused running patterns. Bob Berry, who was a rookie quarterback then, and Rentzel would work for hours after practice. But the kid just didn't have any confidence, and Dutch really started leaning on him. Then he got into his personal trouble. They finally dismissed it in court. He was up on some exposure complaint, but nobody really figured out what it was all about. Lance asked permission to meet with the squad, and we met. He asked us to trust him, and that everything could be explained. He tried, but he really never explained it.

"He stayed on to the end of the season but they had to trade him because of the circumstances. So he went to Dallas. And he became just one of the five best receivers in football. I was glad for him. I always liked the guy. Still, he was never going to play for Dutch."

Enough others did, though, to put the Vikings into the forefront of the 1965 title conjecture. They rolled through the exhibition season and piled into Baltimore, the defending Western champions, on the opening game in Baltimore.

They might just as well have played the game in the Sahara. It was 94 at gametime. The heat may not have beaten the Vikings, but it did nothing to inspire them. By the third period they were out of it, eventually beaten 36-16. On the plane home a half dozen showed symptoms of heat prostration. The most grievously ailing, Larry Bowie was dressed out flat in the plane aisle for treatment.

They came home for the Metropolitan Stadium opener against

the Lions and Harry Gilmer, the Stetson-loving Alabaman who had coached the Viking defense for four seasons. The Dutchman had made mental accommodations to the first-game loss to Baltimore. The Colts were a high-powered football team, after all. At home they were nearly invulnerable. The weather had been abominable for a team that had worked in drizzles and 50 degree chill for three days. He did not want to admit it to the team, but he could understand.

The Vikings were still geared up, therefore, for a title assault. The Mason-Brown running offense had experienced support now from Phil King, the old Cherokee Chief from the Giants; Billie Barnes, one of the Eagle brawlers of Van Brocklin's playing days; and the rookie Dave Osborn. Vander Kelen was in his third year as a backup for Tarkenton. Gary Larsen, acquired in the draft for Jack Snow, the No. 1 draft choice, reinforced the defensive line and Red Phillips was around to put some age on the receiving group. So they would start over again against Harry's Lions. And with the Vikings ahead 29-24 in the final minute, the Lions' Amos Marsh lined up on the wrong side of the formation on a pass play. He not only lined up wrong, he ran the wrong route. The events so confused Milt Plum, the Lion quarterback, that he threw to Marsh in exasperation and completed a 48-yard pass for the winning touchdown.

The only one you could possibly blame at this point was God, and not even the Dutchman had that kind of temerity.

"We'll still beat the Rams," he announced. "One way or another I vow we will beat the Rams."

If God had in fact actually beaten the Vikings in the Lions game, he might reasonably be accused of piling it on now because it rained cascades for the Vikings' first two days of preparation for the game in Los Angeles. "No way," Van Brocklin mourned, setting out the buoys in the deeper ponds at Midway Stadium, "no way can I get these guys ready here in Minnesota for 100 degree football in Los Angeles."

He picked up the phone and called Jim Finks. Six hours later the boys were over the Black Hills en route to Los Angeles. If you use the saturated-sponge theory of how much lousy weather a football team can absorb and still be salvageable for

Sunday, Van Brocklin's calculations were right on the hair. The Vikings won the game on the last strokes of the Coliseum clock when Freddie Cox kicked a field goal.

It was the most emotional kind of revival after the happenings of the first two weeks. They had put it up to Francis in the final four minutes, and he had directed them the length of the field in a surge that was nearly evangelistic in its intensity.

Maybe, just maybe, despite the first two defeats, they had broken away. The field would come back to them. The plane ride home was a four-motored jubilee.

Coincidentally it was my last as a day-to-day recorder of the Vikings' calamities and joys. I left the pro football run at this point for the lesser exertions but larger safety of column-writing. We were somewhere over Lake Tahoe when Francis took the plane's intercom.

After delivering the usual roasting to the authors with verse according to Norman the Apostle, Francis announced the Vikings on this day had awarded two game balls. The second, he said, was for me.

The manual of prescribed conduct with a pro football team at a moment like this is to bury the sentiment under raspberries so thick that neither the giver nor the recipient can possibly be accused of taking it seriously. The professionals' sure antidote for any awkwardness in the awarding of the game ball is to sing, in one raucous voice, a popular clubhouse ballad. It has become the anthem of the post-game presentation. Francis gave me the ball and Hawkins led the chorus:

"Hoo-ray for Klobey,

"Hoo-ray at last.

"Hoo-ray for Klobey,

"He's a horse's ass."

I admit there are kinder characterizations to carry with you through eternity.

But I tell no lie. If you have lived for a while in the peculiar counterpane of brutality, beauty, vulgarity and grace that murals the life of a professional football team, you come to understand the language of the men who play it. When it is time for them to show regard for one another in this rough-shelled culture, it is more comfortable to do it with a deflating wink in the eye and an earthy song on the lips.

They would have to take the house before they would get the ball back.

So the Vikings buried the Giants 40-14 on the next weekend and, soaring once more, immediately were shot down again by Gale Sayers' four touchdowns at the Met, 45-37. Not many football teams in the modern era of the pro game had mounted the kind of flying circus offense with which the Vikings were inciting their audiences and exhausting rival defenses. But they were getting undressed defensively. And the season was just too long to believe they could repair the fences in time to stay in title contention. They got by on a thread in San Francisco where, after trailing 21-0 and 35-14, they overtook the 49ers 42-41 in a football game that was almost beyond comprehension.

But on the following week they made a harmless plodder out of the greatest rusher of all time—Cleveland's Jimmy Brown, defeated Cleveland easily, and then turned aside Los Angeles without stress.

They were driving again, with a 5 and 3 record, and before them stood Baltimore, shorn this time of Johnny Unitas. In the absence of the injured star the Colts would play Gary Cuozzo, a very capable young man but not one to terrify the countryside.

The old allegories and symbols stirred dimly in Van Brocklin's head when all the ready lists were finished and all the films dissected; when the horse, in the lexicon of the bull session, was in the barn.

The Vikings were there at the tolling hour again. This time Van Brocklin made no public declarations of it, nor did he dramatize it in the squad meetings. But if they belonged with the Colts and the Packers in the post-season arenas, they would say so today.

They got plastered, 41-21. Cuozzo threw five touchdown passes, a performance that startled the crowd but did not seem especially surprising to the Viking defense. Defiant and sometimes dominant in the first half, the Dutchman's team was overrun in the second.

At game's end Van Brocklin asked Zamberletti and Eason to leave the lockerroom briefly while he talked to the squad. It was the first time he had ever asked the trainer and equipment man, both highly trusted, to excuse themselves for the post-game observances.

He told his players they had let down their public, and they had let themselves down. He opened the door to the reporters and was quiet, strained and controlled. The only intrusion on the silence at times was the vague sensation of a ticking bomb that Van Brocklin almost always gave off after a losing game.

"Our guys learned today what it means to be outplayed and outhit by a team that wanted to win a little more badly," he said, with questionable accuracy.

"It's why Baltimore is in contention for a championship and why we're just where we are.

"Cuozzo was sensational, but we were in control of the game in the first half and let it slip away.

"We had to think Unitas was going to play, but that wasn't a factor. At times it looked as though we hadn't prepared for much of anything." He did not rage, bluster or scream. It was a civil critique.

With his wife, daughters, mother-in-law and the Los Angeles restaurant character, Johnny (Catfish) Sproutt, Van Brocklin drove to Jim Finks' home after the game for sandwiches and beer.

It had all the trappings of a routine post-game social. Sproutt was one of the itinerant ornaments of the Van Brocklin training camp and practice field, the Dutchman's earliest and certainly his most unflinching and tireless devotee. He was a happy man with a button nose and a crew cut that gave him the rare appearance of a middle-age elf with a gravel voice. His loyalty to Van Brocklin was indestructible. He would spend weeks in camp or in residence during the season, the Dutchman's talisman, confidante, jester and authentic buddy.

The Finks' guests included the general manager's brother and wife. It was a convivial, uneventful evening that lasted until nearly 11 p.m. The blows of defeat always struck Van Brocklin in glancing rhythms, the final jolts postponed by a skin-deep jocularity.

Finks saw the Van Brocklin party to the Dutchman's car at about 11. Van seemed to be delaying the leave-taking and went back into the house for ten more minutes of light postmortems over a beer.

Finks' brother was impressed with the coach's willingness to enjoy the party despite the demoralizing events of the afternoon.

At this point there was no evidence of any imminent blow-off.

But a half hour later, shortly after his arrival home, Van Brocklin telephoned the pro football writer of the St. Paul Dispatch and Pioneer Press, Ralph Reeve; the writer for the Minneapolis Tribune, Dwayne Netland; and me. I was now employed by the Minneapolis Star. Van Brocklin said he would have some kind of press conference at 9 in the morning.

I drove over at the indicated hour, fully expecting the Dutchman to lecture for a few minutes about some projected personnel shifts, maybe a mid-season trade.

He was alone in his office at the Vikings' administrative building in Bloomington's Southtown Shopping Center, a few miles from the stadium. The Vikings public relations man, John Thompson, was in the building but did not sit in. I made no particular note of it at the time. Finks was en route to the airport with his brother and had not planned to arrive until mid-morning.

Van Brocklin grinned briefly and cheerlessly. He looked down at his desk. He was wearing glasses, and seemed strangely professorial and tired, the lengthening chicken tracks under his eyes accentuated. His eyes were faintly reddened. It was their normal texture of the day after a defeat.

"Gentlemen," he said quickly, "I've taken this football team as far as I can. Effective right now I am resigning as coach of the Minnesota Vikings."

I stared at him with just a twitch of the eyebrow. I knew damned well he wasn't kidding, but it was part of the game to make the pretense.

"Let's start over," I said.

"That's it," the Dutchman said. "I've gotten all I can out of this football team. I can't get it over the hump. I'm sorry to do it this way, but it's best for everybody concerned. If you don't think you can do any better, you may as well get out and let somebody else try. I don't have any bad feeling for anybody, I'm just sorry I couldn't give the Vikings fans the championship they deserved."

We all made the gesture of being thunderstruck and dismayed and trying to talk him out of it. But the credibility of the scene already had been strained well beyond the accepted boundaries. It was still legitimate drama, but it was going to shift into inspired burlesque in a few minutes.

I stopped briefly to give Van Brocklin my respects in private before heading for a telephone. He was one for whom men could have a huge affection one day and a guns-blazing hostility the next. For all the flareups and noisy hysterics, most of our working relations and our odd-times social liaisons had been fair to sunny. We trusted each other with confidences and, before a final breakdown a few years later, granted the other the traditional badges of respect in this peculiar business of prides and profanities.

"You don't mean you're out for good," I said.

"I don't see how I could change it now," he replied.

"Well, I want you to know how unbearably normal it is going to be around the league until you find another job, like maybe next week. It ought to be said that nobody in football could have won more football games with a new team. It's a credit to you."

Van Brocklin shook hands, put on his coat, and left the office for home.

It was now my unhappy duty to inform the Vikings' publicity man that he had just lost a coach. John Thompson was out of the office momentarily, however, so I told his young assistant, Tom Vandervoort.

"You had better let the world know your coach has just disaffiliated," I told the fellow. Vandervoort was tall, earnest, spectacled and dumbfounded. "You mean Mr. Van Brocklin has quit?"

"Yes," I said, sympathizing. "I don't want to intrude, but

I'll write a few paragraphs for an announcement if you want, inasmuch as the source has just vacated the building."

Thompson appeared and was duly shattered. I'm not sure he trusted my unsupported evidence, so he got corroboration from Netland and Reeve.

"Did he say why?" Thompson asked numbly. "Also, did he say who's going to coach our ball club against the Green Bay Packers Sunday?"

"He left that," I answered, "unclear."

Van Brocklin's resigning without the courtesy of forewarning the general manager or anybody in the organization may have been terribly gauche, but it was largely in character. He saw it as an entirely personal matter, involving no need for the kind of organizational stage managing he sneered at. He therefore decided to summon his own, first press conference—with the idea of making it his last, at least with the Vikings.

He honestly believed Norm Van Brocklin's style, disposition and methods could get no further production out of the Minnesota Vikings. Events were to prove him correct. And while he did not say it publicly, he believed also that most of the important players on his football team were not willing to make the needed sacrifices.

In this he was probably not so correct.

He was a humbled, frustrated, despondent man, and in this mood it was characteristic of him to behave as a boy. The Vikings' failure in this latest climactic game, he thought, was a rejection by the team of Van Brocklin as man and coach. So he decided he would get the hell out.

Neither Finks nor the owners, nor any reasonable football fan, put that sort of reading on the Vikings' performance. Hearing the news, most of his players sounded relieved. The pressures his mood changes and hovering ferocity placed on the players mounted each year. There is a point of declining returns in the type of incendiary leadership that was the core of Van Brocklin's coaching. He could goad and inspire them with his will and strength and abuse. And sometimes they could vent off their resentments; but as the players got older and the pressure more insistent, the relationship changed. In his later years they lost their unquestioning willingness to follow him. His fulminations and his ego and his defiance of the score had rallied them before but the bombast was getting hollow now, a cartoon. He may have seen the precise moment when he lost the team, and that may have been Nov. 14.

One of his best players looked at the team's 1965 distress in this way:

"I just don't think it was in the cards that we were going to win it all that year. We had maybe 22 good ballplayers. We had the ability to beat any team but we really didn't have the maturity, or one of those 40-man teams. We could have won it, but we would have had to be lucky. I mean REALLY lucky. Injury-free, the bounces, things like that. I look at the Vikings' 1969 team and see the things it had that we didn't in 1965. I don't mean just the stars, I mean guys like Hilgenberg and Krause, the good ones here and there we didn't have to fill in the cracks back then. Mostly, I guess, on defense. We'd score 30 to 35 points a game and be lucky to win."

If the prospect of finishing the season without Van Brocklin caused no great alarm among the players, it shook Finks and the owners. Walt Yowarsky could have coached the team the rest of the way, certainly. But here was the Lord Exalted Head Mentor, the glamor of the team and the symbol of the franchise, ducking out in mid-season.

Finks got the news when he returned to his house from the airport. His wife told him Roz, the office secretary, was on the phone, and Finks replied "fine, tell her I'm on my way in."

"She just wanted to tell you that Norm has resigned," the wife said.

Finks zoomed into the office with 15 plans, all of which proved unworkable. He couldn't get Van Brocklin on the phone. The Dutchman, morose and fed up, had decided if he couldn't be unbeatable he could manage the next best thing and be inaccessible. He took the phone off the hook.

The general manager did succeed in establishing telephone contact after a while and urged the coach to reconsider and come back. Nothing irreparable had been done. He said he understood how Van Brocklin felt but that he had so many friends and the team needed him and—

"I'm sorry, Jim," Van Brocklin said. "I'm finished."

I was preparing to leave the Viking office when Finks called me aside and asked whether it would do any good if I made a personal call on Van Brocklin to help talk him out of it. I had a serious doubt whether it was in the best interests of either Van Brocklin or the Vikings for Van Brocklin to return, and suggested instead that Finks telephone Warmath or Rollie Johnson, a television executive with whom Van Brocklin was close. This Finks had intended to do.

He told Warmath: "This guy has made a helluva mistake. I'm sure he'll listen to you as an outsider. I think he really wants to coach this team but feels hurt and down for some reason. I'm going to be talking to our owners in a few minutes. It would help if you tried to convince him he made a mistake."

Van Brocklin called Finks in the afternoon. They talked once more, Van Brocklin still insisting it was impossible for him to reconsider. Finks left his office late in the afternoon to have dinner with Ridder at a boat and yacht club in suburban Mendota. Warmath and Johnson talked to Van Brocklin. So did his old coach with the Rams, Joe Stydahar, by telephone. "You've done a stupid thing," Stydahar said. "The only thing to do now is admit it and get back on the job."

Van Brocklin reached Finks by telephone later that night at the yacht club. He had made a mistake, he acknowledged, and would like to return. Finks and Ridder drove to Van Brocklin's house on Medicine Lake. The Dutchman was still looking depressed, but was back on the rolls by now and the discussion was largely academic. He would meet with the squad in the morning and try to explain it.

The team was gathered at Midway for its regular 10 a.m. Tuesday morning meeting, without intimation that Van Brocklin planned to return. The air was curiously meshed with befuddlement, relief and regret. There were also a few hangovers induced by a Monday night party at the Rand bar and restaurant in St. Paul, where some of the athletes had improvised a ritualistic beer bust to suit the drama of the day. It had a tone that accommodated both the mourners and the celebrators. After a time it was hard to distinguish among them. Even Van Brocklin's sympathizers welcomed the chance to valve off steam. There was a certain fatalism laced through the bacchanalia, not unlike the post-battle binges of the dogfight survivors.

But they looked less than gallant the morning after, and the team's confusion took a new turn when Van Brocklin was spotted through a doorway entering his office.

After ten minutes passed without further emanations from the coaches' office, Motormouth Tom McCormick, the backfield coach, emerged bearing a shoebox.

"This is it," mumbled one of the vets. "They're going to let us vote on whether to take the Dutchman back. The odds are bad. Goldwater would have a better chance."

The election rumor was spiked immediately. The shoebox contained players' mail shipped over from the Bloomington office. A minute later Van Brocklin entered. "I made a mistake," he said. "We all do it. I did what I accused some of the players of doing. I did it because I didn't think I could take you men any further. Well, it's over the dam. We've got to pick up the pieces now and put it all together."

The ones who had played under Van Brocklin for years had seen him so exultant in the morning and on the verge of incineration in the afternoon. But from this day on some of them would never again give him their full trust and allegiance. In a sense he was down off Olympus now, and from here on the old rigid coach-player relationship was going to be a game of one-upsmanship.

"I think," the veteran now says, "we were all aware that the Dutchman realized he had done something foolish as far as his tactical control of the situation goes. But whatever was wrong with his approach to the team really hadn't changed. So now some of us were going to kick the hell out of him, I mean by not being momma's boy when he demanded it — the same way he kicked the hell out of us.

"I know it hurt him to have to admit what he did. For two or three weeks he stayed pretty much away in practice, sort of sitting on his haunches, and smoking and squinting like he does, not saying much.

"The Packers blasted us the next week and so did the 49ers the next. And after we lost that bad to the 49ers, the Dutchman called us a bunch of quitters. Would you believe it?

"Well, you can't accuse the guy of being inconsistent on that score. I'm convinced we won the last two games mostly because the Lions and Bears were amazed that we showed up at all."

Bud Grant, with Jack Patera, in the traditional sideline posture of the Metropolitan Monuments.

Measurement against Green Bay: Bud and Joe went for it on 4th down at their 27, and made it.

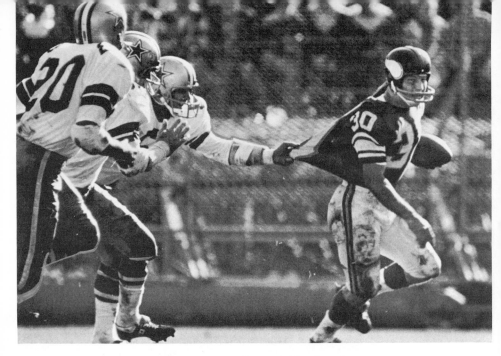

Bill Brown and the vanishing laundry.

Six men in white clutch in tangled confusion at departing Clint Jones.

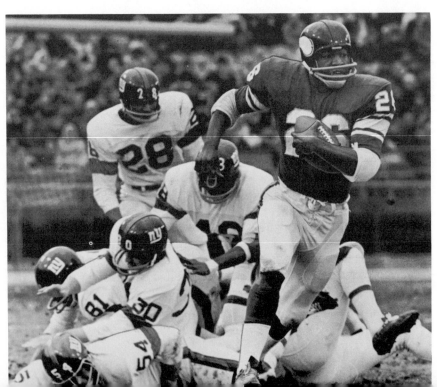

In their natural habitat — the blizzards and icefields — the Vikings were unbeatable in 1969. Larsen and Marshall maul a San Franciscan.

Moose Eller overpowers a blocker and buries Roman Gabriel for a safety in Vikings-Rams divisional playoff.

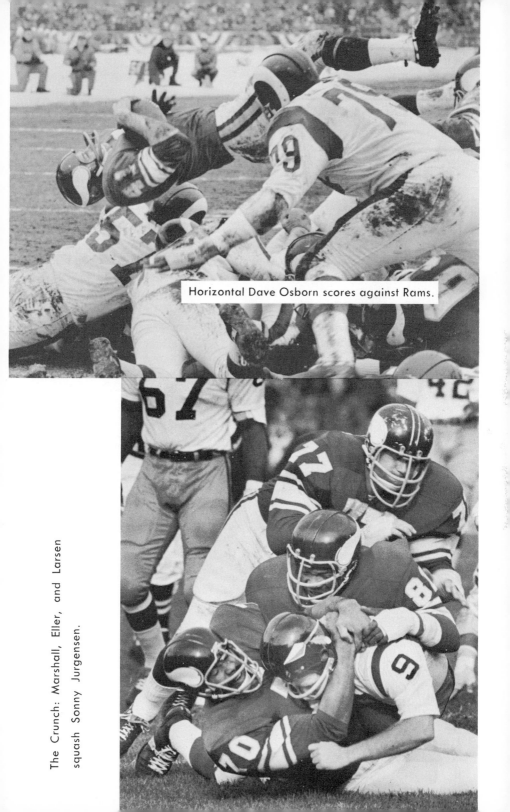

Horizontal Dave Osborn scores against Rams.

The Crunch: Marshall, Eller, and Larsen squash Sonny Jurgensen.

The man called Zorba hollers his cadence above the crouching heavyweights in the Super Bowl.

Joe Kapp hurdles (again) Jim Nettles for a score against Rams.

After the brawl, the battered knight and his public.

Chapter XIX

"It is impossible for me to return to the Vikings with a clear and open mind." — Francis Tarkenton, Feb. 9, 1967.

Professional sports is a continuing soap opera where the personality collisions frequently upstage the deeds of the huffing knights and dragons on the field itself.

For this reason the Van Brocklin-Tarkenton blowup had a lot of competition in the arena of melodramatic encounters between heroic figures. But there was a Shakespearean property to it that lifted it well above the routine teeth-gnashing vendettas of the liniment rooms.

In any cataloguing of the Vikings' corporate assets in the winter of 1967, Norman Van Brocklin and Francis Tarkenton unquestionably would have been listed No. 1 and No. 2, the exact order being open to the latest Standard and Poor indexes and the usual voluble debate.

He had barely visible protection for half his career. Yet Tarkenton nonetheless had produced some remarkable statistics and a national renown as a hairbreadth escapist. He was one of football's top half dozen ticket lures, less for his artistry than his frolicsome gall.

Somewhat to the dismay of Van Brocklin, however, his rabbity style had withstood the success of the 1964 season and the threat of normalcy it posed. Francis still free-lanced and scrambled, not as much as in his early years but often enough to appease his adventuresome heart and to remind the customers and the cameramen that he was one of a kind. This is not to suggest that Francis cast the needs of showmanship ahead of the demands of the ball game. But once in a while, it was a close finish.

Van Brocklin got to be increasingly fond of pointing this out, and eventually decided that what Francis really was at bedrock was a selfish football player.

With Finks, he resolved in the early winter of 1967 to trade this quarterback who had thrown 113 touchdown passes in six years, completed 53 percent of his passes and had the mentality and seasoning—if not the orthodoxy—of a great one.

Their relationship for most of the six years had been essentially friendly, and flavored with mutual respect. Even after they had broken, Van Brocklin did not discredit Tarkenton's football intellect and his nerve, although he spent a lot of time wondering about the quarterback's priorities.

Tarkenton, on the other hand, esteemed Van Brocklin as a football man to the end—and still does now, as a ten-year hierarch already being nudged by notions of retirement.

There the affinities end. In the separate undertakings since 1967 Van Brocklin and Tarkenton seem happily rid of each other, although the thought that some day they might be thrown into each other's arms again on the same team is almost too delicious for the football buff's lymphs.

Until late in the season of 1966, their public frictions were rare and temporary. Tarkenton and Van Brocklin had minds closely attuned to the basic elements of tactics and strategy, and the young Georgian was usually a loyal field subordinate.

Despite his huge reservoir of experience and savvy, Van Brocklin did not object to advice, from his quarterback or his assistants. His record on accepting such counsel was mixed. But he recognized in Tarkenton an imaginative football brain, and in later years they talked as tactical equals.

They did some hassling. There was a memorable scene on a plane in 1963 when, after the Vikings had lost a game decisively, Van Brocklin walked up the aisle to where Tarkenton was sitting with Hawkins and accused him of worrying more about Tarkenton's image than the welfare of the team.

Tarkenton stood up and told Van Brocklin, jaw-to-jaw, "If I can't play for you, then get rid of me." He also told the Dutchman what he thought about the coach trying to call him down on an airplane in front of the rest of the players.

Van Brocklin usually spared Tarkenton the kind of vituperation he would lay on other players, but occasionally they would collide at squad meetings the final year, briefly but explosively.

By this time the Dutchman was convinced his team's competitive dive in 1966 (it ultimately finished with just four victories) was largely due to a don't-give-a-damn attitude among the veteran players instigated by Tarkenton.

Tarkenton's closest friends in his final years were players of the quality of Tingelhoff, Bill Brown, and Grady Alderman. The suggestion was advanced by some of Van Brocklin's friends in the media and on the fringe of the club family that the Tarkenton bloc did not always play with life-and-death fervor because of its mounting disapproval of Van Brocklin.

The idea seems absurd on the face of it. Brown would have been a gung-ho competitor at the junior prom. His pals contended he was the only man they ever saw who probably made a contest out of his first good-night kiss. Tingelhoff was an all-pro annually, with cause; and Alderman never lost his reputation around the league as a class player and man.

That most of the vets were now disenchanted with the Dutchman was unarguable. Van Brocklin could see it, and he could also see that some of the coaches—on a staff undergoing increasing turnover—no longer gave him the personal allegiance and friendship he craved.

In the end the qualities that made him a great player and remarkable coach through five years of struggling with a new football team brought him down—his single-minded passions, his churning will to dominate, his ego. The men he once inspired and scared into performance sometimes beyond their physical capability no longer submitted, or believed him, by 1966.

There was one, fugitive moment of final fulfillment for Van Brocklin and Tarkenton, when their six-year partnership reached the full measure of its promise. In mid-season the Vikings played the Packers, then the champions and striding toward another title.

It was a football game of the type the classicists revere. It was hairy-chested stuff with no accidental, whimsical shifts in trend or temper. It had the concise qualities of the military campaigns of the drawing board, conceived by two rare football mentalities, Lombardi's and Van Brocklin's, and executed by disciplined veterans.

Tarkenton scrambled virtually not at all. The battle was waged almost without error. It was ball-possession football carried to the last decimals. Each team controlled the game for nearly a quarter at a time, an extraordinary throwback to the land wars of another eon. The Vikings did it with Brown, Mason and Osborn, the Packers with Elijah Pitts and Jim Taylor, but both of them did it with the grunts in the front lines. Jock Sutherland and Bernie Bierman would have called it the greatest football game of the decade.

Tarkenton directed it without tactical blemish. When he passed, he had both the time and the disposition to stay in the pocket. He threw 16 completions in 26 attempts. And, in the final quarter, he rallied the Vikings to 10 points in long drives with an offense that posed no mystery to the best defense in football, except how to stop it.

The Packers might have had the unsettling sensation of looking into a mirror. They had won with that kind of football for years. This time it beat them.

And in the aftermath the papers and the bar talk back home were full of Tarkenton's great day in Green Bay, and the Dutchman sizzled a little about that.

He sizzled even more the following week when Francis threw for five interceptions against the Lions. In conversations with Ridder and other owners, Van Brocklin began to insist that Tarkenton was never going to get the club off the ground, that he was interested in personal glory, that he was erratic and no leader of men.

On Dec. 4 the Vikings played their final home game of the season, in the snowdrifts at Metropolitan Stadium against the league's rookie franchise, Atlanta.

Whatever dissensions existed on the club, the Vikings reasonably should have won the football game by three or four touchdowns.

Tarkenton looked forward with some eagerness to playing in front of a television audience of Atlantans, his hometown neighbors. The coach, he assumed, was aware of this natural ambition.

The coach, however, decided this might be the appropriate time to grant Tarkenton a day of rest in favor of young Berry, the struggling second-year quarterback who might be called upon for larger things in 1967.

Berry, he decreed, would be the quarterback-in-custody of the Vikings' game with Atlanta. His explanation was that Berry deserved the trial, the Vikings were headed nowhere in the race, and that the coach had important personnel decisions to make for 1967.

To whispered suggestions that he was also sticking it to Tarkenton in a spectacularly public rebuke, Van Brocklin replied with a wounded glare. "I don't check the television programs," he said. "Berry had the chance coming, and once I gave him the ball, he was going the whole way. It would have been a lousy thing to take him out when he got behind."

The Vikings lost to the newest team in football, 20-13, in their final home game, under miserable weather conditions, with their Pro Bowl quarterback sitting on the bench.

For the first and only time in his coaching career at Minnesota, in Ridder's judgment, Van Brocklin had allowed his personal demons to affect his coaching decisions in a way that burlesqued the product and humiliated the organization.

"It was a disgrace," the publisher told other owners. "One way or another somebody around here is going to see to it that it doesn't happen again."

Dutch gave the ball back to Tarkenton the following week and they beat Detroit 28-16 with three touchdown passes. In their last game together they lost 41-28 to Chicago, against whom they had started it all six years before with a victory that only Tom Swift would have dared to imagine.

New York, Van Brocklin and Finks agreed, was the most fruitful marketplace for a Tarkenton trade. The Giants had the then— unloved Earl Morrall for a quarterback. They were sinking in the hearts of the Manhattan football crowd as well as in the standings. Moreover, New York was a show-town that surely would admire Franny's peculiar matinee gifts.

The Giants were aching for a box office personality to distract New Yorkers in their growing fascination for the Jets' Joe Namath.

There was nothing available that came close to the box office quotient of Francis Tarkenton. And Tarkenton, Van Brocklin and Finks informed the Giants' Well Mara late in December, definitely was available.

They talked twice, the second time in February. New York was about ready to conclude the trade. For Tarkenton the Giants would give the Vikings their first and second round draft choices in 1967, their bonus choice in 1968, and a tight end they planned to acquire from Baltimore, Butch Wilson.

Rumors of these imminent transactions reached several interested people, among them Tarkenton. He had already had a long soul-breasting talk with Van Brocklin after the Atlanta game. Their differences seemed resolved. He seemed adjusted to playing for Van Brocklin again in 1967, although it was clear all around he would not have been heartbroken by a trade. His critics later contended he forced the trade to New York, partly in pique but mostly out of his admiration for large green bills. Francis undoubtedly has the weakness, shared by a few million people. But he appeared to be reasonably mollified after he had another six-hour reconciliation session with Van Brocklin in early February. He assumed they were great pals again. Then he ran into new trade stories on the West Coast and returned home, fuming.

On Feb. 9 Francis Tarkenton decided in Atlanta he would blow all remaining bridges with Van Brocklin and the Vikings. He wrote a letter to the five directors, Finks and Van Brocklin, announcing his disaffiliation.

"Because of the events of the past few months, and my feelings toward a number of things," he wrote, "it is impossible for me to return to the Vikings with a clear and open mind."

"As you know, I have tried to subdue these feelings and erase them from my mind, but it has been impossible.

"Feeling as I do, I am sure this decision is the best for the Vikings, you and myself . . . I hope you and the organization understand that nothing can be done which would change my decision."

All hands were predictably confounded. Not the least of these was Van Brocklin, who got the news on his return with Finks from New York, where they had reached a general understanding with Mara on terms of the trade.

Tarkenton knew perfectly well he wasn't going to retire from football. He also knew he had a stomachful of Van Brocklin and was through with the Vikings. In addition, he knew he was a property big enough in pro football that neither the owners of his Minnesota contract nor the NFL could afford to let him go idle. It would have invited the monopoly sniffers.

On another day, the Tarkenton letter might have caromed off Van Brocklin and produced nothing more than another phone call to Mara, announcing, "Go ahead. It's a deal."

But Van Brocklin was embroiled in staff problems. Lew Carpenter, his end coach since 1964, was finished with the Dutchman. The newest turmoil involved Tom McCormick, the talkative Irishman whom Van Brocklin had befriended when they played together with the Rams. McCormick was the good humor man of the Viking staff. He had once endeared himself forever with the offensive backfield by telling his wards—in the midst of a losing streak—to break all training rules the Friday night before a game and get themselves loosened up. To the bachelors he recommended a good blonde and quiet springs.

The therapy was remarkably successful, the Vikings winning that weekend in overwhelming style. In the interests of ongoing discipline and for certain hygienic reasons, however, Van Brocklin advised McCormick to find other prescriptions.

In later years, McCormick squirmed under the errand-boy duties that Van Brocklin would assign him, and deeper resentments developed. Van Brocklin ordered McCormick to meet him at the airport on his return from New York. It was then when the Tarkenton news reached the incoming coach.

Ridder met Van Brocklin shortly afterward and reviewed the Tarkenton letter. The Dutchman's frustrations were building. There was the coaching staff, a losing season, the Tarkenton trade, the hangover of his 1965 resignation, the Atlanta game—and now the Tarkenton letter. "Maybe," he told Ridder, "I'm just a pioneer-type coach, good with a new team. I don't think it's going to work any more. I think I better get out."

Ridder had never lost his respect for Van Brocklin's vast football competence, the power of his will or the human qualities that Van Brocklin often submerged under his competitive ferocity or obscured with some of his explosions of spite, or his dark suspicions.

Yet he understood that Van Brocklin had to go, for the peace of mind of everybody close to him. "Why don't you think it over and we'll get together tomorrow," Ridder suggested. "We don't have to do anything right now."

Van Brocklin drove home, and considered. He met the next day with Ridder, Finks and others. Momentarily he seemed to waver. This brief spasm caused some consternation among the management barons because they, too, had removed all bridges by now.

It got down to a settlement on the contract. Van Brocklin's had four years remaining. He was then getting in the neighborhood of $45,000 a year with bonuses that could inflate that to $60,000. Because he was resigning, however, the ownership had no obligation to settle with him.

Still, they had all lived with him intimately and agreeably, for the most part, despite his eccentricism of the last two years. He had delivered more for their organization on the field than they had expected or hoped. Accordingly, they offered him $100,000, or approximately half of what the face value of the contract called for.

Van Brocklin seemed embarrassed and distraught. He said it was too much. "Why not let us be the judge of that?" Ridder said. Subsequently, however, the Dutchman insisted on a lower figure, in the range of $75,000.

They shook hands. "Some day, and not long from now, maybe," Ridder said, "I think you'll realize you made the right decision. You will always be a first-rate football man, coach."

The room was silent. Van Brocklin put his hand to his eyes and brushed away the moisture. He nodded, and they left together.

In the aftermath, there were attempts by Van Brocklin's well-wishers to rewrite history in some manner, to revise the libretto of what happened, to make the Dutchman the innocent victim of a conspiracy laid by Tarkenton.

This bothered me, as one man close to both disputants at the time and familiar with the interplay of their vanities and ambitions. I didn't mind the attempted canonization of Van Brocklin, although he never needed it or deserved it. I did object to the indictment of Tarkenton as an alleged provocateur who broke up the team in a willful and self-serving campaign for money and glorification.

Van Brocklin cut his way through pro football's jungle to become a great player on nerve, intelligence and ability. He was and is a very good coach. But when he was grieving about Tarkenton's devotion to personal interests, he must have forgotten about his own such devotion in Los Angeles ten years before.

As long as he commanded the loyalties of his ballplayers and made them better men with his furies and his nose-thumbing at the odds, Van Brocklin was a great leader. With the Vikings, something went out of him when he stepped out for a day in the middle of the 1965 season. They feared him less, followed him less ardently.

He is the last man in football I would consider a competitive quitter. But for all of the mental toughness in him there is also much of the adolescent, who likes to be liked. When his furies spilled over and offended and alienated people who were once his friends, both players and coaches, their sudden enmity seemed to him a repudiation of his values and a humiliation to his pride.

Nobody pushed Van Brocklin into leaving the Vikings—the owners, fans, writers, players. Tarkenton did not push him. There is in the makeup of this football man, who is maddening at times and impossible at others but admirable in other ways, a capacity for self-injury. Whenever he has been hurt or humbled, the man who brought him down was Norm Van Brocklin.

Strangely, the players who footballed under him remember his flights into practice field apoplexy almost with affection. Having survived them, they look on the whole exercise now with the forgiving nostalgia that distance almost always invokes.

"The guy," one of his vets said, "was a 21-carat original. I never loved him. He bad-mouthed a lot of guys. You almost had to change water to wine to get Van Brocklin to give you a good word. But you felt like a million when he did, because you knew you deserved it. He was funny as hell, though. For instance he had this thing about taking on the weather and not babying yourself. He wouldn't let anybody use handwarmers.

"Francis tried, and Van Brocklin almost had a fit. The second year he found a box in Eason's training room, unopened, because there was no way Eason was going to break those out—and he had them thrown out. The box was buried deep under some junk, but Van Brocklin found it.

"I saw his Atlanta team playing Baltimore last fall, and it was snowing and raining and just the most awful day you can imagine. The Atlanta team was out there freezing their testicles off. No capes, no nothing. And old Dutch is bundled up miserable in that red parka and he's got that cigarette sticking out, the whole bit.

"So I see Flatley on the bench. He suffers pretty good, anyhow. He's looking at the other side and sees how the Colts are coming off the field. They all got capes and jackets and nice toasty heaters, and Flatley's standing there on the sidelines jumping up and down to keep warm with his hands jammed under his belt.

"I know what he's thinking, about the time Roy Winston was trying to keep warm on a zero day at the Met. Roy is a Louisiana boy, you know. He is neurotic about cold weather. When Van Brocklin wasn't looking, he'd always get his hands somewhere to keep them warm. So this time he's got to run out with the kickoff team, and it's really, brutal cold. He runs out there with his hands under his belt, and Van Brocklin blew his stack.

" 'Winston,' he howled, 'get your goddamned hands out of your drawers.'

"Well, that's the Dutchman, I guess. I remember him best from Bemidji. After a tough workout, he'd try to get a little close to us and say, 'Men, I know you're all nervous and emotional about making the team, so tonight go ahead and stay out to midnight and drink beer and blow your brains out if you want. Some of that is good in training camp. You have to relax.'

"So the next morning if somebody would miss a signal and hit the wrong hole, the Dutchman would just run your ass off. And sooner or later he was bound to yell out, 'All right, if you're going to drink beer, you're damned well going to pay for it.' "

I can hear it yet.

Chapter XX

"We didn't have a punt-return play in, but we sure knew how to stand at attention."—Viking player in Bud Grant's first season.

Jim Marshall's eyes were glazed and his faltering voice bore witness to some terrible visitation. His audience was the supply corps of the pro football training camp, the lockerroom attendants.

"Gentlemen," he declared, "you will not believe what our ball club, the fearless purple and white, has been doing for the last half hour out on the practice field under Gen. Grant two days before an exhibition game!"

One of the whirlpool corporals ventured a guess. "Windsprints and rope drills after two hours of scrimmage?"

"Wrong," Marshall announced, "one more try."

"You have been watching old film clips of the 1934 Gopher-Pittsburgh game on wide screen," another offered gamely.

"Wrong again," Marshall disclosed. "Gentlemen, for the last half hour the Minnesota Vikings have been doing close-order drill, by the numbers. We have learned how to stand at attention, at a 45-degree angle to the scoreboard, breast-to-breast on the hashmarks, with our helmets cradled in our arms."

Marshall was about to lapse into the reveries of another imaginary life—Jim Marshall, Paratrooper—in which he could visualize himself as a bloused-boots veteran of the airdrop at Remagen, his hard-toed combats shined to a mirror polish and his packed chute beside him.

He might have, except that Harry Peter (Bud) Grant happened to walk in behind him, and silence erupted here and now.

Harry Grant's first few weeks with the Vikings in Mankato in 1967 were accorded the same hushed stupefaction as a visit from another planet. Except for a handful of football nomads who had made the grand tour of the NFL, the Vikings were peopled by the ballplayers Van Brocklin had housebroken, nurtured and carrot-trained.

To most of them Van Brocklin was, for six months of the year, more than a football coach. He was a property of life, like the air, water and sunburn. When you took Van Brocklin from the Vikings you were somehow changing the balance of nature for 30 or 40 people. It was not that they were dismayed as much as they were disoriented.

The change in the disposition and style of the Head Overseer was almost shattering psychologically. It was as though Ivan the Terrible had been replaced by Calvin Coolidge.

"Van Brocklin," observed a lineman who labored under both administrations, "hit a football team like a landslide. Grant comes at you like a glacier."

"We tried to get some kind of book on him from Hackbart and a few others who played under him in Winnipeg. They told us he never said much at squad meetings, and that he had the damndest Mickey Mouse rules that he used to bring-about squad discipline. They told us he almost never raised his voice and that sometimes when you talked to him you get the feeling somebody in the sky was taking it all down on concrete slabs because it sure as hell didn't seem to be registering on Bud.

"So he got down to Mankato, and it was the craziest sparring you ever saw. A lot of the vets didn't like Van Brocklin but they knew in their guts he was just about the sharpest football mind in the business. Bud they just knew by reputation, that he had some great record coaching up there around the Arctic Circle with 12 players per team, three downs and maybe a couple of seals. In other words, this was the NFL. Bud played in it, but back in the days before the Marlboro Cowboy. Nobody knew Bud and nobody knew his assistants. He seemed like an all right guy but he was distant and quiet and cool.

"So they had Bud Grant on probation as a football man. He

was a little cagey about putting in his new squad rules, but little by little they crept in, and it was a party.

"Everybody on the team accepts them now, because they know it isn't just so much chicken by the coach but the idea of discipline and common sense and all the rest that Grant got across later. But at the time, you can't imagine the horse laughs.

"I'll never forget our first exhibition game under Grant. We didn't have time in training to get our punt return play in, but I'll be damned if we weren't ready to stand at attention when they played the national anthem. Not just standing respectfully like we've been doing all our life, but with full military bearing with exact 45-degree angles to the flag and everybody standing exactly on the yard stripe or lined up perfectly on the sidelines.

"So help me, we were convinced Grant had flipped when he lined us up the first time at Mankato. Milt Sunde, Don Hansen and Ron Acks had just come back from the National Guard, so he commissioned them to be instructors.

"We all lined up like we were going to do a relay or something. So Bud says, 'Stand at attention,' and you'd be surprised how many guys didn't really know how. So he brought out Sunde, Hansen and Acks. Hansen acted as a sort of drill instructor.

"Would you believe he spent 15 minutes a day teaching everybody how to stand?

"Well, about this time Bud told us about the coaching rules. First of all, there was no smoking in the lockerroom and team buses. You could only smoke in the can, in the biffies. At halftime in those first years the men's room looked like a volcano. You could see huge mushrooms of smoke rising above the stalls.

"Then it was just one cigarette, I repeat, one, after squad meals. Then Bud banned smoking in small dining rooms, when we were on the road. Notice I said small. If the ceiling was high enough, or it was air conditioned, you could smoke, but if the room was small, no. It was okay to smoke in the Marriott in Chicago, but bad in the place we stayed in Dallas. It got so that you had to be a surveyor to know whether it was all right to smoke.

"Bud's idea was 'smoke if you have to, but be sure you don't bother the men who don't want them.' You can't argue with that, but the whole business seemed so highschoolish that we used to spend our spare time in the lockerroom thinking up new Bud

Grant stunts. We figured we had seen them all until we found out you couldn't have cookies on the airplane.

"You could have sandwiches, pie and two beers apiece after the game, but you couldn't have cookies."

Harry Peter Grant was nothing if not a well-regulated man. He believed in the orderly process, the virtues of self-control, moderation in appetites, and winning football games. In Harry Grant's carefully-ordered world, they all meshed together. He came down to Bloomington from Winnipeg fully expecting the snickered asides. In the lockerroom ribaldry he would be likened, on alternate days, to Captain Queeg and Mickey Mouse.

Grant decided he could endure the clubhouse burlesque, that it was part of the price of walking in behind the salty-trooper emotionalism of Van Brocklin. He would let his own personality, his style and his professionalism stand on the record, given a reasonable time to blend them with the team's.

Finks telephoned him a few weeks after Van Brocklin's resignation. The general manager had made the gesture of interviewing two or three others, Bill Johnson of the San Francisco 49er staff and Nick Skorich of the Browns' staff among them. He respected both highly, but made the overture largely out of consideration for mutual friends who had asked him for the courtesy. Neither Finks nor the Viking ownership had much question about the identity of the next coach.

Grant had turned them down seven years ago before the Vikings offered the job to Van Brocklin. He was successful as the coach and general manager in Winnipeg. There was further success and stability ahead. And anybody taking the job of coach with a rookie franchise in the NFL was heading indisputably for ulcer gulch.

There would be opportunity enough years ahead, he reasoned —possibly in the immediate wake of the man who accepted the job Bud Grant turned down.

With Van Brocklin gone, Tarkenton going and their survivors in various phases of confusion, Viking football in the winter of 1967 was in a shambles. And yet, the poets suggest, out of shambles marble monuments occasionally rise.

Grant was the unanimous nominee as the incoming marble monument.

But was he available?

Harry Grant, man of measured logic, considered the credits and debits of a move into the big leagues. He had just signed a five-year contract at Winnipeg. He was comfortable, prosperous, a dominant figure in the provinces.

Against this, he placed an uncertain future in the National Football League. It was in character for Bud Grant to consider, "What are my chances of being successful? Because if I'm not after a couple of years, I'm a dead duck." He posed the dilemma in that precise language.

The Vikings in 1966 won four football games. The exuberance of their first rush at the league's gentry had been spent in the Van Brocklin-Tarkenton trauma. Some of their best young talent of the early years had peaked out. Rip Hawkins had retired, Tommy Mason was ailing, and Tarkenton was headed for New York—in exchange for a fishbowl-full of draft choices that at the moment were only numbers on the blackboard.

In other words, the new coach was starting out with a loser, No. 1; and with a loser that was going to be quarterbacked by a second-stringer, Ron VanderKelen or Bob Berry or one John Hankinson.

Harry Grant's practical mind told him to stay in Winnipeg.

But he was a football man from the beginning, and only ultimate destination for a football man was the NFL.

"How many years will you give me?" he asked Finks.

"Almost as many as you want," Finks said.

"Three years," Grant replied.

"We'll give you more than that," Finks said.

"I don't want it. If I can't establish something with the team in three years, I'm never going to do it. Three years it is."

Finks declined to pursue the point. He had known Grant for years, as a rival in the Canadian League and as negotiator at the player market. He understood Grant's stubborn intellect, the single-minded devotion to winning that burned evenly under his public reserve.

His subsequent biographers assumed it filtered by osmosis from Grant's college coach, Minnesota's Bierman. It probably didn't. Grant had the same reluctant admiration for the old sweatbox maestro as most of Bierman's pupils. But he was an athlete of such prodigious gifts and versatility that he really never listened very hard to Bernie and certainly was never scared by him.

He insisted on playing baseball in the spring and thus automatically started the fall season with the fourth team, a club joke because there was no other end within five light years of him. Nor did he bust his glands in the practices. Bierman used to seethe with the frustration. He wanted to fire Grant a half dozen times, but you do not kick off the best athlete on the team when you want to get to the Rose Bowl.

Nobody ran more penance laps in Minnesota football history than Bud Grant.

In his last couple of years of competition, Bud's practice field zeal did improve. There was never any question from his freshman year on about his competitive grimness in the games themselves. He played end both ways, with force, ingenuity and instinct. He pitched a baseball and rebounded a basketball almost as well, and before the end of his senior year he was confronted with the quandry of what to take cash for first—football or basketball.

He compromised by planning to do both, first basketball with the Lakers and then football with the Philadelphia Eagles. By his second season in 1952 with the Eagles he was one of the best in the business. The Eagles were appreciative but not very rewarding. So Bud Grant went to Winnipeg, where they doubled his pay, and five years later named him coach, at the age of 29, to succeed Allie Sherman. His teams won four western playoffs and six Grey Cups. But now, in February of 1967, they would ask on Hennepin and Lowry: "Can the guy coach an 11-man team?"

This is what the guy was thinking:

"I didn't believe I had to come in here and win seven games the first year. If I thought I had to do that, or come in behind a championship season, it might have been a little different. But I was going to have a chance to develop this thing. It wasn't good to be stepping in without the No. 1 quarterback, Tarkenton. But the quarterback is not the whole team. As a matter of fact, the defense was my main concern when I took over. But we didn't have to set the league on its ear the first year. Yes, I know a lot of people said we were coming in completely ignorant of the NFL and the personnel, and our own players, for that matter. But it was still football. The personality-types and the problems are the same whether you're coaching in Mankato or Manitoba. I never worried much about that.

"I was aware that my style and temperament were different from Van Brocklin's. I also knew that I wasn't going to go in there the first day and tear up all the old policies just to put mine in. But I expected the wisecracks when I put in the smoking rules and some of the other things they call Mickey Mouse. They'd get used to them.

"Look, when I got into coaching I had no ideas about it. When Winnipeg offered me the job, I was about as unprepared as anybody, except I was 29. I could play two, three, maybe five more years. But if you want to get into coaching, the best place to start is head coach, right?

"I started from scratch. People ask me how I acquired my coaching methods and disposition. I couldn't tell you. I didn't draw any kind of a map. I mean I didn't decide overnight to become stone face or old iron eyes or whatever picture the fans eventually got of me on the sidelines. I just learned things that were good for me as I moved along, and for the team.

"This business of petty disciplines. Yes, there is some military psychology in it. And I think the greatest testimonial to it—always remembering that you don't want to make a fetish of it—is that most players eventually can see what it's done for them.

All right, let's take a little thing like don't walk on the grass here or there. It's an unconscious thing. We hope it will carry into the game when the real discipline is needed. It's like your kid, when you try to get him to hang up his clothes. You've got to do it subconsciously. You can't harp at him all the time. You've got to create an atmosphere or something close to it so that he'll WANT to hang his clothes up.

"We've got 40 people, football players who are competitive, emotional, highly intelligent, egotistical. We've got to take these 40 people and make them into a team. Let me tell you. It's about as tough a job as there is in sports because they are all of different racial, religious and social backgrounds. Yet they all have got to have a common goal, and they can't turn it on suddenly when they go onto the field. You have to build this up in all your living habits and training habits, eating, sleeping, living together habits so that this is not a big step when you carry it onto the field, but just another, natural step.

"This no-smoking business. I've really got nothing against cigarettes. I'm not a crusader. I play a game, I suppose, when I insist on the rules about smoking. I want them to know it's important for a group of men to accept rules of self-sacrifice because they are important for them as a TEAM. Maybe discipline isn't the right word. The habit of doing the right thing unconsciously, maybe that's it. You march in the military because it teaches you to react to orders, to submit yourself to the group.

"I didn't want to put in all of this right now. We all wanted to get a chance to get acquainted. But some things I just didn't want to keep postponing. For example, we'd go on a road trip and get into the other town at 1:30 or 2:00 p.m. So we'd have a workout and it was 'See you at 11 tonight, here's meal money.'

"Some of the guys would go downtown and have a couple of beers, have supper, see a show, have a couple of more beers, come back at 11 o'clock, and say 'Howdy, see you in the morning.' Maybe a few of them would go out the window after the 11 o'clock meeting.

"Well, a lot of teams do that. I don't judge anybody else's system. The only one I'm comfortable with is mine. We kind of went along for awhile, then we began to have dinner together, which was a step. This meant they couldn't go to Toots Shors in New York or wherever they wanted to eat. But what is wrong with some restriction on the player's personal life the night before a game? I don't think this footloose stuff does any good for the football player psychologically or the football team. And I certainly know it doesn't do them any good physically to have two, three, four, five, six beers or what else before a game.

"So we said we don't want it, and if we find it, we'll take appropriate steps. Watching them come in glassy-eyed for an 11 o'clock meeting with a football game at 2 the next afternoon didn't make any sense.

"Well, some of them said, 'I've been here for five years and we did this all the time.' They would dress up, put on nice clothes and spend their money and time, and this was their bag. And I said, that's fine, but I tried to explain that if they really couldn't give up one night a week for the amount of money they're getting

paid, to concentrate on football, maybe they were meant for some-
place else. We have a meeting at 11 o'clock the night before the
game. And we want to talk about something. We're not just going
to come in and tell all about the girls on the town, the stories and
whatnot. We are going to talk about the game tomorrow and we
are going to bed with it, and it'll maybe give us that much more
tomorrow to work with, a little edge. If we don't win some ball
games, maybe the players won't buy it—which, I suppose, is what
made it tough all around the first year when we won just three
games.

"I don't say this is the only way. It just happens to be our way.
I guarantee they are going to think about football the night before
a game. And if we can show them that's the way we're going to
prepare, then we're going to ask them to do the same thing. And
after three years, I might say they have done it. We're not checking on them. They might have a beer or two, but if I find them,
they know it's going to cost them. And if I don't find them, well—
I hope I never do. I never have."

So he wasn't Calvin Coolidge at all, walking among his
platoons of helmeted skeptics at Mankato in the summer of 1967.
He was Amos Alonzo Stagg, Bud Wilkinson and Jack Armstrong,
all wearing the same earphones.

Whatever identity he later took on among the inquisitive ballplayers—this remote man who looked like the sheriff from Kenora
—the first thing he was was late.

It was almost unimaginable that Bud Grant, the meticulous
man of timetables and litanized order, should keep the whole
camp-bound cavalcade of cars and buses waiting for 10 minutes
in Bloomington.

"I'm sorry," he blushed, striding on board, "I was fixing my
kid's bike. I lost track of the time."

Fixing the bid's bike, on his first day as coach in the NFL.
Well, it tracked. Nothing shakes Bud's priorities. When you tell
the kid you're going to fix the bike, CBS can wait.

"I was relieved," observed Jim Finks, "that it wasn't the
lawnmower."

They later grew to understand him. But in his first exposure
to NFL coaching, the Vikings gave Grant the same wary distance
they would give the undertaker walking into a fraternity smoker.

They thought the man had taken the wrong bus on his way to Mt. Rushmore, not as a tourist but as a permanent bust.

Chapter XXI

*"Grant would tell you it's all right to knock hell
out of a guy, as long as it doesn't cost you. Always a
practical guy, Bud."—Dale Hackbart, defensive back.*

Having mastered the intricacies of standing at attention, the
Vikings now focused their energies on learning Bud Grant's
offense.

Their initial chore, they discovered, was to find it.

Bud Grant's first-year offense with the Vikings was so fundamental it could have been run by the Burroughs Elementary School
BobCats. On certain days in November, in fact, the audience
would have sworn it was.

For this it is hard to fault Grant, in retrospect. But not many
of his veteran players, the incumbents from the Van Brocklin administration, were so charitable when his spare hieroglyphics first
went up on the blackboards at Mankato.

He knew there was going to be a transitional problem in putting in new terminology, new concepts, and new patterns. There
was nothing especially original or complicated about any of it, but
obviously it was going to be different.

There was also the matter of allowing time for the team and
coach to adjust to each other, for the coach to learn first-hand the
capabilities of the athletes, and for the players to condition themselves to the new personalities of the coaching staff.

They were also going to have quarterbacking problems the
first season, no matter who handled the job. Grant concluded almost immediately that the holdovers, VanderKelen and Berry, and
the rookie candidate, Hankinson, were limited people. If they
couldn't cut it, he would bring in somebody new. If it was some-

one new, everybody was starting the season as a stranger—the coach strange to the league and team, the team unsure of the system, and the quarterback ignorant of just about everything that mattered—the coach, the team, and the system.

And if the new quarterback came from Canada, he was also going to be ignorant of the league itself.

The tolerant hearts, therefore, could forgive Bud Grant for not incorporating half of Avogadro's Trigonometry Tables in his first-year playbook.

And they did—a couple of years later.

In the addled summer of 1967, however, the post-Van Brocklin Vikings and Bud Grant agonized through the eerie atmospheric side effects that always follow the storm.

"I never knew how it was to be in the eye of the hurricane," one of the men recalls, "until Bud Grant came in behind Van Brocklin as coach.

"When I think back on it, it was really a wrenching experience. I'll tell you where you felt it the most—in the film sessions where you'd look at the other team's offense or defense, or review your own game films.

"Van Brocklin used to provide a running commentary. In fact, if they ever taped Van Brocklin's narrations in the projection room, Bob Newhart would be out of business as an amateur. He wasn't always funny, you understand. He was downright brutal sometimes. But when you remember it, the whole thing kind of breaks you up. When he was looking at the other team, he always had some observation or tip or warning, or he'd be calling some great pro like Ditka 'a pussy' or something like that to let you know he was human, in case you'd forgotten. But it was the whole smear, a critique.

"So now Bud Grant comes in and turns on the projector, and all you hear is the whirring of those little projector wheels or somebody belching every so often. It's like the old silent movies are back. You watch for 30 minutes or so, and Bud leans back in his chair and says, 'Any questions?'

"Nobody has got any questions, and you have to think one of two things:

"Either we are the smartest football team ever assembled, or everybody was waiting for the Tom and Jerry cartoon."

"As far as the offense he laid out, for most of the veterans it was the same thing as going from college calculus back to counting toes. Not the basic formations. Everybody does pretty much the same thing except Stram in KC and Landry in Dallas. It was the small variations, the individual blocking, the refinements, where there was a difference. Van Brocklin really had a sophisticated system of blocking changes, where the linemen could switch their blocks on the fly.

"Bud didn't put much of that stuff in. I feel a little sheepish about saying this, but some of the linemen actually used Van Brocklin terminology in the first year when they wanted to change blocking to suit a changed defense, because they didn't have any of their own in Bud's offense.

"Well, all that has changed now, but in the first year it was just open house, you seemed to be milling around. A guy who changed a lot of that fast, incidentally, was Jerry Burns, when they got him from Green Bay. I don't downrate Bud Grant as a football coach. I think the job he did moving that Viking team of 1967 all the way into the Super Bowl three years later has to compare with anything Vince Lombardi did. But he did it in a way completely different from the way Van Brocklin would have—if Dutch ever could have. Van Brocklin would have done it up there in the front tank with his ivory revolvers and kicking everybody in the ass.

"Grant did it the staff way, and the staff really wasn't whole until they brought Burns in there to shape up the offense. For one thing, the Vikings in Bud's first year never really knew how to handle a blitz. You remember how terrible Joe Kapp looked in that game in Atlanta that year, getting blasted by the linebackers and really smelling out the joint. Well, it really wasn't Joe's fault at all. The team just didn't have the blocking switches to handle the blitz, and it bothered a lot of guys.

"But I'll tell you where Grant is a good coach. He never stopped being Bud Grant. I mean, he believed in what he was doing, and that eventually he would get through to the players. The whole thing was a little unreal for a while. Bud came in with that crew cut and military bearing and quiet voice. Somebody said it looked like they just chiseled him out of the North Shore cliffs on Lake Superior.

"Sometimes you'd ask him a question and he'd just look at you dead pan, so that you didn't know whether you had green teeth or offended his family. They started calling the squad room Grant's Tomb. On the sidelines he'd stand there with his cap and those goddamned earphones and there was no use saying anything to him because he couldn't hear you.

"But even after that rough first year when we won only three games and tied three, the guys started coming around to him, because they saw that he was fair with the players. He gave every man a good shot. I think the thing that impressed them even more, maybe, was that he treated the guys decently. He never abused a man on the field or humiliated him. He would say things to individual players in meetings or on the field, but never in a way to make it sound like the guy had just evicted his mother.

"Don't get me wrong. Grant isn't any little boy blue. Winning is just as important to him as it is to Lombardi or Van Brocklin or A. J. Foyt. The guy who isn't willing to adapt to Grant's ideas of team discipline or just doesn't dig that college-coach style finds other employers pretty quick. Paul Flatley was one of those. Paul and Grant just didn't gear together. Flatley wanted to smoke when he felt like it, and he liked to go out for a show and some drinks the night before a game. 'If you're 100 per cent sharp and ready to go on Sunday afternoon,' he'd say, 'what the hell difference does it make? Grant figures everybody who plays football for him ought to think and act like a high-school kid.'

"Anyhow, I know Flatley went in to see him the day after the last game of the 1967 season and told Grant what he thought about his rules and that he wanted to be traded. I understand Grant told him that a trade wasn't in their plans, and Flatley was so mad he took his family to Colorado to live in the off-season. He seemed in a lot better frame of mind when he got back, and he worked awfully hard in the summer camp in 1968.

"And just before the start of the season Bud cut him.

"I never saw a guy so mad in all my life as Flatley when he left town. But when Van Brocklin and Atlanta beat the Vikings and Grant two years later in that mudpie fight in Atlanta, there were two guys in hog heaven—Van Brocklin and Flatley."

There were other departures among the discontented. Most of the vets shrugged off Grant's first season as either a private penance or some elaborate practical joke by fate. His remoteness, the dogged devotion with which he pursued his rinkydink rules, his silence in the meetings and, despite all that, his self-possession and serene belief that he knew where they were going—all this made Bud Grant faintly unbelievable to the older dudes.

When he ordered Fred Cox to kick a field goal in the final minute of their opening game, at a time when the Vikings trailed the Rams by 32 points, the old guard of the club was convinced Bud in truth did operate by the constellation Ursa Major or some other mysterious lights.

For awhile he was an easy caricature in the clubhouse. They pictured Bud as the coach from Mars, and they would go 'bleep-bleep' in furtive yips on the practice field. He didn't help the image by being so deliberate in his halftime counsel during the Browns' exhibition game that the Vikings did not show up for the second kickoff and got docked 15 yards for delay of game.

They lost a lot of football games, but they began to notice, as the season waned, that Grant's critics may have been smiling but the other teams weren't. They lost eight games in 14 (they tied three besides winning three). This meant that with a coach and quarterback virginally strange to the league, and without a good receiving corps, and with all of the syndromes of a switch from Van Brocklin football to Grant football, the Vikings had been beaten in only little more than 50 per cent of their games.

They took a second look at the sheriff from Kenora; and his rules seemed a little less funny. And they remembered most of all that during the squirmy weeks when they were losing and catching the derision from the fans, Grant stood without fluster and talked to them as professionals. Now they could come out of it with a little more professionalism.

This they understood, and listened. Nobody, perhaps, listened quite as penitently as the free-booting Badger whom Grant himself had signed nearly 10 years before, Dale Hackbart.

Hackbart was the man with a democratic outlook on professional contracts. He signed all available. As a result, in one and the same year he was under contract to the Pittsburgh baseball Pirates, the Winnipeg Blue Bombers, and the Green Bay Packers. The Pirates gave him a $10,000 bonus to play with Grand Forks of the Northern League but were losing enthusiasm for Hackbart as the next Ralph Kiner when Hackbart suddenly became the object of a custodial fight between Winnipeg and Green Bay.

Grant himself pursued the much-coveted gladiator to the very gates of the border in 1960 to preside over his signature on a Winnipeg contract. After which, Hackbart signed a Green Bay contract. This result was that Lombardi had to pay (1) Hackbart, as the signatore and (2) Grant and Winnipeg as the wounded parties.

By the end of the 1967 season, Hackie had advanced a niche professionally. He had gone up from the level of a six-year pro football mediocrity to that of a widely-suspected cheap shot specialist whose primary credits were penalties totaling more than 100 yards in 1967.

At this stage of transition, he decided maybe Bud Grant was worth a hearing.

Hackbart was a happy-souled character with unusual athletic gifts but scant sense of direction. A gangling quarterback as a collegian, he was consigned to the secondary at an early professional age. He came to the Vikings in 1965 with no great reputation as tough guy.

"I had known about Van Brocklin, though," he recalls, "and I talked to some of the players before I went to camp. They said he likes a hitter, and this is maybe what I had not been in the past. So I decided I would hit everything that came near me.

"I think this sort of impressed Van Brocklin but it did not make many friends for me. I had four or five fights with Bedsole and a couple with Jerry Reichow. I suppose it was pretty primitive. I was trying to make the ball club, and the only way was to bust a few people up. So I hit them coming downfield, and I hit them wherever I could. I think Van Brocklin liked it, although he concealed this pretty well because right near the end of training I got cut.

"I didn't blame Van Brocklin. He had some other guys. I went back to Winnipeg and played for Bud for a while and showed my impartiality by getting cut there, too.

"But I made it with the Vikings in 1966, and in 1967 I really got pretty wild, I guess, Bud's first year.

"I remember hitting Dave Parks of San Francisco out of bounds one time; and Gale Sayers of the Bears as he was going down, and it cost us the ball game because they went on to score; and I tackled Jack Snow and broke his nose, and he claimed I slugged him. So I got to be sort of a marked guy, and it really came home in a game with the Browns.

"That was the game I clotheslined Gary Collins in the end zone with us leading 10-0. I guess I really decked him. As a result, they put the ball on our one-yard line. Bad things started happening to me about then. Our defensive captain, Lonnie Warwick, got so mad at what I'd done that he was still standing there chewing me out when Cleveland got up on the line and snapped the ball. They gave the ball to LeRoy Kelly and ran right over Warwick and knocked the bejeesus out of him. So now he was really mad because he not only got creamed while chewing me out but the Browns scored. So now he chewed me out all the way down the field, over to our bench, and right into our dressing room at the half.

"I figure I was out of the woods with that, but early in the third period they called a sweep and here come their two guards out of there — I think Gene Hickerson was one of them — and they have got eyes only for me. The play is going one way and they're coming another. They chase me for 30 or 40 yards downfield and practically into the stands. The only thing that saved me was the brick wall. They had to slow up or they would have taken it with them.

"But it was even worse in the game with the 49ers. Dave Parks, their flanker, was playing with a couple of broken ribs. The first guy that hit him was our cornerback, Mike Fitzgerald. Parks went out for a few plays. He came back and I got him on the sidelines, several series later, and landed on his back. He was really in pain. Well, it was one of those things that happens when you go full-bore. They gave me a penalty for hitting him while he was out of bounds.

"So we exchanged the ball a few times and they were on offense again. It was just a routine play, off tackle. I remember coming up on the play, the guy was down, and I stopped. I just about had my hands on my hips and Walter Rock, their tackle, came flying through the air and buried his helmet into my chest, right in the sternum.

"It knocked the wind out of me, and I was lying there and moaning and I did not let him know that I was hurt. I got back up and went back to the defensive huddle. I was just trying to catch my breath in the huddle, and Warwick was standing there and he was saying, 'for Christ sake, shut up so the guys can hear the signals.'

"I mean, how's that for sensitivity?"

"I'm sure Rock felt he had evened the score between Parks and me. The reason I can say that is that he was absolutely right. I hurt for six weeks after.

"It took me a year under Grant to smarten up. I think a lot of guys started doing that the next year. He told us you may as well classify the league into three divisions—the lower, middle and top—and that we would know we were advancing if we could beat the teams in the divisions above you. He began to reach the guys when he talked about how to play smart football— that you could actually get rid of the mistakes that beat you by working on them and controling your actions and using your head. I think the team started to take on some of Grant's attitude in 1968. We played it cooler. We learned you can play tough and aggressive football and still keep your emotions under control. I'll tell you why we learned that. Because if you didn't, you were going to be on the bench or some place else.

"So he would tell you you could knock the hell out of a guy, but don't do it if it is going to cost you. Always a practical guy, Bud.

"A lot of the players had the same kind of attitude I did. I mean Marshall, Eller, Warwick, a lot of them. We led the world in penalties in 1967.

"What it meant for me personally was that I toned down in 1968 and got just one in 1969, in a game where I wound up as an innocent victim, which was the worst blow of all.

"We were playing the Packers in the University of Minnesota stadium and I chased Elijah Pitts all the way across the field. Wally Hilgenberg knocked him out of bounds. I hit him on a sort-of follow-through and got 15 yards. I came off and Grant grabbed me right away. He said he thought I had learned not to do that stuff. I said, 'it's the last time.' Grant said that he had no doubt about that. That was right about the time I got my bell rung by Forrest Gregg, and it was a shame, because I was just a bystander. Warwick should have taken the blow, actually.

"Bobby Bryant intercepted the ball and had fallen down. He got up. He started coming up field so I started looking for somebody to hit. I was just going to block Gregg when Warwick hit him head on. Gregg went down on his knees. I pulled off because, well he was on his knees and he weighed something like 260 pounds, and there just ain't no sense in hitting a man that large in that condition.

"So I jumped over him. The films showed that I put my hand on his head like so, using it as a brace. I vaulted over him and hit the ground, rolled over and got up. It showed that in the films, but as you know there ain't any instant replay on the field for Forrest Gregg to see me innocently jumping over him. All he saw was me getting up after somebody belted him. It was a case of the sins of the past returning to haunt me, I suppose. But there wasn't any ghost wearing No. 75. It was Gregg all right, and he's got the biggest damn forearm you ever saw. I saw it just as he was driving it into the birdcage I was wearing, the one with the bars down and across.

"If I didn't have that birdcage on, he would have flattened my nose beyond repair. I felt my neck snap back, and I was actually knocked goofy. He knocked me silly. Stunned me. They said I was on the sidelines talking like a bird.

"I talked to him later, and though I didn't figure it was my fault, I don't guess it hurts a guy to apologize. It took him a little while to cool off because they had kicked him out of the game, and that might have hurt the Packers. The thing is, you don't want guys like Gregg carrying any grudge. It tends to take some of the joy out of this game.

"He retired again this year, I noticed. But he retired last year, and came back. Like I told him, I bear absolutely no animosity."

Around the lockerroom they contend that within one more year and a course at Cambridge, Hackbart may put in for the British ambassadorship.

"I owe my modest successes," he said, with controled detachment, "to the fine example of our leader."

Sew no choir boy collars yet for Dale Hackbart, however. He is getting older, and he may not play regularly, but not many people in the National Football League let it all hang out so publicly and recklessly on kickoff plays. His tackle on the Los Angeles Ram runback man, Ron Smith, in the divisional title game will rank with the stark cold-blooded assaults of the decade. Smith caught the kickoff near his goal line, took two strides upfield, and veered obliviously into the oncoming Hackbart at the 12-yard line. He was all but congealed by the impact.

The officials nearly penalized the Rams coach, George Allen, for allowing an unarmed man in a combat zone.

Chapter XXII

"Football is a kid's game, it's fun. Only we play it with grown men and big cameras and millions of people paying $6 a head to watch."

—Joe Kapp, Quarterback.

He was oddly cast as a messiah. His battlefield voice had the timbre of a breaking logjam, and his jaw testified to the ravages of at least one collision with a beer bottle and a thousand more with blitzing linebackers.

When he walked it was with a happy caballero swagger made up of equal parts of gusto, defiance and knobby knees; and in full gallop he resembled an angry butcher pursuing a sausage thief.

When he passed, all that was predictable about the trajectory of the ball was that it would come down. Its flight occasionally was marked by tangential wobbles, making it appear dangerously out of control.

These and other random imperfections conspired to stir within him a genius for being underrated and sporadically scorned. It was a condition he suffered with tolerant restraint, and a sympathy for the misguided. After eight years of playing football on the high tundra of Canada, he moved about with the bearing of a man to whom most of the disasters of life have already happened.

He was a large man, Joe Kapp. He confronted the world with a round, bronzed and inquisitive face that invited friendliness. But his belligerent forearms often found their way into the ribcages of surprised defensive linemen not accustomed to arguments from quarterbacks.

He might have sprung from anywhere out of the roistering frontier west—the sawmills, the oil fields, the dusty street shootout, or the traplines. Where he came from, in truth, was the Mexican-American shanties of California, and he would never forget it. He belonged as much to John Steinbeck and the Grapes of Wrath as to Pappy Waldorf and the California Split T. If he didn't know how to play football, he might have led a grape boycott. He was a man of appetites, compassions, venture, and spouting optimisms. He wore a helmet instead of a sombrero and he might have eaten caviar instead of refried beans, except that he preferred not to because wherever he wandered on the football prairie he was a man of the folk. He was their delight and sorrow, their head conquistadore one week and their lugubrious Sancho Panza the next.

In an extraordinary way, Joe Kapp was part football player and part eminent domain. There were stars whom the fans gave the respect of distance, their gaping detachment—John Unitas, Gale Sayers, Jim Brown. There were others they envied and therefore told them to show-me—Paul Hornung, Joe Namath, Sam Huff. There were still others they purely idolized, like Doak Walker.

Joe Kapp they commandeered and integrated into the neighborhood. He was communal property. He had no charisma nor vainglorious glamor. They liked him best when he rode around town in his 1939 LaSalle. They suffered most when the coach would send Joe back out for another series after two straight interceptions, when everybody in the park could see the defensive backs were flipping coins to decide who was going to intercept the ball as it fluttered earthward. It was bad enough they flipped coins. BUT TWO OUT OF THREE?

His passes did not always flutter with the Vikings, nor even very often, but just often enough to create an invigorating sense of suspense among the audiences and the receivers. In Canada, especially in the earlier days before the savage enemy rushes had exacted their attrition, Joe's passes almost never wobbled. He could—and, of course, often still does—zoom the football with velocity and character. It was not unusual for him to fire 60 yards crossfield for a five-yard advance. He had that control and power. On the football field he was a zestful, uncomplicated physical person, a 6 foot 3 inch, 215-pound heavyweight who somehow happened to play quarterback. He might have played any other position. There were skeptics who suggested now and then that he should have.

He looked on football as fun and games, a gambol in the pasture for which people paid $6 a seat to watch. He knew it was a make-believe war, all that violence and those grim vows and that big money. But he played it both ways, as a grenadier-for-hire and as a rollicking playground brawler.

His Dagwood Bumstead gait with the football amused his rivals until he piled into them. After the word got around, nobody messed with Joe Kapp. He was a Big John character, serio-comic at times because of the blunders that his complete earnestness and bravery would lead him to. Very few high-price athletes stumbled so publicly. But as much as any man who has ever played before the millions, he performed with a fearlessness and utter commitment to the men around him that honored his every action, even when he was flopping.

People he met quickly gave him their affection. He struck them as one of those precarious circuit riders who travel a thin street between the canonizers and the lynchers. Once in a while the twain met in the same game, and there was hell to pay, especially for Joe.

He was the son of a Mexican-American mother and a German-American father. It was a heritage that did not surprise at least one admirer who characterized Kapp as "a guy who comes on like Poncho Villa and goes around end like the Rhine — slowly but inevitably."

Despite the money pinch in his childhood and the predictable alley fights, Joe Kapp believed himself ordained for success, in whatever endeavor. But wherever Joe Kapp went in San Fernando, Salinas, Newhall or Berkeley, a ball of some description was at hand.

He was one of the very best high school basketball players in California and certainly one of its most formidable football players. They gave him a scholarship to California, and he responded by making the basketball team and taking the football team to the Rose Bowl.

It was never settled as to which displayed Joe at his truculent best. On his one appearance as a basketball player in Madison Square Garden, a fight broke out between the California team and its rival. An armistice intruded before Joe had time to sufficiently defend the Golden Bears' honor against his chosen opponent. To guard against any such future dereliction, Joe walked up to the other and introduced himself:

"My name," he said, "is Joe Kapp.

"Look me up if it starts up again."

As a footballer he was a winning quarterback, although the mention of his name did not always paralyze the opposition out of hand. Nor was he surrounded by All-Americans. But he threw and ran hard enough to attract the curiosity of one Jim Finks, then the general manager of the Calgary Rough Riders of the Canadian League. The Canadians were the hit-and-run shoppers at the American football counters. Ten and 15 years before, when they competed actively for some of the high priority NFL and AFL draft choices, they splurged on one or two players and filled the rest of their squads with Canadians and American discards.

Like everybody else in the recruiting wars of the 1950s and 1960s, they used the wiles of the marketplace. Somehow the American pros got the impression, before their drafts, that Joe Kapp was already boxed-up for Calgary. It was not clear who planted this impression, but Jim Finks reputedly was an enthusiastic provincial gardener. Nobody drafted Joe higher than 17th in the NFL, and he signed with Finks.

Joe Kapp arrived in Canada with immediate plans to capture the dominion. His first setback occurred in a Montreal saloon after an exhibition game. Kapp walked in innocently and ordered a beer. The bottle arrived from an unexpected angle, in the hand of an enraged teammate later found to be mentally unstable. The bottle smashed into Kapp's jaw and shattered, sending blood spurting out of his face. Kapp began swinging in self-defense. Other squad members restrained him and tried to stem the bleeding. Finks himself drove the stricken young quarterback to the hospital. They put 100 stitches in Joe's jaw and eventually got it back together in a general sort of way.

Wooly new versions of how he got his jaw scars accompany Joe Kapp in his suspenseful progress through life. Fatalistically, he never tries hard to discourage them.

"The people," he shrugs, "are entitled to their legends. I never knew what provoked the guy. He came bawling to me the next day that it was a mistake, all a mistake. I told him we both ought to be grateful for small mistakes. If the bottle would have landed a couple inches lower he would have got my jugular vein, and the whole Canadian blood bank wouldn't have saved me."

Finks traded Joe to Vancouver two years later in 1961 in an effort to build his own team. Joe was the quarterback in British Columbia for six years and for a time ranked right with the Mounties and Lake Louise as a prime Canadian resource. His team won the Grey Cup in 1963, a year in which Joe was named the most valuable player in the league. He played through 1966, contented enough but never really shaking off the ambition to lay his boots in the bigger goldfields and shorter endzones of the American professional leagues. His wanderlust was further goaded by a messy coaching situation at Vancouver.

Accordingly, Joe decided that legal technicalities should not impede the larger design of pure justice. So he signed a contract with Houston of the American Football League. Under this arrangement, Joe would play out his option with Vancouver in 1967 and then transfer his loyalties to Houston in 1968.

This scheme was met with vigorous approval in the front office of the Houston Oilers but very little ardor in the front office of the British Columbia Lions. Vancouver saw so little merit in the plan, in fact, that it suspended Joe and told him to go to hell.

It also suggested the same destination for Houston—although Texas critics might argue this was no real choice at all. Vancouver threatened to sue the Oilers for alienation, conspiracy, misrepresentation, and several other offenses against the monarchy.

Joe Kapp obviously was not going to play for Vancouver in

1967, and that was a fact. He also was not going to play for Houston in 1968, and that was a blessing.

At about this time Harry Peter (Bud) Grant was surveying his uneven ranks in Mankato. In some measure the camp resembled a replacement depot. Tarkenton had departed, replaced by half-back Clint Jones, the All-American halfback from Michigan, and Bob Grim, a running back-flanker from Oregon State. They would be joined a year later by Ron Yary, the mammoth tackle from Southern Cal, and two years later by Ed White, the college-educated blacksmith from California.

None of this, however, seemed quite to counterbalance the 20 touchdown passes the club came to expect annually from Tarkenton. Grant did look admiringly on the agile vastness of the rookie tackle Alan Page. He was the bounty of still another off-season trade—the one of Tommy Mason and Hal Bedsole for the Los Angeles Rams' No. 1 draft choice (Page) and Marlin McKeever, the tight end.

Something, however, appeared to be missing, Grant sensed.

"To put it in simplest terms," he said, "it was a quarterback."

He concluded that Vandy had only a mediocre arm and, after four years subordinate to Tarkenton, was victimized by the second-string syndrome that is a very definite hazard in the pro football leagues. Bob Berry would have to battle his lack of size forever and John Hankinson could not play big league football.

Grant was not surprised when Finks reached the same conclusion simultaneously. They could have bargained around the league. But in late August in the NFL a football team is lucky to find an available quarterback who can hold the ball for extra points.

They decided to collect on all of their old debts among their pals and rivals in the dominion and enlist Joe Kapp to quarter-back the Vikings. They did not expect Joe Kapp to win the title for them in 1967. They did expect him to have better luck with flying beer bottles and, maybe, to steal a few games here and there in the construction of a better football team for 1968.

Finks called the Vancouver Lions' president. He agreed it really was a raw deal and an affront to the queen what Houston tried to do by signing Kapp. And that if Kapp wasn't going to play for Vancouver and couldn't play for Houston, wouldn't it be nice if all parties except the contemptible Oilers could salvage something by giving Joe a place to roost—namely Minnesota?

The Lions' president named the salvageable figure. Finks winced, but said he thought it did have a round, strong solidity to soothe all lingering grievances. In the end, and in various forms, it came to well over $100,000—including the compensations the Vikings made confidentially to teams like Calgary, Winnipeg, Edmonton, Toronto and a couple of others who agreed to waive Joe out of the league.

The negotiations were narrowed to the Vikings and Joe's attorney, who prolonged them enough to insure a largely catastrophic season for both his client and the Vikings in 1967.

By way of proving that the passage of three years had not lessened his fondness for the economics of disaster, the lawyer did it all over again in 1970.

The prognosis, any football man of discernment could tell immediately, was pretty horrible. Kapp joined the Vikings a couple of weeks before the start of the season. He didn't know Grant's coaching, Grant's system or the prefix number of his headset. He didn't know the Vikings, the receivers, Mick Tingelhoff's snapback quirks or the number of lakes in Minnesota. He didn't have the mistiest notion about the habits of the NFL defensive backs, information that is as basic and indispensable for the quarterback as the aisle numbers are for the checkout boy.

He didn't know how to handle the blitz in Grant's offense, which made the mystery just about unanimous. He was also somewhat out of shape from idleness during the legal skirmishes. And, to complete the lamentable inventory, his voice was hoarse, making it tough for the flankers to understand him.

Joe's first response to these discouragements was to advise Bill McGrane, the Vikings' public relations man, on arrival from Canada:

"My intention is to burn up this league."

"Immediately?" asked McGrane, impressed.

"No, you always have to go through a familiarization process. I'd like to get acquainted with my new teammates, first."

There is nothing like a fresh breath of dynamic thinking, Kapp decided, with which to break the ice in new surroundings.

His first view of the Vikings was at a Friday night exhibition game in Cleveland's Municipal Stadium, where the purple heads scored a psychic breakthrough by nearly hypnotizing 80,000 people into a deep and bottomless sleep while defeating Atlanta.

A tactful man under his outgoing exterior, Kapp decided not to confide to Grant and his new lockerroom neighbors his earliest suspicions about the Viking offense.

Still, Joe Kapp could not restrain a small confidence here and there that he was ready to seize the NFL by its very tendrils.

"The first time I met Joe," Hackbart remembers, "was right after that exhibition game in Cleveland when we got back to the Holiday Inn at two in the morning. He was rooming with McKeever. They had a couple of beers over there, and I walked into the room and introduced myself. I just got the impression that Joe was going to take over and he was the leader and he was going to run the whole show.

"So I figured this is just one helluva accomplishment, since Joe has been with the club for only six hours. So I said I was glad to hear that, but that it might take a couple of days at least.

"Don't get me wrong. There are guys who you will listen to when they talk that way and guys you just brush off and tell them to dry up. Kapp got a kick out of football, you could tell that right off. I knew he played eight years in Canada, so he's no fuzzy kid. He's a good beer drinker and he's sociable, and you could see he was respectful of the others, so you don't put a guy like this down right away even though he hasn't put on a jock yet for this club.

"He asked about the players on our team and asked what kind of league it is, and then he just came right out and told me that he was going to make a hit in this league. He was just going to do it. He said straight-out he was going to rip the league up. And even if I didn't believe it, I could tell he meant it, which counted for something, anyway. The only thing I said was 'you know, you are going to have to make a believer out of me, because there are a lot of players that come into the league with that kind of attitude, and a lot of them that have not made it.' But the point is that when Joe talked like that, even before he put on a uniform, it didn't bother you because he wasn't a wise-ass or some slick talking clubhouse politician.

"But I just don't think he realized how tough it was going to be trying to recognize defenses, getting his own offense down, even learning the faces of the guys he was playing with. The things every other quarterback in the league was doing by second nature, Joe had to think out while he was doing them."

Frequently during this thoughtful process an enemy tackle would intervene and Joe would complete the problem lying in a crumpled position and looking at third and 18.

But there was an unquenchable elan about this football beachcomber, a stubborn romance that conjured images of the hard-knock wayfarers of history — Marco Polo, Death Valley Scotty and Sam McGrew of Lake LaBarge.

He was the troubled but unflappable helmsmen, in that first year, paddling about with indestructible optimism at the very moment he was leading everybody in the boat over the waterfall.

He had the corner lot kid's pure affection for playing football, but eight years of dodging third-down ambushes had given him a faintly hunted posture. The gunfighters who sat with their backs to the wallboards would have understood.

His teammates accepted him almost immediately. It took the fans at least one year to comprehend him and at least another to grant him equality. But Joe confronted this lack of adulation with abiding calm and faith in ultimate justice.

With the fans, his first hurdle was being compared with the departed Tarkenton. "I figure," he used to say, "I can't scramble like Tarkenton, but I got to move around now and then. I may not run with much speed, but I make up for it with a lot of desperation."

His response to the cool inquisitiveness of the Sunday parking lot tailgaters was the smiling chumminess of his Mexican-American temperament. He had one of those well-stitched but sunny faces that reflect a forgiving attitude toward the iniquities of the world.

They would hear him calling his play at the line of scrimmage in a loud, authoritative, raspy voice. It might have been classified as tequilla-tempered baritone. They would see the enemy defenses constantly blitzing and threatening to blitz, trying to confuse the stranger. The defenses might have spared themselves the energy. During his first year with the Vikings, Joe was confused coming out of the lockerroom.

And they would see Joe in that run-from-daylight stride, moving without much grace but a certain inspired urgency.

Joe would roll to the right. He would start in slow gear and seem to throttle down as the traffic congested. His primary receiver was covered. His secondary receiver was covered. The enemy would hit Joe twice and wait for him to fall. He would stumble about in a controlled disorder, and then he would see Red Phillips in the end zone and throw off balance.

The ball did not have much thrust at this point, but it did reveal some symptom of guided flight. At times, astonishingly, it would settle in Phillips' arms.

And afterwards, on some of the better days, he would stand in the stadium parking lot, socializing with teammates and his tentative new public. A chattering blonde would come up to him and ask for the autograph of the new matinee celebrity.

"Aren't you the quarterback, Al Capp?" she would ask.

And Joe would view her evenly, his Baja smile bespeaking the charity of the ages.

"It's Joe, lady," he would say, "Joe Kapp."

And as she trailed off he would remark to sympathizers, "It's okay. People have trouble with my name. At least she didn't get an 'r' in the last name, like some of them do."

But the ballplayers took an earlier reading on this heavyfooted nomad from the mountains. He might not chase Unitas out of the league, they decided, but he was man enough to play with them, all right.

By disposition and calling, Kapp was a happy mixer. If he was going to be their quarterback (and it was generally understood that he would replace Vandy after a decent acclimatization) he would have to get to know the Vikings in the only way that was permanent — in the mauling and stomping on the football field.

Within a week of Joe's arrival Grant was surprised to hear a general yelping and gibing whenever Kapp took over at quarterback in the passing scrimmages.

"What he didn't know," Kapp tells now, "is that I made some side bets with the guys that whoever intercepted a pass from me got a buck. And if I beat the defense for a touchdown, I got a buck. I just thought it was up to me to show that I wanted to belong, to get in on the inside horseplay. I mean when you want to quarterback the team and you come in cold like I did, you have to let them know how you tick and what kind you are. If they don't buy it, you're out of luck. It's not that you try to make an impression. All you do is try to join up, to sign in. I think they understood that.

"So when I'd come in there, you'd hear the defense crowing, 'let's get some of this guy's money' and all kinds of noise. Well, I threw a couple for touchdowns but the biggest noise came when Warwick intercepted one and he took off down the sidelines like Gale Sayers, so I went over to cover and I hit him a shouldershot. I'm sure I didn't shake him up much. But in these bets for laughs, you understand, it's your personality that comes through a little. It just has to if you want to lead the team. And I wanted to lead that team, even if most of them didn't know me from Adam the first few weeks.

"I'll tell you how I look at football. First, it's a kid's game. You can't take yourself too seriously all the time. I mean people are starving in a lot of parts of the world. Christ, they're starving in this country. So what is this game we're playing? It's basically a game for the kids with runny noses. Only we play it with grown men and big cameras and millions of people who pay $6.00 a head to watch it. A hundred million others spend all Sunday watching it, because it is supposed to be some kind of micro-what the hell ever the word is, a micro-something of the big bad violent world. But the world doesn't end Sunday night, no matter who wins. So that's why I don't have trouble finding time to have a joke in the lockerroom.

"But now I'll say this. Once you decide this is your profession, even though you don't have to buy all this violent world bull, there is only one thing to do in it, and that is win.

"If you're a quarterback coming to a new team like I did, you have to have acceptance. So you just try to project a little. It's not much different than trying out for your high school team.

You just go out there and play the best way you can. The quarterback's job is to provide the pass, the same in Salinas, Berkeley, Calgary, Vancouver and Metropolitan Stadium. It doesn't make a damn how you provide the pass. Listen. All this business about me not looking pretty as a quarterback, or throwing end-over-end passes. You know how much that fazes me? Not a goddam bit. I played with good clubs, bad clubs, in sunshine and blizzards in Canada, and I knew when I came into the NFL that I could pass. I have picked teams apart and I can do it any day of the week, given the time and the receivers. So I think I can do it when I have to, I mean provide the pass. I feel I can throw on the run, if that's in our program, which it is; and do some bootlegs and roll-out type of stuff. I think I can throw deep and hit the sidelines stuff. I'm not saying I can do it alone. Christ, football is nothing without the whole bunch. I mean when you get that beautiful inner relationship.

"But when things don't work out, there's one thing that I will do and I have done all my career, and I'm not the guy to take off in terror before I look. But if there's nothing left, I will run. Maybe I should do it a little more because sometimes I get over-optimistic and try to force the ball through. I may look bad running, but I can usually make some yards. And I don't go for that first-down and fall-down business, either. They pay me to advance the ball as far as I can. I don't worry about getting hurt.

"So I thought about all these things when I came down to the Vikings, and I decided I wasn't going to change my philosophy any. I play for me. I try to be honest about it. I don't play for the coach, the fans, the press, anybody. I play for me first.

"That may sound very selfish and make me look like a hypocrite when I say football is great only when everybody is involved, like 40 for 60 minutes. But I'm talking about the satisfaction it gives ME first, to be with a winner. I think if everybody goes into it that way, you WILL be a winner. The real selfish guy is the one who is worrying about his statistics, or how he looks, or if he's going to get the rap. I don't want those guys on the ball club. I don't want to be anywhere near them.

"Yes, I had some troubles getting off the ground. There was

our own offense, learning it and then trying to do something with it, because it was pretty fundamental the first year. Then the other guy's defense and personnel, especially my ignorance of the cornerbacks. I begin a game now, I look at the corners, and I start right away. What kind of help are they getting from the linebackers or other defensive backs, underneath and on top. How good is this guy on the corner? Has he got guts, and if he doesn't, that's where you start. Right there. That's going to get you something. It's the toughest position, cornerback, ever invented.

"But once you get some working knowledge, a takeoff point, the rest comes fast. But this business of reading keys can be overdone. Some of it really is a lot of b.s. Sooner or later you find out which way they are going and you drill the football. That's what you do. You drill the football. Just like on the playground.

"But now let's say you got the thing going, and we get back to this thing about the team and everybody rolling together. Let me tell you. A long ball to Gene Washington may thrill me and Washington and the fans and Grant and it's lovely to have six points on the board. But you know what the real thrill is in this crazy business? I'll tell you. It's one of those long ten-play drives. This is the really great thing for an offensive team in football, because the guys who get the satisfaction are those big number 50s and 60s and 70s out in front of you. This is no phony rah-rah stuff. It's the truth. Nothing holds a team together and makes it whole, like one of those drives.

"It tells you your guys on the line are the hitters. You don't score this time with a thoroughbred like Gene putting a move and some steps on the defensive back and it's all over. You score because 11 guys are hitting. It's a great feeling. I don't know, it's like a carpenter putting all the nails in and putting the chair together, or the cabinet, or whatever. And the best feeling is not when the big roar comes and Brownie goes into the end zone and Freddie comes out there to kick, but the best feeling is RIGHT WHEN IT'S HAPPENING. You can feel it in the huddle—the guys want to go back there and keep it going. Right then, right there. Lombardi called it love. He was pretty close to it. You trust these guys. And when it's over, they're the ones you want to celebrate with. I mean they're the ones you want to be with right after the ball game. The fans coming on the field and all, that's no good. I think the treatment a ballplayer gets in Minnesota, now, is just about tops. But frankly, when the fans run onto the field and try to be part of the ball game, so to speak, even though their intentions are good and they want to grab you and shake your hand, why it's just a pain in the ass. People can get hurt, and besides, the guys you want to shake hands with are the guys with the purple shirts."

With his outgoing nature and willingness to oblige, Kapp presented no personality problem to Grant, or VanderKelen for that matter, the man he was trying to shoot out of a job.

Through the first six weeks, in fact, Vandy was his most valuable tutor. They talked about defenses, where X team was vulnerable, what it meant when the Packer free safety made this move or that. He counseled Joe willingly, aware he was hastening his departure not only as the Vikings' interim No. 1 quarterback, but probably from the payroll.

"What good would it have done to play it cagey," Vandy remarked. "Kapp was one helluva confused guy when he joined the team, and I don't blame him. He was decent to me, and there was no reason to hold anything back. If I was going better, I might have had some reason to resent his moving in. I never could get going early in the season. And I didn't in 1967. Kapp wasn't exactly wearing out the scoreboard himself. I suppose you can say we were advising each other, but maybe consoling would be a better word."

Chapter XXIII

*"When Carl Eller would leap high and lift his arm
skyward to thwart a forward pass, he did it with the
appearance of a scriptural avenger."*

And so it was that late in the game on Friday night in Los
Angeles, with the Vikings' trailing by 39-3, they sent in Joe Kapp
to pay his professional courtesies to the Rams and the NFL after
eight years in the Klondike.

The Rams' defense regarded the curiously-determined intruder
with a minimum of fright.

"Here comes Sgt. Preston of the Yukon," one of the linebackers
announced hospitably.

With his latent feeling for the dramatic occasion, Joe paused
for some suitably respectful greeting to mark his introduction
to the imperial Rams of The World's Greatest Football League.

Scanning the secondary to see that the audience was attentive,
Joe declared:

"Screw you, Rams."

There is no evidence that the Rams took any special umbrage at
this unflattering decree. Kapp wasn't the first to make the
suggestion, after all, and the ball game did seem pretty secure
from any stray miracles.

Still, in the spirit of genial combat, they flattened Joe on the
nearest available play.

Bud's decision to kick a field goal in that game with a few
minutes left and the score 32-0 was the public's first intimation
that the new coach was going to try his level best to avoid rash
decisions and reckless conduct.

Football audiences later came to understand Bud, to see — sometimes with a limp resignation — that there was always some gray, obstinate logic hovering over even his most obscure decisions.

After being grossly abused by the Rams all night, he reasoned, it was important to the team psychologically to get SOMETHING on the board. The wisdom of this course was lost on all of the back-home folk. They were disoriented to begin with in the absence of television (late-night line charges and all) and were trying to muddle through by radio. It didn't bother the players, especially. Nor did it a year later when Bud met that ultimate test of all champions by showing his ability to repeat. He had Freddie kick another field goal again with the score 33-0 in favor of the Rams and a minute or so left.

By then, in late-season of 1968, Bud had converted most of the skeptics on the ball club and he had won enough games to change the prevailing disposition of the home crowd from one of fitful drowsiness to hopeful tolerance.

Methodically, at fan club meetings, he gave the professional's explanation of his strategic caution. They listened politely but still rolled their eyes a little when he finished.

To them, Bud made maddening moves that seemed to ignore the most rudimentary needs for some kind of spark that would relieve the smothering stodginess of his team's performance. He ordered a punt in one game with the team trailing by 11 points and in posssssion not far from midfield, with 3½ minutes remaining. He went for field goals when the fan's gambling heart throbbed for just a wisp of daring to rescue him from the dreary mathematics of the professional's manual of odds.

"How much of a gamble is it," the fan would mourn, "when you're in last place?"

The Vikings once conducted a splendidly-executed land offensive that carried them 80 yards with the score 17-0 against them and eight minutes left. It was a brilliant stroke except that it consumed five minutes and had everybody in the stadium climbing the wall except George Halas and the Bears' defensive line.

Grant did not specify that the drive should consume five

minutes, of course, but there was something about the Vikings' destiny in 1967 that made it appear that way. Their every action seemed influenced by some devious dark cloud. Against the Cardinals they blew an 11-point lead with 7½ minutes left. Against the Packers they lost to a field goal with 10 seconds remaining after they had the lead and possession of the ball with a little more than a minute to go. And each time they seemed to have exhausted all known avenues to blow a game or the lead, they would surprise their adherents and discover another.

The fan's frustration gradually expanded into a form of the free-for-all shakes. Each Sunday afternoon become a countdown to neurosis.

On Nov. 10 it reached the stage of absolute contagion when the Vikings' suicidal urges collided with those of the Detroit Lions. Before it was over, everybody in the park—the Vikings, the Lions, the fans, and the sponsors—were willing to settle for a tie, if this was the ultimate price of escape.

By that time the Vikings already had tied two games and had developed a wily versatility in avoiding both victory and defeat.

The Lions had no such experience, but they balanced this disadvantage by being a pretty lousy ball club. Nonetheless, the Lions had towering handicaps to overcome in shooting for a tie. For one thing, they finished with a 17 to 7 advantage in first downs and a 366-to 177-yard advantage in terrain.

And yet Detroit managed to achieve a 10-10 tie with enviable aplomb. This they did by fumbling 11 times, a feat never before performed in 47 years of professional football.

Eleven fumbles by the Lions left the Vikings virtually stymied. It was now almost impossible to visualize a team—the Vikings— not being able to win a game in which the opposition blundered that extravagantly.

But they reacted to the challenge with unhurried dignity and a seasoned tread. And the fans, at first almost engulfed by indifference, were caught up in the rising tension. Could these two teams overcome the mutual peril that seemed to put first one and then the other on the verge of winning?

The Vikings were the first to answer. With the score 10-10 they launched a drive that carried to the Lion 35, within field goal range. At this very juncture when success threatened, they recovered smartly and started a majestic march in reverse.

They swept all before them, and then they started on all behind them. Irresistibly they moved backwards, in progressively larger leaps, rebuffing all efforts to contain them. Joe lost seven on a blitz, then he lost nine. By now they had full momentum. Machine-like, they moved toward their own goal line.

The odds were against another long loss, however, because everyone in the arena knew the Lions were going to blitz again. The Vikings prevailed nonetheless and got Kapp thrown for another, culminating loss of 13 yards. This made a first down unreachable even for Bobby Walden, the punter.

So now the hand of opportunity turned irrevocably to the Lions. They had already fumbled 10 times, tying the record. It was so bad their kickoff man had to place the ball three times to start the second half, because it kept falling off the tee. The question was: Could the Lions do it again now, in the clutch?

Joe Schmidt sent in a play and the messenger returned hurriedly to the sideline, looking suspiciously like a man telling the coach: "The fullback says he don't WANT the ball."

But he got it and, naturally, fumbled.

It went that way all year with the Vikings.

And yet Grant held them together because he felt in his bones his low-key, plodding football in 1967 was right for the team even if it didn't produce much in the winning column. The transition gaps were too big, emotionally and philosophically, to allow him the luxury of go-for-broke football. It could have made his football players a weekly laugh-in around the league, which they were not. They could take the sighs and the snickers and the incipient jeers toward the end of the season, because there was quality in the team and, Grant was convinced, much character.

Kapp would have to be part of that. And Kapp was bridling a little because Grant restrained his swashbuckler's heart in the interests of keeping the ball in the park.

They lost football games, but they were acquiring something unnoticed by the fans and sometimes even by the coaching staff. And this was a tough-minded trust and loyalty to each other.

It began to express itself in the hard times of 1967 and reached fulfillment when the ball finally bounced right for them in 1969.

It revolved initially around Eller, who was maturing in his emotional outlook in a way that matched his enormous physical strength, and Marshall, Tingelhoff, Alderman, Mackbee, Warwick and Winston.

From the beginning the blacks had meager representation on the ball club—once past training camp. Aside from Marshall, the ones that did make the roster were usually hanging on precariously and were never able to achieve a role of spiritual leadership.

Marshall could have. But in his early years he was saddled with financial problems and moved by airy spirits. The combination made it hard for him to qualify as a social stabilizer.

By the mid 60s, however, the Vikings discovered one of their problems may have been the distinctly white cast to the roster. So thereafter came Jones and Washington and Reed and Henderson, Page, Harris, West, and others.

There had been black-white problems on many teams. With the Vikings, they were minimal. The black leaders — Eller, Marshall, Mackbee — mixed well with the whites. Most of their parties were integrated. Marshall, in fact, was the club's social lion. His house parties often brought in people like Kapp, Kassulke, Alderman, Brown, Dickson and other whites; the Negroes plus the neighbors and a couple of vagrant parachutists now and then.

But, as much as anyone, Eller wore the cloth of leadership for the Viking defense. In his early days he was a leisurely, irresponsible boy-giant, capable of athletic deeds beyond almost all mortals in hip-pads. But he fell into spasms of aimless football. So do almost all rookies, surely. But Eller had so much size, strength, and mobility his errors seemed to demand special explanations, because he was a very special athlete.

They called him Moose. Almost all of them liked him, first for the easy adolescence with which he carried his strength, but later for his willing acceptance of the obligations that went with his competitive stature.

"In the years when things were going bad," Mackbee said,

"I remember we used to meet quite often at Carl's apartment—
I mean, the defense. We would get some booze and wine and
sit around after the game playing a little nickel and dime poker
and talking it out. We knew the offense wasn't going very good,
but we also knew it would get better and we had to hold our
own outfit together. Carl was great at that. He grew up pretty
fast. Pretty soon you found out there was a lot of stuff inside
this guy. What Grant was saying, I mean about keeping under
control, not doing anything to detour you from what was ahead
of you Sunday afternoon, Carl was saying in another way when
it was just the guys talking."

And so by 1968 Carl Eller was just about the best defensive
football player in the league. He had leveled the dip-and-soar
graph of his performances. Now he played not only with extraordinary power but reliability. And nobody in the National
Football League delivered that surmounting stroke of the great
competitor—the big play—as often or as indelibly as Carl Eller.

He would knock down passes, blocks kicks, recover fumbles,
and make open field tackles on the pass rush with a style and
sudden violence of a force of nature. When Carl Eller would
leap high and lift his arm skyward to thwart a forward pass,
he did it with the appearance of a scriptural avenger. The
spectacle had a statuesque quality. It would rarely be forgotten
by audiences who saw Eller at those times when the stakes of the
game and his personal avowal had aroused all his power to a
full commitment.

The realization that he was capable of these achievements
stimulated in the onetime poor black submissive kid from South
Carolina a new self-assured independence and reach for horizons.
He let some air into his personality. He started dressing as he
damned well pleased. He was mod and flamboyant but tasteful—
the New Breed. He went to Hollywood, and he may be an actor
yet. The kid who used to have trouble telling the sports writers
how - real - good - it - felt now would deliver very articulate and
thoughtful postgame critiques.

And finally he became the Bud Grant kind of professional, the
man of well-managed fervor on the field and detachment afterward. The Super Bowl loss appeared to be no personal tragedy

to Carl Eller. No doubt it bothered him. But the professional didn't wail or agonize or burp on the floor. He said the other guy played a helluva game and had a better day today, and we may be able to beat him the next time around.

All this was not entirely accidental. Grant, in a small way, abetted Eller's rise in esteem in the lockerroom. The big man had always been popular. Grant nudged him to new responsibility. Because he saw Grant's need and felt his man-to-man overtures, Eller responded. Men drew around him, not ostentatiously, but in the dozens of ways that athletes will when they feel respect and fondness for man who can produce in the crisis.

There was this kind of chemistry working in 1967, and it all seemed to froth over in a slapstick explosion one Sunday night at a team party. It could have meant a longterm squad civil war on another team. But with the Vikings it came to acquire the trappings of a Wagnerian ceremonial-turned-comic opera, wherein two antagonists met and hurled themselves at each other as the symbolic chieftains of separate realms. And when the contest over they retired with heads still aloft but eyes largely blackened and the realms still more or less in place.

A scenario like this could only mean that Kapp and Warwick were cast in the roles of the contending titans.

Warwick was the middle linebacker and the defensive signal caller, a tough, poverty-haunted kid from the Appalachia of West Virginia. He had huge shoulders and a gnarled, furrowed, weathered face. He played as though forever grateful somebody had given him a chance in pro football—and as though he might lose everything if he did not knock the head off every passing fullback. He could have been a bouncer or a coal miner, but he had nerve, ambition and an athletic instinct. And he hit like a boxcar.

"I've had a few battles, I admit," Joe Kapp recapitulated, "but this one had to be the goofiest.

"We played the Packers that day and lost 30-27 on a field goal in the last minute. I fumbled the ball. I was responsible. They won after I fumbled the ball. I had lost games before on a personal play of my own, but this was the first time in many years, and it was the first time it happened in the NFL.

"So I went home and drank some tequilla, with my wife. Now I like tequilla, of course. I call it a truth serum. I don't drink to excess. But I find tequilla an interesting drink.

"We had a party at the home of a suburban guy who follows the team. I always make the team party because I think that's a very important part of football. You should have a little party or some kind of discussion, or celebration. I don't care what you call it. I think there's a buildup from Monday through Sunday, and when it's all over, even if you lose the game—even though it's not a happy situation—there's a get-together with the players. This is the real enjoyable thing to me, talking to the players after the game. They are my people, the ones I believe. And in my years of playing I'd never missed one of those.

"But I felt so bad about this game that I thought about not going. I was just going to stay home with my wife and let the thing drain out of my head.

"But we went to the party and Lonnie and I started talking. He was one of the guys I really hit it off with. We have the same kind of disposition, I guess. Anyhow, he went out of his way to help me get situated when I moved to Minneapolis. We sat down many times and went over defenses. He would go over linebacker plays and tell me how they played it in the NFL and what I could look for. He was just a great help to me.

"So we were talking now in this recreation room of the guy's big house and I'm telling Lonnie it was my fault we lost the game. Now Lonnie wouldn't buy that. He was saying the defense was just as much to blame, and I'm saying it was the offense, me, that blew it. And it sounds like we're two of the greatest guys who ever lived, trying to puff the other guy up. But we keep at it, see, and pretty soon one of us is saying 'what the hell do you mean you got it figured right and I don't.'

"Before you know it we're eyeball-to-eyeball and nose-to-nose being such great, considerate guys. The trouble is I'm owly when I've had one or two past my limit and so is Warwick.

"He likes me but he can't figure out why I'm so goddamned stubborn. All of a sudden it looks like we're going to fight. So it proves we're not smart. I'm saying 'Lonnie, you're not giving me any out. I got to stand here and not let you run me.'

It looks like we're going to have a fight right in the basement.
Well, I'll say this. If Warwick was nice I wouldn't want him
on my team, because you've got to have him like that. I like him
like that. He's what you want out there, a guy that will fight you
to the bottom of the pit. We got other people like that, though
they control themselves a little better than Warwick and me, I
mean guys like Osborn and Brown. If you gave those two guys
baseball bats, they would take on the Viet Cong.

"Well, we went outside and I kept saying, 'Lonnie, this is
dumb.' He wanted to fight in the basement but I said 'no let's go
out and give me some room to run.' You know, trying to gag
it off. But now we're outside. It's fall and we're in the leaves.
The moon is up and we're out there in the goddamn fog like
we're in the Hounds of the Baskervilles. And, yeah, it's midnight.
I tried to spar and keep away from him, but he's a powerful
man. We both got hit. He put a mouse on me and I got a little
mouse on him and knocked his teeth loose just a bit. It was about
a two-minute match. He ended on top of me. I couldn't move.
And then Winston came out and was sort of refereeing and
sweeping up and eventually all of our good old buddies busted
it up.

"Warwick phones me the first thing in the morning. I wasn't
awake yet. He said we better go see the doctor, for our eyes,
you know. So we did. We had coffee and went to see the
doctor at Midway Hospital. My eye was closed and his was half
closed.

"I told Warwick, 'listen, this is going to get out, so let's go
see Bud.' We went into his office and told him what happened.
We both had bought the big sunglasses. His first words when
he saw us were 'What's all this Hollywood stuff? Take off your
glasses,' and I said 'No, we'd rather not.'" And we told him
the story. You know Bud—I don't think he'd look surprised if
the sky fell down. He just pointed out how ridiculous it was for
the two signal callers of the team to be standing out in the
middle of a lawn knocking each other silly.

"I mean when you come to think of it, it was pretty silly.
In addition to that, it hurt like hell."

With their dignities intact but their eyeballs purple, the two antagonists headed for a doubtful fate in the lockerroom at the hands of their peers.

Chapter XXIV

"Never chew out a player in front of his friends and teammates. It embarrasses him. Besides, you may be wrong." — Bud Grant's old coach.

On Sept. 22, 1968, Harry Peter Grant summoned John Beasley to his side in mid-afternoon in Milwaukee and told him:

"Tell Joe to go for it."

Was John Beasley surprised? Were the Green Bay Packers surprised? Did the Arabs expect to lose in six days? Was Calvin Coolidge throwing in with the radicals here in Milwaukee?

He was. For one play, anyhow. It may have been forgotten in the tumult of the Vikings' NFL championship celebration 15 months later. But in some odd, miniscule fashion it helped get them there.

Bud had stabilized the Vikings, but at harsh cost to their pugnacity. He was getting them disciplined and smarter, but they had lost the take-it-to-them impetuousness of their earlier years.

More than that, they had come to type Bud Grant as a football prude, a man with the right principles but no spirit of adventure. Football, a lot of them thought, ought to be more than slide-rule theories about percentages.

So on Sept. 22 The Minnesota Vikings led the Green Bay Packers 16-6 halfway through the third quarter. The Packers had just scored a touchdown and blown the extra point. But they had the look of resurgence. It seemed to heighten when the Vikings fell just short of a first down at their own 27-yard line.

They now stood at fourth down and two inches to go at the

27. They had a 10-point lead. The manual in this situation lists two options: (a) punt and (b) punt further.

Beasley bounded into the huddle. "The coach says go for it."

Joe Kapp, riverboat gamesman, lifted his helmet earflap ever so slightly to make certain Beasley had not said "throw for it," which undoubtedly would have been the best of all worlds for Joe.

Still, he had to admire Grant's stamina. Cautious old Bud had held out pretty long, at that, before bowing inevitably to Joe's theories about the football of joy. He was happy to see Bud Grant confirm his judgment.

Joe decided to call a quarterback sneak.

He grabbed the ball and shambled into the left side. LeRoy Caffey saw him coming and gathered him up on the line of scrimmage. Joe stopped, squirmed some more, and stopped again. They gave Joe three inches and the first down.

I have seen it run 25 times on replay. Each time I see the official signal first down I am convinced the official's old man fought with Zapata.

Whether the official still thrills to the saga of the Mexican revolution, however, his first down decision actually was irrelevant. The Packers could have taken over and scored, but they would not have won. Without trying to, Grant had suddenly humanized himself. Every rinkydink quarterback watching television would have gone for it, and everybody in the huddle would have done the same.

No professional coach would have, though; except, improbably, Bud Grant.

Was it one of those goony whims to which even the most self-possessed are entitled.

Don't be silly.

"Here was a situation," the man said, "where if we had punted the ball to them, they would have had good field position plus that momentum they had built up. A first down at the point would mean a tremendous lift for us and a loss of momentum for them. We had to do it. We weren't going to beat them playing defense the rest of the way."

Thus did Bud's good gray logic almost bury the Vikings' first redeeming act of whackiness in more than a year. But not quite.

No matter what happened in Milwaukee, they were more sure

234

now, a little looser with Bud, secure enough to kid his regular-army rules. Somebody wearing a string tie would walk by him in the training camp corridor and ask impishly "wide enough, coach?"

Mackbee started playing a little game with him. "Bud, now, he's different. He figures he has to be a little apart. So in breakfast in the morning he will walk right by you and he will not say anything. He's not putting you down but that is the man's style. I always say something to him. I say anything that will make the man answer. Maybe I just say 'good morning.' Now, that is a tough one not to answer. So I have this game. I respect him as a coach but I am not afraid of him, and I thought maybe his style of not saying anything was intended to instill some fear."

If the football team was more relaxed, it was also deeper, stronger. Grant had explained Joe Kapp's 1967 troubles by pointing to his lack of a full summer camp with the team. He would get it now, Grant reminded the restive partisans, and he also would get some interesting competition.

The Vikings had traded for Gary Cuozzo in the off-season, giving New Orleans their No. 1 draft choices for the next two seasons. Cuozzo was one of the hostages to the pro football star system. He had been locked into obscurity for years in Baltimore, first by Johnny Unitas' greatness and then by the conscience of the Colt management and staff. The Colts kept playing Johnny well past the time when his injuries had reduced his once pre-eminent skills to the commonplace. Cuozzo could have quarterbacked the Colts then. As a matter of fact, he quarterbacked them remarkably well in his few full-game appearances.

But by 1968 his exasperations clearly dictated a change of environment. He was a reserved, likeable and highly-intelligent young man, a Phi Beta Kappa with a side interest in dentistry. He fought against the condition that has afflicted scores of promising young quarterbacks. This is the second-string complex symptomized by lack of opportunity, a mutual loss of confidence by the player and the veterans he must try to lead at sporadic moments, a jaded outlook, and a growing feeling of martyrdom.

Cuozzo went to New Orleans to quarterback a new team but seemed both uninspired and prone to injury. He was essentially a standup, in-the-pocket passer. New Orleans rarely gave him a pocket, which meant he did not often have the luxury of standing up—or even sitting down without risking destruction by enemy rushers.

The Vikings' willingness to surrender two first round draft choices for him suggested that the management was not intoxicated with Joe Kapp's longterm prospects. Grant, however, had a completely free mind on his choice of quarterback for 1968. Eventually it came up Joe Kapp. He was more durable and, despite his lapses, he was The Leader. The players gave him the full, coarse, ribald allegiance that is conferred only rarely in this gruff society. They did love Joe, his cornball pronouncements about the team, the way he would get ready for a game—moving about the lockerroom, actually shadowboxing like a fighter.

And they liked Gary. They played for him, respected his cool earnestness. He had a good arm and a feel for tactics. But he was injured often, sometimes when his consistency had him on the verge of moving Joe out of the job. The relationship between the two was even, amiable and professional. Joe's arm-waving congratulations to Cuozzo, in games where the younger quarterback had replaced him, were neither strained nor hypocritic. Kapp had no doubt he should have stayed in the ball game. But when your team is moving, you do not stand around on the sidelines and sulk.

And so they were building a base for a run at the title, the 40-man depth with which the Packers and Colts used to dominate the game. They were doing it faster than either their loyalists or the rest of the league realized. They were no great football team in 1968, but neither were the others—Green Bay, Chicago and Detroit—in the Central Division, and an 8-6 record pushed them into the divisional playoff against Baltimore.

Events in the Super Bowl were to prove that Baltimore was no gargantua, either. But in the rain and morass of its municipal stadium the Colts were still well beyond the reach of Grant's football team, in spite of Kapp's extraordinary courage, will and plain belligerence. He threw nearly 50 times. They red-dogged him and pounded him and ran him into the ground. But they did not run him off the field. He refused a proffered Colt hand once, and in the final, inconsequential minutes he got one last atoning touchdown that told the Colts Joe and the Vikings would be back.

When it was over Kapp had to be dragged, not fully conscious, into the Viking dressing room. It was no forced melodrama for the cameras. He really could not walk unaided. His face was spread with the greasepaint of the warrior, mud fused with blood. His eyes were half closed and he could barely talk.

The little equipment manager, Jimmy Eason, looked on him from the other side of the room. He had tended to him the whole game, seen his slow physical deterioration under the hammering of the Colt line.

Pro football undoubtedly is over-glamorized at times. It is smeared with Madison Av. veneer, arty stop-action TV photography, slick-magazine language, and stuffy philosophical insights into the game as a microcosm of humanity. But anybody who has stood on the sideline for the 2½ hours of a big league football game will testify to the one prevailing truth of it—the unremitting physical force and authentic violence in it.

"I never saw a tougher man in all my life than Joe Kapp in Baltimore," Eason said.

Grant walked up to Joe. "Any other team, Joe," he said. "You could have beaten any other team today."

Kapp's reddened eyes momentarily flared. He understood the coach's considerate gesture, but he refused to be congratulated. "We weren't playing any other team," he said.

"I'll never forget Dave McMillan, my university basketball coach," Bud Grant would say. "He used to talk to me about coaching. He was an old Scotchman who had the business pretty well figured out. 'There are two things,' he said, 'if you're ever going to coach. Never chew out a player in front of his friends and teammates. It embarrasses him when you don't have to embarrass him. Besides, you might be wrong. And so you protect yourself both ways. Take him aside.' Then Dave would kind of whisper to me as though saying something very confidential. 'Take him aside, and he'll listen to you. If you talk to him in front of his buddies, he has got to show disdain for you. He's got to show his teammates that he's really not listening to you. This is what he does to maintain his pride. The second thing is to tell him something nice. Tell him something that lets him know you think he's worth talking to. Tell him what a hell of a job he is doing. You perk him up. You get his attention. Then, Buddie, let him have it.'

"So when people ask, 'how do you set your relations with your players? I think I may have borrowed Dave's ideas on that. You remember your own playing days, of course. And the rest is your own disposition, your own temperament. You have to admire your player's pride. But I don't try to get close to the players. I don't think they are buddies of mine. I think I can establish a communication with them without being a funny guy in practice or without hollering at them. If I can show them, prove to them by performance that what I'm saying can make them a winner, they will listen.

"I don't spend a lot of time talking at the film sessions. This may have bothered some of the players at first. My feeling is that there are players who can't relate well other than on the football field. With some fellows, you can go up and draw on a blackboard, but they can't transpose that very well in their minds. I'm talking about the line spacing or the timing—things like that. They lose perspective. They may not be seeing what we are seeing because we've spent years doing this and they have not. But when you put them in their natural arena, the football field, it comes clear. So why do it all twice if you do not have to?"

They were listening to Grant. He had taken them to the division playoffs, and there weren't many Mickey Mouse choruses in the showers now or bleeps on the practice field. He had told them to cut down the silly penalties—they had, and they were winning. He told them to THINK, THINK ALL THE TIME— and they were thinking. Their character was changing. They were coming to mirror the coach now, with his stolidity and his obsessive control. He was reaching them with a message that may have been a Boy Scout slogan in the past but which swiftly and dramatically shaped them into a genuine whole with identity and character.

He got them believing that nothing matters but the team, that one submerges himself for the many. It was syrupy to some of the outsiders, but it worked. And it worked partly because they had a quarterback whose every action and word on the field was the essence of this code.

Bud Grant, in short, was a salesman. He convinced his people that what was best for the team coincided with their own personal interests. He turned his special teams—the kamikaze desperadoes on the kickoff and punt teams, the field goal and extra point units —into a corps of musketeers aching for a chance to go out and run under the ball. They were in action 20 percent of the time, he said. They covered 60 percent of the field. Games rose and fell on their performance. They believed it, not because it was part of the routine to believe it, but because it was true. They even had a Richard the Lion-Hearted, the drawling Arkansan Jim Lindsay, to fight their battles for them and psyche them up in the huddle and the sidelines.

The players never got close to Grant but they saw that he had a private personality not unlike their own—he was an artful practical joker known to dump buckets full of water on drowsing journalists at poolside. He hunted and fished and was a very normal person, a practical man as a coach. He appreciated they could not all be all-pros and he went from there to maximize what they did best. And yet he did practice a type of guilesmanship on both his players and outsiders. For example, he exploited his reputation for reserve by letting others talk themselves into awkward silence. They would ask a question and, while Bud would stare motionless in the standard position of The Muse, they would attempt to fill the silence with their own answer, and suddenly Bud was one-up. "Nobody," a friend said, "practices conversational counterpoint as well as Bud Grant."

His ship, now, was just about secured.

Lest there should be some misunderstanding, however, no football team or training camp is ever going to be mistaken for a choir boy assembly. Nor were the Vikings, even under Grant.

There was the saga of the love-deprived linebacker who had the curfew system all figured out at Mankato in the fall of 1969. Despite the risks—Grant's standing fine for overnight departure from the premises was $500—the linebacker felt the reward justified the high hazards. The reward measured 38-24-36 and wasn't going to be in town long.

Slipping out at midnight, he headed unerringly for the lady's nest. There he awoke in the morning in time to discover he might just be able to make the training table breakfast at camp.

Unluckily, his absence had been duly noted by the curfew sleuths.

"That will be $500 for being out of the dorm," Bud Grant said in his role as head magistrate.

"I'm sorry, I had it coming," declared the miscreant, leaving.

"Just a moment," the magistrate intoned. "It will be another $50 for missing breakfast."

The bankrupt linebacker repaired to his room.

"There's just one thing I want to know flat out, roomie," his partner asked. "Was it worth $550?"

The linebacker regarded his roommate with the eyes of a man too stricken by events to be bothered with the obvious.

"Roomie," he said, "I wouldn't say it was the greatest evening. As a matter of fact, I would rate it somewhat down the list, because of the unusual circumstances."

"In other words," the roommate said, "you would classify it, for $550, as . . ."

"Fabulous, man. Just fabulous."

And quite suddenly, in 1969, they had their football team. There were Kapp and Brown and Eller, Alderman, Tingelhoff, Osborn, Marshall, Warwick, and the other vets. There were the young vets like Washington, Page, Jim Vellone and Beasley. Men like John Henderson and Paul Krause who came in trade or in the hunt for new geography.

Here was Dave Osborn, a weather-chiseled boy from the prairie who played football as though the routine dive play was the culmination of the American dream. He was incredibly tough and intense, a blocker, a runner, fearless and committed. They brought in an All-American, Clint Jones, to play halfback and everybody expected Dave Osborn to disappear. But four years later Dave Osborn is still the Vikings halfback. He has no great finesse or speed. But he is perfectly capable of taking the head off any complacent defensive tackle.

He was, if you remove Kapp as a character unto himself, the symbol of the Viking offense. Its people, Brown the fullback included, were not very showy or renowned.

Alderman had been in the Pro Bowl a number of times but would not be instantly recognizable anywhere outside his living room. As a blocker, he performed the one surmounting duty of the pass protector, and that was to maintain contact. Rival defensive ends would say there is not a play that goes by when you do not think you could overpower Alderman, to throw him aside. But by the time you break off contact with him, the pass has been thrown.

Tingelhoff was one of his confidantes, a contemporary, one of the near originals. He had won more honors than the rest—all-pro five straight years—but in his droll country style he would kid the anonymity of the offensive center. He had played on bad knees, with fractured ribs, grotesquely swollen ankles. He was a good head, and the men he played with would put their lives on him.

Beside him were Milt Sunde, the so-dedicated, so-willing Joe Palooka type whom the Vikings drafted as a token to Murray Warmath and later thanked themselves a hundred times; and bald Jim Vellone, limited and aching much of the time but a very resolute man; and Yary, the young Californian with his great strength; the tight end Beasley with his willingness to mingle with the head-hunting linebackers; the tackle Doug Davis with his quiet competence and strength.

But out on the flanks, of course, were the individualists, chiefly Gene Washington. Joe Kapp's label for him was The Thoroughbred, and he came with all the skills and nuances of personality the word suggests.

Within three years, no pass receiver in football attracted larger crowds of enemy defensive backs—three, to be specific, in the Super Bowl. He had the hurdler's speed and the basketball player's jumping power. He had height, acceleration, instincts and unplumbed reserves of natural talent but strangely he did not really know how to catch the ball very well when he became a pro. At Michigan State they did not throw that much. And he did not catch much with the Vikings in his first year, behind Flatley. This disenchanted Gene Washington, who has much faith and confidence in Gene Washington. But it did not take Kapp long to discover that Washington had the kind of speed and range to make any pass in the ballpark a potential touchdown, regardless of the number of people covering Gene Washington or the number of flops the ball made in its struggling descent.

He came to the club well-adjusted to his potential for stardom, and he had not been stampeded by it. The pros will say he is not especially good at running with the ball despite his speed, and that he is not especially nifty. But what made him a championship receiver was the simple truth spoken by a bushed defensive back from Green Bay: "About the time you figure you're going stride for stride with him, he's ten yards by you. He doesn't look like he's running that hard. And he doesn't look that way going into the end zone, either."

Henderson was a slender, dignified young man who had no such heraldry as Washington. Just the reverse, in fact. He came from the Detroit Lions in 1968, about a day after his reputation arrived in camp. Henderson was a man who allegedly did not like to catch the ball in a crowd. He was tested soon enough, and it turned out to a bum rap. The only thing Henderson lacked at Detroit was opportunity.

They now had serviceable spare parts for the offense that the Van Brocklin Vikings didn't—Oscar Reed, a bustling fullback of low gravity and remarkable traction; Bobby Grim, the full-service receiver and back; Cuozzo, a Jones who was now not only available but dependable; halfback Bill Harris, Kent Kramer the end, and Bobby Lee the young quarterback and punter who won or saved at least two games in 1969 with his stormy weather kicking.

There also was Ed White, the dumpy young Hercules of the squad, a rookie lineman from California. Pro football is the Muscle Beach of bigtime althletics, populated by strongarm characters. But on the Vikings, the others all looked on Ed White in envy and sometimes in trepidation.

"That boy," declared the wary Louisianan Roy Winston, "is a caution. When I'm playing linebacker in scrimmages, I'm not very conscious of many offensive linemen, individually I mean. But this White, now, I like to stay advised of where that man is at all times."

At a time when White's reputation was still not fully established, Vellone promoted an arm-wrestling contest in which he matched his fellow Californian against all available scoffers. His first contestant was Alan Page, a man hugely endowed with biceps and wrists with the power to tear unabridged dictionaries. They sat down on the lockerroom floor with their arms on a bench. It was agreed Hackbart would count to three to signal the start of the bout. Page already had himself psyched to a high level of combativeness. Sweat gushed from his forehead when Hackbart reached "three."

In five seconds Page's arm was under the table.

Three or four others were thrown into the arena, but White dispatched all without as much as a mild grunt. Whereupon Hackbart cast off all restraints of modesty and volunteered to meet White himself—provided he could use BOTH hands.

With a smile of cordiality, White turned Hackbart three ways and then tastefully dumped him on his back. "The only way anybody is going to beat my boy," declared Vellone, "is if the Vikings draft a gorilla—and even there my boy would have a shot if he ate enough bananas."

Page may not have won the team arm-wrestling title but he was strong enough to play with Eller, Marshall and Larsen. Without dispute it was going to be the best defensive line in the NFL. On certain days Eller was a defensive line by himself. Marshall did not have Eller's strength nor impact but he did have great acceleration and range. Page was the young businessman-mauler, a player of great power but without sustained passion. He played under control and at times almost casually. But when required he usually delivered, very often painfully and sometimes spectacularly.

Larsen was the defensive line's concession to the old social order, an integrated white man. They ribbed him about it and he enjoyed the teasing. He was a big, Nordic ex-Marine, durable physically and completely savage as a competitor. He seemed to enjoy hitting people. His success against enemy running plays tended to free Marshall and Eller for their all-out assaults on the pass rush. Together, the four of them on their best days were a portrait in mayhem. And they were never better than in the fourth quarter of their conference title game against Los Angeles when they hounded and mangled Roman Gabriel and the Rams' offensive line into exhausted futility.

For months the newspaper and magazine authors groped for the appropriate label for this hostile group. The public's inventions were more interesting—The Four Thors, Lavender Hill Mob, etc.—but by common consent they became The Purple Gang.

Behind them they had Warwick, the furious mountain boy; Wally Hilgenberg who, like Henderson, played with the fever of a man reprieved; and Winston, a backwoodsy sage from the cane-brake, not big but very powerful in the arms and shoulders, a wise battlehorse seldom slickered by a fake or influence play.

Grant played his defensive backs in hordes, five at a time in passing situations, and he had good ones. Kassulke and Sharock-man and Hackbart were the hard-heads; Mackbee, the nervy, un-predictable one who got into the league and stayed on pure exuber-ance and feistiness; Krause, the canny, finesse player; and young Bobby Bryant, whose sense for the ball and limber acrobatic move-ments produced interceptions by load-lots before he got hurt in mid-season.

Kassulke and Sharockman were the living evidence of the old-pro's proverbs about paying the price to play in the league.

He seemed almost impervious to pain, Kassulke. He was a roughhouser with a busted nose and a toothy laugh, and he was the foil for the clubhouse gags because he had such a beautiful and genius-level wife. But on the football field he would beat the hell out of everybody in sight. This was what got him into the league and kept him there. He had spent a career challenging the 220-pound tight ends, the Mike Ditkas, John Mackeys and Ron Kram-ers, and the stitches on his face and the scar tissue in his legs testified to it.

Sharockman bore the same signatures. He had played with concussions and fractures, with blood in his mouth and numbness in his hands. There were times when he could barely see and others when he could not stand upright. He had taken the fans' jeers in the old days when somebody's mistake, his or another man's, meant the familiar spectacle of Sharockman chasing a flanker into the end zone. But he was still around 10 years later, and when the ones in the trade called a man a good professional, they were thinking about a man like Ed Sharockman.

With them were Dickson, Steve Smith, Jim Hargrove, Mike McGill, Mike Reilly, Charlie West the runback man, and of course the man who had won more Viking football games than any five others, scored more points, and stubbed more toes—the cracker barrel schoolteacher, Freddie Cox.

Grant had all these with which to shoot for the Super Bowl in 1969, and a staff of aides—Burnes, Bob Hollway, Bus Mertes, John Michels, and Jack Patera — that must have been good because Bud spent two years getting it together.

With this formidable cast, the Vikings flung themselves at their first NFL opponent in 1969—Tarkenton and the Giants—and blew the ball game in the last quarter.

But they did not lose again for three months.

Chapter XXV

*"There ain't a most valuable player. There ain't no
Santa Claus and no red-nosed reindeer, either."*
                                                    —Joe Kapp.

Sentimentalists in televisionland were beginning to feel sorry
for Francis.

The Vikings had him by 13 points into the fourth quarter and
it was anguish for any disciple of the brotherhood of man to watch
Francis trying to pass in the face of an onrushing tide of flesh
represented by Eller, Marshall, Larsen and Page.

I don't think Francis during his Viking years ever considered
his physical safety so jeopardized as to justify a plea to the spirits
of his Methodist forbears. I am convinced it came time for such
invocation in Yankee Stadium.

Nothing else could explain how Tarkenton—now trailing by
six points with two minutes left—completed a pass to the Viking
10 at a time when he was sprinting in horrified flight toward the
sidelines, about to be devoured.

The Giants had third and 17 on the Viking 43. Tarkenton
dropped back and was immediately surrounded. He escaped
toward the left sidelines, oblivious of the receivers far downfield.
For several years Tarkenton had wondered openly when the re-
wards of his early life as an Eagle Scout paragon would come to
him. A helpful providence chose now.

Francis paused one count ahead of the galloping Viking pursuit and threw blindly toward the end zone. His objective, he admitted afterward, simply was to relinquish the ball. He was not
throwing at any identifiable body, friendly or otherwise; and he

was not throwing at any fixed object, such as the end of the stadium. All he was doing was throwing the ball as far as he could.

By raw accident, it came down in play somewhere near the Vikings' two-man patrol at the 10-yard line. The Vikings dutifully batted the ball down. Before it reached the ground, however, it flopped onto the chest of Butch Wilson, the Giants' tight end who was both very horizontal and very amazed. He clutched the ball in self-defense.

A couple of plays later Tarkenton's touchdown pass beat the Vikings out of the game their whole organization insisted was the one they had to win to fuel their championship drive.

Joe Kapp did not play against New York, having been un-horsed by Cuozzo's strong performance late in the exhibition sea-son. Joe had been injured, to be sure, but he was ready for New York. Faithfully applauding Gary on the sideline, he was still able to reflect in his idle moments on Grant's new daring spirit. Grant had to be daring, Joe concluded, to risk playing a crucial football game without Joe in the huddle.

Well, they started over the next week in Metropolitan Stadium against the Colts. They had last seen each other in Baltimore, a year before. The Colts were charging the dressing room, the new conference champions. Joe was on his knees in the mud, dazed, spent and bleeding. But he would not forget this moment. He honed it and ritualized it and imbedded it in his mind.

Carefully, he declined to share his retaliatory vows with the world, or the Colts. Baltimore accosted him with the same de-fenses, the same frequencies. They were going to send the double safety blitz at him at the right tactical moments, in effect loosing nine men on the quarterback. They were wagering they would smother Joe before he could throw deep downfield or slip the ball to the outside.

The Vikings' game plan blew the strategy apart in minutes. Kapp WAS getting time, and the receivers were chewing up the remnants of the Colt secondary exactly as the manual said they would.

It was El Dorado for the conquistadore, a never-never land for the boy with the ball. He threw to Osborn 18 yards into the end zone and then the bomb, 83 yards to Washington, and then to

Grim and then to Kramer. The crowd, although smitten, was not in convulsions because it could not fully grasp the immensity of Joe Kapp throwing for 306 yards and a 31-7 halftime lead over the National Football League champions.

Somewhere, in some unnoticed skirmish, somebody broke a bone in Joe Kapp's left wrist. He felt pain. But 300 yards in one half and four touchdowns! That was Nirvana. They gave him a needle and a pat on the rump and sent him back in.

They brought in Gary Cuozzo in the second half when the demolition of the Colts seemed complete, and Gary immediately broke his nose. It may have been a coincidence, but don't bet on it. The world, or whoever runs it, owed Joe Kapp this afternoon of unearthly deeds. Not just a good day, but a day for all of Joe's rivals to look on and despair.

He kept throwing, to Washington for 42 yards for his fifth touchdown, to Beasley for one for his sixth.

Among all of the duly embalmed football players in professional history only three—Sid Luckman, Y. A. Tittle and Adrian Burke—had thrown seven touchdown passes in one game.

With 7½ minutes remaining at the 15-yard line, Joe Kapp called one final pass play. He appeared to call it quickly. His meditations at that moment are not recorded—but there was always Bud and those field goals. Kapp drilled it for Lindsay, and there he was. The ball was in the end zone with Lindsay.

So Joe Kapp, from Salinas and the Canadian provinces and a thousand scrimmage fields from California to the Great Lakes, was a sure-enough immortal.

It finished 52-14. There were no gasps of exhilaration from Joe Kapp, or Pat O'Brien speeches. Nor were there from his buddies. But Mick Tingelhoff, langorously knotting his tie an hour afterward, remembered the old canon of Van Brocklin.

"Some day we got to get over the hump," Tingelhoff said, almost in benediction. "Nine years it took us. We got over the hump today."

As though exorcised by this one-game-in-a-decade, all of the blunders and bad hops and lousy calls suddenly vanished from the team's Sunday inventory and transferred supernaturally to the other bench.

They won football games on strength and stubbornness, behind the Purple Gang and Tingelhoff's offensive line. But they also won when their fumbles remarkably turned into touchdown runbacks and when Freddie Cox was their only offense. They won on Bryant's interceptions and Lee's punts. They won on Kapp's great days and on his fizzling days when Cuozzo relieved. They won with a minimum of bravado and a maximum of schoolbook efficiency and square-collar discipline.

An NFL scout who watched them for a month described the phenomenon:

"I've seen them for four games," he said, "and I swear that watching that outfit play defense—is like going to an execution.

"The head coach just stands there on the sidelines without moving a lip or even a nostril. He doesn't even adjust his headset. The natives are raising hell in the stands and the scoreboard keeps lighting up, but Grant stays planted in front of the bench at a 20-degree angle to the sideline, and every time there's another light on the board it's like another jolt at Sing Sing.

"Even the Packers, with all that discipline from Lombardi, still showed you a little flareup of emotion. These guys dismantle you very calmly and impartially so they'll all have enough time to get home and play with the kids or diagram a few plays or whatever they do for excitement."

His exasperated judgment was not totally deserved, but it was in the ballpark.

And yet no team run by Joe Kapp was going to be completely free from the brash impulse. They won their division title in the Thanksgiving snowstorm in Detroit, gave Bud the championship ball, and sang the hoarse lockerroom ballad for him. They now faced Los Angeles in the regular-season preliminary to the December game for the conference championship. It was textbook football again, and the Vikings were going to win it. But in the third quarter Joe rolled to the left and trundled downfield to be confronted with the crouching Rams' defensive back, Ritchie Petitbon.

The alternatives here were to try to elude Ritchie or squash him. Disdaining mortal options, Kapp flew OVER Ritchie. They discovered later it was an illegal hurdle. The information reached the officials a few months too late. The play nourished a touchdown drive and etched a trademark on Joe. With this boyish, beanfield gyration Joe Kapp had removed the dull-beige complexion his team presented to the national public. They had some lilt now, some personality.

They went 12 straight games without a loss. Their home games became exultant social pageants, a gathering-of-the-clans among the tailgating thousands in the parking lots. In a literal way the state of Minnesota had not experienced this kind of ardent togetherness since wartime.

There used to be a sort of hunkering reserve with which Minnesota crowds watched their football. For many years they greeted a Viking victory with the same unboisterous approval they gave the arrival of nightfall on the prairie.

It was transformed by Kapp, the winning streak, Eller and The Purple Gang, and the civic nuttiness of viewing winter football in snowmobile suits. It came to be a Mardi Gras in the snowfields of the stadium; the tailgaters saluting their warriors with snowmobile helmets high and jumper cables clinking in harmony.

It was all quite mad, and totally incomprehensible to the millions who were watching on television.

The Vikings did lose once more before the Super Bowl, in the seascape of Atlanta's municipal stadium, 10-3 to nobody but The Dutchman Himself.

The rainstorms and the uncharted fathoms of standing water made the ball game a burlesque. Grant removed Kapp from all potential hazards—fractures, concussions, and drowning—before the end of the first half. But no matter. The conditions were impartial. The Dutchman deserved what he wrought.

He allowed himself no post-game public jubilance. He credited his kicker, Billy Lothridge, with winning the game and said nice things about all concerned. He took three questions from the assembled reporters and vanished into the walls. The new, austere Dutchman. A pity. The old one, the one who used to call himself "a surface guy" was much more believable.

On the eve of the Super Bowl, however, he was one of just two NFL coaches who bothered to telegram good wishes to Grant and the Vikings.

But before that were the Rams, and the Browns. The Browns in the league championship game went without much protest, 27-7. They played the game in near zero weather. The Browns did not especially admire that. Nor could they expunge the memory of their 51-3 disaster in Met Stadium six weeks earlier.

But the Rams—now there was bona fide theater, the libretto of giants in collision.

By then the fans had acquired a doctrinaire faith in the might of the Gang and a fairyland belief in the stardusted power of Joe Kapp. He said the words and performed the deeds of a man touched by wands. If they liked him before, they loved him when he refused to accept the Fan Club's most valuable player trophy with the explanation that was gladiator's creed in every gruff, honest, nongrammatical syllable:

"There ain't a most valuable player and there ain't no Santa Claus and no red-nosed reindeer either."

But he was trailing after two periods, by ten points. He was being outgunned by Gabriel; and Eller, Page, Marshall and Larsen clanged uneventfully against the Rams' offensive line. Trailing a team of the Rams' strength and poise, ten points down with 30 minutes to play, they were looking at odds of better than 10 to 1.

Grant spoke economically to them at halftime. He did not minimize the seriousness of their situation, but he reminded them the game was still very much in hand—and they had not come all this way, all these years, to lie down now when the gold was there before them.

They came out deliberately, silently. They did not expect what now filled the arena. The crowd was alive and booming. With one unsolicited, swelling declaration the fans lifted and escorted their professionals onto the field. It reached to the insides of tough, cool mercenaries who, after all, were once the kids with the runny noses who played the game for fun.

Kapp still threw for an interception. But his defensive line rubbed that out. And Kapp was now hitting the target. The crushing line battle started to swing to the Vikings. Kapp got his team ahead 21-20. They kicked off and Hackbart buried Smith on the 12-yard line. Gabriel was thrown once at the two. Then Eller, caving in the right side of the Rams' protection, interred him in the end zone for the safety.

With a minute left Page intercepted at midfield to choke the Rams final offensive, and it was over.

They mobbed Joe and the Vikings at the finish, and they stormed the goalposts.

But the thousands who accompanied them to New Orleans stood around in a mourners' chorus a few weeks later when the Vikings expired in the Super Bowl, 23-7.

They went into it the same Methodical Men who had dispassionately crunched the NFL. There was something in the occasion that might have demanded more. Perhaps Kansas City of the still-noisy and resentful American League, had it—the right pitch of emotion to harmonize with the brawn, the desired flow of the adrenalin-of-defiance.

On the other hand, maybe all they needed were Jan Stenerud the kicker, the defensive power of Buck Buchanan, Aaron Brown, Curly Culp, Bobby Bell, the others—and Lenny Dawson and the multiple offense.

The professional verdict from the players and their coaches afterward was that the Chiefs' shuttling formations did not bother the Viking defense, that the Vikings were aware of everything Kansas City would send at them.

Being aware, though, cannot quickly change the habits of a career. Having a picture of a play does not necessarily solve it when it is run by flesh and blood. Grant had made the same point himself in another context. If the Vikings really were not surprised by the Chiefs' diversified offense, they deceived a lot of people in the Tulane Stadium.

Stenerud kicked three field goals, Charley West dropped a kickoff on the Viking 19, and Mike Garrett scored from the 5. It was 16-0 for the Chiefs at halftime before Al Hirt and the British Army took over.

But in the third period Kapp rekindled the spirit of the Met. He passed to Beasley, then to Brown, then to Henderson and then to Reed, and Osborn ran it in from four yards out. With 25 minutes to go, they trailed 16-7.

Right here, Grant was saying. Right here is where we take them.

It might have been. But the Chiefs slickered Eller once more on an end-around with Frank Pitts, and when Otis Taylor broke through first Mackbee and then Kassulke on a 46-yard touchdown pass from Dawson, it was the finish.

With eight minutes to go Kapp went out with a dislocated shoulder, the symbolic fall of the leader.

He sat numbed and desolate on the sidelines, with the pain and the failure at this very last rung of the 10-year climb, for Joe and a football team.

Just a game for kids, a fun game that shouldn't be all that end-of-the-world. Except that it was.

In the dressing room they gave him privacy, and drugs to dull the pain. His teammates in the lockerroom spoke with no elaborate grief or shame. They had made too many mistakes and Kansas City was a better football team today, period. Francis was there with consolations. The thousands of telegram signatures hung emptily from the concrete walls, and Grant said it would all be okay tomorrow—and in 1970.

Months later he would offer a post-mortem:

"We felt our defense was tough enough, that we could hold anybody. Nobody was going to drive the length of the field against us. If we didn't gain a yard, we could put them in the other end, and sooner or later we would get something on the board. We would play tenacious football. We felt if we got the opportunity we could move and score. We believed we could exploit the mistakes of others and minimize our own. This is how we felt about our football in general. Kansas City confronted us with a great team. The only thing I said was 'now don't think anybody is going to be deceived by the fact we are 13-point favorites. Be prepared to play a Green Bay-type of game, a Detroit-type. Back and forth, rock and sock until something breaks open.' They had a history of playing more bad football games than we did. We had played a whole season in which we made only two misplays that cost us, against New York and Atlanta.

"So we went down and fumbled two times, Henderson on our first drive and Charley West on that kickoff. I think the ball Henderson fumbled after catching it in their end was the only fumble he made all year. Charley West has very good hands. So what do you make of it? They had three interceptions. I can't blame that on anybody in particular. Their linebacker stole one and Joe hung up another. We had a pass interference by Sharockman, those missed tackles and six penalties—by the team least penalized in our league. What it came down to was that against a truly great football team we played our poorest game of the year, from the standpoint of the errors we made. I suppose you can say they had something to do with it, and I would not argue. No, the multiple offenses didn't hurt us. It's still football. We knew about their formations, what they run from them. Yes, Eller was beaten on the end-around. He wasn't fooled. He was blocked. Their guy came around and made a great play. He got the angle on Carl and not only blocked him but knocked him down. And you very seldom see that happen."

So neither for Carl nor the Vikings, nor Joe Kapp, were there fountains of champagne in New Orleans or moonbeams on the canal. It was as true for Joe as the others. There wasn't any Santa Claus, after all, and no red-nosed reindeer—and no gold on Bourbon Street, either.

Chapter XXVI

"I still look in awe at the big names, even though I knocked the hell out of some of them."—John Campbell, pro football player.

The final wage for the pro football player's striving and sacrifice may not be in the playoff split at all, or the championship diamond on his finger.

Stripped of its ad agency overlay and high-powered merchandising, there is a nobility to this game. It is present not in the contrived postures of Spartan fierceness you see on the magazine covers and in the pre-game shows, but in the fraternity of the men who play the game.

There is no disputing that we tend to invest the whole fabric of pro football with too much grimness, an Olympian life-and-death gravity that is often too thick for the non-convert to digest.

But there are times—such as the Vikings' comeback against the Rams in Metropolitan Stadium—when it is truly moving and transcendent because the emotions it stirs on the competitors are naked before us. And we have an unforgetable sensation of being not only witnesses to the drama but participants in it.

To the player, the reality of the game is the struggle on Sunday, yes. But just as much as this are the fatigue-soothing beers in the bull session, the 240-pound rookie unable to resist crying as he leaves the lockerroom after the coach tells him he cannot make the team, and the season's last plane ride home.

An ex-sailor named John Campbell from Wadena, Minn., and the University of Minnesota, joined the Vikings in 1963. From there he went to Baltimore, Pittsburgh and back to Baltimore. He has not been a great pro football linebacker, but when healthy he has been a good one. He is a man of intellect, sociability, and a sharp edge of irony, and he will make it as a businessman when he is finished as a football player.

But no life will ever touch him with the emotional jar of pro football or evoke its bittersweet memories of pain, winning, manhood and comic despair.

"You just have that feeling of rapport with everybody in pro football," John Campbell said. "It's that kind of fraternity because you know exactly what the other guy went through to get where he is. You go through the anguish of the cuts. I've seen veteran players dressing in tears when one of the other veterans they played with for five or six years got cut. You have ties with these people. Hell, when I got cut in Pittsburgh, I looked over and there was a guy who had taken my job, and his eyes were watering a little. We'd been friends for three years.

"You just can't throw that aside and say it's a cold hard business. It is that, maybe the greatest business in the world, but probably the worst profession. I say that because anybody who thinks pro football players have a career is a fool. You better get something else ready for you because you get a head knock or your knee goes the wrong way, and it's over. I've seen players who have been in the league for eight or nine years, and the only thing they have to show for it is $5,000 in an old bar and they're getting robbed blind of that.

"I know there are a lot of guys who get themselves established in the off-season, but a lot don't. Here's a guy whose been in the league four or five years. He's got plenty. Don't worry about it. Winter and spring are for relaxing. He can play another year, and another. The old male ego always says I can make it another year and I've got plenty of time to get serious about an off-season job.

"The game is pride and money. A lot of people say it's a body contact sport. Bull. Dancing is a contact sport. Pro football is a collision sport. That's why you wear all that stuff and why they keep improving it. The helmet, in fact, is the best weapon you've got. At the university I used to love to crack back on people and just lower that headgear and knock their jocks off.

"They used to put elbow pads on to protect your elbows, and they fell down. Now they tape pads on your arms and keep them wrapped until it's just like a baseball bat. If you come out of the backfield and they bang you with one of those, it gets your attention.

"People will talk about the violence in the game. I'm not one to say it doesn't have a lot of it, and I mean honest, gut-shaking violence. But the fan always relates those wide-open collision tackles with his own body, his own physical condition. He sees himself taking the blow and wonders how they do it. The ball player has conditioned himself to it, physically and emotionally.

"So I've always said I'm not that impressed that I'm a football player. I never thought of myself as a career player of some kind of star. Every year I've gone to camp I've said 'thank God I'm here.' I've been happy to be associated with people like Unitas, Bart Starr and people like that. To me, I'm still from Wadena. I never did get to the point where I thought, 'well, I've really arrived.' I still looked in awe at the big names, even though I knocked the hell out of some of them and was a player rep and all.

"It's never been easy, especially the first year with the Vikings. Don't kid yourself that they don't test a new man in pro ball. Bill Brown was my special inspection agent in camp. He'd come up to block me and end up tackling me, because it was easier for him that way. So I kicked him in the guts once and Brownie said he's going to beat the hell out of me. If that doesn't worry you, how about Harry Gilmer, the defensive coach, then coming over and saying, 'you gotta get OUT THERE on that end sweep.' I said, 'I can't, he's tackling me.' And Harry said, 'well, okay, it's all right by me, but he's screwing with your pay check.'

"So the next time I said, 'Bill, if you do that again, I'm going to kick you right in the crotch.' He snorted something at me, and a little later he said, 'it's okay, it's all part of the game.'

"So I made the team and we were friends. And, do you know, four years later, when I was with the Steelers and we played the Vikings, he came out there blocking for Osborn and I'll be damned if the son of a bitch didn't tackle me again."

"I almost died laughing. You tell yourself then that if he comes out again, you're going to touch him up around the head or something, but you don't want to try to hurt a guy. Brownie, I mean, isn't hurting you if he tries to hold. They all play that game, me included. All I'm saying that it's tough to earn a salary in pro football by honoring thy rule book. That's why they invented six officials and they may have more yet, for all I know.

"The ballplayers police each other pretty well. You'll get a guy who thinks he can get away with the cheap stuff, or maybe he picked on some pigeon the week before. One of your guys, very early in the game, will get down with him and tell the man: 'Look, you try it one time like we saw on the films and you are in for one helluva long afternoon.'

"What happens is that each team tries to set the tone. Who's going to be the hitter? Who's going to win the battle of the hitting? By the large, this is the team that will win the ball game. Me, I've got to let that tight end think: 'Don't tell me this S.O.B. is gonna be this tough ALL afternoon?' If I get him thinking that way, I've won. If on the other hand he just knocks me all over my can on the first couple of plays, I've got to be thinking: 'Another 15-rounder today. Nuts.' That's what Jackie Smith of the Cardinals and I used to do. You can't believe the things we did to each other. We were tripping, ripping jerseys, biting, just beating the daylights out of each other, and doing everything but playing football until one of us would say 'aw for Chrisesakes, let's knock it off.'

"But we didn't. He came off the line one time and I was trying to cover for the safetyman. Charley Johnson threw the ball to Smith. The only way I was going to stop him was to grab his jersey. He went up for the ball and the jersey stretched two feet. He came down with it laughing, and I laughed, and so now we understand each other a little better. Mutual respect, right?

"Well, the next time he came off the line, he saw I wasn't looking and he turned around the belted me in the mouth and knocked out seven fillings.

"Now, you have got to call that mutual respect compounded. We speak to each other now, cautiously.

"But I think that it's basically true most of the pros don't take that extra shot that could put a guy out. Hit hard, Jesus yes. In college there's a lot of cheap fouling that can really hurt. In the pros you try to think about that, remembering the other guy's got to earn his money, too.

"You learn to live with the pain. It's a condition of the game. Players have different pain thresholds and it has nothing to do with manliness. Mine happens to be pretty high. We were playing

Atlanta a few years ago and I got hit from the blind side. I went down to catch my fall and Errol Linden fell on top of me. I felt a helluva jolt. I got up and my arm went in four directions. I just grabbed my wrist, put it between my legs, and rocked back. Snap. Snap. It snapped back in and I went off the field. The doctor said I was an unholy stupid to do it, but that I had set it perfectly. The arm was broken and the elbow dislocated. All I thought about when I got up from under Linden was 'my God's my arm's not right, I got to get it right.'

"The fan watches all that colliding and pictures himself getting hit, like we've said, but he doesn't picture himself going through three months of tough conditioning, taking a lot of cracks. Your head hurts and subconsciously you say 'this is part of it, my head hurts, I can't see, I got spots all over, but this has happened before. I'll get over it.'

"The fan, now, will be washing windows and fall off the ladder and hit his head, and he's fuzzy and he may think the world is ending. The pro ball player just happens to live in another one.

"And it's one you'll never, never forget—mostly because of the guys in it."

The crowds can only sense this. Sometimes they try to become part of it. This may explain why by the thousands they mobbed Joe Kapp after the Los Angeles game. Joe Kapp, the improbable legend. For them it was as much an act of contrition as a gesture of gratitude. The dirty-faced professional knew in his heart that some of them might be jeering him one week later, but the knowledge did not lessen the impact of the occasion. He wept. And not because he was being glorified by the crowd, but because Tingelhoff and Eller came up to him with grimy hands and pumpkin faces and hugged him and kissed him.

And this, as much as the money they bankroll, is the crystal of the athletic ideal in pro football. They DO sacrifice. The one permanent reality for them is not the tinsel of TV and countdowns, but the trust they place in each other.

A hard-knuckled, sweaty love DOES grow up among them, in the grind and worry of the training camps and in the locker-room. But it is never more vivid than on a frozen field when the reliance one man places in the man squatting and grunting beside him on the line of scrimmage is utter and complete.

This is why in the year of 1969 the unstylish roughneck with the scars on his chin was the leader of his team. It does not matter if he can or does repeat in future years. There are thousands who will remember the sight of the midfield mob-scene when the clerks and plumbers and brokers and schoolboys clutched at Joe. They had booed Joe Kapp before and maybe they would again. What they were telling him now was from Kipling: "Though I've belted you and flayed you, by the livin' Gawd that made you, you're a better man than I am, Gunga Din."

Maybe Joe was wrong.

For the football player, when the scoreboard explodes with the numbers for your team and the thunder comes down from the bleachers, and the big black man with blood on his face shakes your hand in the huddle, maybe there is a Santa Claus, after all, and one of those reindeer, too.